PASSPORT
TO THE IMPOSSIBLE

A Missionary's Incredible Journey with God

PASSPORT
TO THE IMPOSSIBLE

A Missionary's Incredible Journey with God

JIM WOOLSEY

Foreword by Evangelist Jimmy Swaggart

JIMMY SWAGGART MINISTRIES
P.O. Box 262550 | Baton Rouge, Louisiana 70826-2550
www.jsm.org

ISBN 978-1-941403-22-8

09-129 | COPYRIGHT © 2015 Jimmy Swaggart Ministries®

16 17 18 19 20 21 22 23 24 / BVG / 11 10 9 8 7 6 5 4 3

TABLE OF CONTENTS

FOREWORD

In 1985, Frances and I were invited to visit the Soviet Union. Jim Woolsey and his wife, Jean, traveled with us, along with a few others. At that time, Cold War tensions between the United States and the Soviet Union had reignited between the two super powers, and talks to eliminate missile build up were in the air. Two years would pass before President Ronald Reagan would stand at the Brandenburg Gate and call for Mr. Gorbachev to tear down his wall, and two more years went by before that wall fell.

For us, the mid-1980s were an extremely busy time for this ministry, and we were pressed on every side with the demands of advancing world evangelism. I thank the Lord for the help of godly men like Jim Woolsey, who, at that time, headed up our international outreach efforts. He did an excellent job, too, getting the telecast on in about half of the countries of the world and translated into any number of languages. We saw a harvest of souls that was unexcelled. In fact, I think I can say without fear of exaggeration that Jim Woolsey was instrumental in helping us to see the greatest harvest of souls in history. I realize that's quite a statement, but I believe it to be true. Of course, it was made possible because of two things: the anointing of the Holy Spirit upon our efforts and the modern technology of television, which enabled us to reach untold millions with a single program.

We were both so busy that the only time I really heard from Jim was when he needed the go-ahead to push the telecast through in another country.

One of those times was in 1987, about two years after our visit to the Soviet Union. I was working in my office in Baton Rouge, Louisiana, when my secretary said, "Jim Woolsey is here and wants to see you." Of course, I told her to show him in immediately.

He sat down, looked at me intently, and then proceeded to say the most far-out statement that I had ever heard another human being utter. He said, "Brother Swaggart, I think we can get on television in Moscow, Russia. Furthermore, I think we can get on TV-1." At that time, TV-1 was the propaganda channel for the Soviet Union. It went out over 7,000 television stations, covering all 15 of the Soviet Republics.

As I listened to him tell me this, I wondered, "Does he know what in the world he is saying? He is talking about the Soviet Union—the very heart of atheism for the entirety of the world! It is the monolithic Soviet empire! They don't even believe in God, and they hate everything that originates from the West."

So I asked Him, if this were possible, what the monthly cost would be. He told me what he thought it might be, and, to be frank, when I heard the figure, I swallowed hard. Yet I knew in my heart — of course, I did — that this would be one of the greatest miracles in the history of man.

In fact, if there could be a present-day extension to the book of Acts, what Jim Woolsey helped to carry out and make possible would be among the great experiences recorded.

So I gave Jim the go-ahead and a year later, he was able to get the telecast on in Riga, Latvia, which was a part of the Soviet Union. Getting on in Latvia was a miracle in itself, but still, I remember thinking to myself, "Moscow? Over TV-1?"

By now, Jim had probably made some 35 trips to Moscow, meeting with their television executives and refusing to take no for an answer.

Then, in 1989, he got a yes and, miracle of miracles, we began airing the telecast over TV-1 out of Moscow. We aired there for more than three and a half years and, as stated, saw a move of God that was unexcelled.

During that time, I received a phone call from a preacher with whom I was not acquainted. He said to me over the phone, "Brother Swaggart, I have just returned from Moscow." He went on to explain how every six months he and a group of other preachers went to Russia and invited pastors from all over the former Soviet Union. They paid the way for the Russian preachers so that they could engage in an intensive weeklong study of the Word of God. In a particular service with more than 100 of these pastors present, he matter-of-factly asked each pastor to stand and give a short testimony of how he had given his heart to Christ.

He said, "Brother Swaggart, 90 percent of the preachers who stood up that day — some now pastoring churches running several thousands of people — all and without exception said they were saved as a result of the telecast." He added, "I thought you would want to know." Of course, we wanted to know, and we were so thankful for his phone call.

As the telecast went out over the former Soviet Union, translated into Russian and, as stated, covering the entirety of all 15 Soviet Republics, the Lord gave us the greatest harvest that we had ever witnessed or experienced to date.

What was done in Russia at that time, I must say unequivocally, was not brought to pass by my faith, but rather by the faith of Jim Woolsey. This is just one of the stories of the miracle 1980s respecting what the Lord helped us to see and accomplish. We give Him all of the praise and all of the glory.

As you read more of Jim's stories captured on these pages, you will find, I think, that the entirety of this book presents a collection of miracles — miracles of the same caliber as those recorded in the book of Acts.

Jimmy Swaggart

PASSPORT TO
THE IMPOSSIBLE

"But Jesus beheld them, and said unto them, With men this is impossible; but with God all things are possible."

— Matthew 19:26

PREFACE

This book originated from a sincere desire to make known from a first-hand eyewitness account the great working and operation of the Holy Spirit. This move of God is taking place in a portion of the global outreach of Jimmy Swaggart Ministries (JSM) that has literally touched multiple millions of hearts and lives around the world.

What you will find in this book is not the story of some religion, church, or denomination. It is really an eyewitness account of the "acts" of the Holy Spirit through Spirit-led men and women who confronted impossible obstacles and situations for the cause of Christ, while trusting Him to fulfill His plan.

This book is really not about the writer so much as it is about the Holy Spirit and His mighty work among men who attempt to reach a lost and dying world with the gospel of Jesus Christ. As well, it is written so that the slain Lamb of God may receive all of the glory and credit. The writer just happened to have had the privilege of traveling millions of miles around the world with Him and being present when the Holy Spirit carried out these incredibly awesome acts of His.

Prayerfully, the writer has tried to recreate events, locales, and conversations from his memories of them. Conversations in this book are retold from the writer's recollections in a way that evokes the feeling and meaning of what was said and may not represent a word-for-word dialogue. However, the essence of the dialogue is accurate. Also, due to the nature of some incidents, the names of individuals may have been changed to protect or maintain anonymity.

The writer has tried not to embellish anything in this book. In fact, he has opted to downplay the events as you can appreciate from the simple language used to give you just the facts of each miracle of His grace to advance the cause of Christ throughout the earth.

It is the author's desire that the reader's faith in Christ not only be challenged by these events recounted here to believe God even more than ever, but also that the reader will in some way also *"grow in grace, and in the knowledge of our Lord and Saviour Jesus Christ"* (II Pet. 3:18), *"unto the measure of the stature of the fullness of Christ"* (Eph. 4:13).

With the above understanding in view, I present to you *Passport to the Impossible: A Missionary's Incredible Journey with God* as part of the 20th century's Acts, Chapter 29. Of course, the book of Acts in the Bible only has 28 chapters. It is the Holy Spirit using each one of us to continue His writing of Chapter 29 right here at the end of the church age, this age of grace.

"But the people that do know their God shall be strong, and do exploits" (Dan. 11:32).

THE MANDATE

"Jim, I want you to put our gospel telecast on every national television network in every country of the world that will air it. As the international director of this ministry, you can carry this task out any way you feel the Lord directs and leads you to get it done. If you have to travel to each country, then travel. If you have to call long distance, then call them, but God has given us this mandate to take this gospel of Jesus Christ into every nation of the world."

It was Evangelist Jimmy Swaggart speaking emphatically to me in his deep, baritone voice. He was giving this directive on one of my first days of work at his worldwide ministry headquarters in Baton Rouge, Louisiana. This man of God did not ask me if there were any questions, and I did not ask him for any clarifications. I knew exactly what this meant. For nearly 20 years, the Lord had been preparing me as a missionary for this daunting role, although I still felt woefully inadequate for such an impossible task.

A MOVE OF GOD

I was certain of this: God had already begun a huge move of the Holy Spirit unparalleled in church history and was using this man to spearhead it under the anointing of the Holy Spirit. How did I know this? I had been a missionary with the Assemblies of God up to that moment for more than 15 years and had already lived on the foreign field in Peru and Guatemala for that length of time. I had seen and experienced firsthand what this God-called, Spirit-anointed ministry had done in the hearts, lives, and homes of hundreds of thousands of people.

As a missionary in Guatemala, with my wife, Jean, and our four children — Curtis, Kimberly, Kevin, and Shauna — we had the privilege of putting the Jimmy Swaggart gospel Spanish telecast on one of the national TV networks and establish the JSM Guatemala outreach office. We were immediately inundated with mail from viewers who had prayed with Brother Swaggart during the weekly telecast and had given their hearts to Christ.

As each letter told us, people were getting saved from the very first telecast. In just a few weeks on the air, already 3,000 letters a week were flooding into the outreach office in Guatemala City. The letters were stating that the senders had just gotten saved, and they were asking for Brother Swaggart's follow-up booklet in Spanish, *What Must I Do To Be Saved?* They also wanted to know where they could go to church. This was unheard of heretofore. There had been another ministry from the United States that had a so-called gospel interview-type television program, but they only received one letter a week from viewers, if that many.

In a few more weeks, 8,000 letters a week were pouring into the JSM outreach office from first time viewers! I was sure of this: A move of God had started in Guatemala by the Lord using Brother and Sister Swaggart. Little did I know at the time that the Lord would have me be a small part of that same move of the Holy Spirit in the entirety of the world!

Now, here I was in Brother Swaggart's office hearing him tell me: "Take this gospel telecast into every nation of the world." As I left his office that day, I thought, "Lord, who am I to carry out such an impossible task? Most countries of the world are closed to the gospel due to communism, religion, dictators, and the powers of darkness."

The Lord only reassured me, "My grace is sufficient. Trust Me."

With this, I hope that as you start reading the pages of this passport, it will become *your* passport to an adventure of increasing faith in the only wise, true God who can do anything and surmount and conquer any obstacle. If our faith will just continue to look to His Son, Jesus Christ, and what He did for us at the Cross of Calvary, we will see His mighty works carried out by the power of the Holy Spirit. Everything we need is found only in the Cross of Christ — His finished work there. The Cross alone is the means by which all things come to us from God. As a result, our faith must rest in that finished work. With this done, the Holy Spirit, who functions entirely and only through the parameters of the sacrifice of Christ, will help us greatly both in life and living. We are just mere recipients of this grace of God by faith alone so that, *"To Him be glory both now and forever. Amen"* (II Pet. 3:18).

It is in this spirit that *Passport to the Impossible: A Missionary's Incredible Journey with God* is handed to you, the reader.

Missionary J. B. Woolsey
January 10, 2015

INTRODUCTION

PASSPORT TO
THE IMPOSSIBLE

"I am crucified with Christ: nevertheless I live; yet not I, but Christ liveth in me: and the life which I now live in the flesh I live by the faith of the Son of God, who loved me, and gave Himself for me."

— Galatians 2:20

INTRODUCTION

The following is a reprint of the interview article, "Jim Woolsey: My Strength Made Perfect in Weakness," taken from the magazine *Sword of the Spirit*, April 1986, Vol. 2, No. 7.

A LESSON IN HUMILITY, a reflection of servitude, a man who stands awed, even amazed, to excitedly tell you the stories of the events that happened in his life and his work with Jimmy Swaggart Ministries to get the gospel out to all the world. This and much more is what crosses your heart as you listen to Missionary Jim Woolsey as he warms your spirit with his sincere motives for serving the Lord.

Missionary Jim Woolsey, director of Jimmy Swaggart International Ministries, is the first person to admit about himself, "I'm probably the least qualified person to do this." Yet in his unboastful spirit, his department, in its achievements, can speak for itself:

The foreign outreach of Jimmy Swaggart Ministries is now involved in 189 countries of the world in some way and now maintains 65 international offices, all under the direction of Brother Woolsey.

The Jimmy Swaggart gospel telecast now covers 135 countries of the world with a total weekly program potential viewing audience of over 260 million people. (This being a very conservative figure means that this number of people around the world have access to the telecast if they want to view it.) The weekly telecast is now produced in 13 different languages that are aired over 1,600 television station networks.

The JSM ChildCare International (JSCCI) is now involved in 46 countries of the world — helping to educate, clothe, feed, and provide medical attention to over 250,000 needy children on a daily basis — helping to build 106 schools to date and involved with a total of 216 schools in the Third World countries.

The JSM medical ministry is now operating on four continents with over 50,000 people being treated in some way each month, also allowing the gospel to be ministered to them.

Then there are the 540 missionaries stationed in 189 countries of the world that JSM is currently helping substantially toward their monthly support.

JSM is involved with 196 foreign missions' projects that are currently in progress — churches and evangelistic centers being built and Bible schools under construction.

When God spoke to Brother Swaggart and said, "Take the crusades to the great cities of the world where you have television. I will stir entire countries and save multiple thousands of people," it was to Brother Woolsey he turned and said, "Since we have this mandate from the Lord, I want you, Jim, to choose the countries we will go to for nationwide crusades

where we have been on television and set them up, organiz-
ing the pastors and leaders of the work in each for these crusades." So, besides maintaining all of the above, he has been
in charge of the foreign crusades in each country ... no small
task, to be sure.

This incredible amount of work is all handled under Missionary Jim Woolsey's area of responsibilities. I sat in his
office, while interviewing him, wondering what has enabled
this man to handle all of this, but more importantly, to wonder at his ability to personally travel over 750,000 miles last
year and successfully convince these countries (many who
are anti-American as well as anti-Christian) to air the precious gospel of life.

He spends a total average of 2,000 hours per year in the
air flying to the different countries of the world and, at the
same time, 2,000 hours per year on the ground working in
meetings and coordination of the over 65 JSM international
outreach offices located throughout the world in the same
amount of countries. He personally handles over 5,000 television contracts. To do this, he confessed, "I really only get
about four hours of sleep every night, seven nights a week
for years now. The outreach offices and TV networks on the
other side of the world call to do business over the phone in
the middle of our night here." I wondered if it could be his
years of experience as a missionary and serving the greater
part of his time in Peru and Guatemala (over 15 years).

Or could it be his expertise in laying out his plan of attack
like a professional salesman?

"No," says Missionary Woolsey. "It's actually by faith and the leading of the Holy Spirit. I really don't know how it works, but it all falls into place."

He began to explain that all he does is pray over a large globe in his office until he gets impressed by the Holy Spirit at what country he should visit. Then, off he goes with no appointments and many times without even contacting any missionaries in the area (many of whom doubt that the airing of the program can be done).

Of the last 50 countries visited, he has had no preset appointments in 48 of them. "I just ask God, and each time the Holy Spirit gets me in to see the head man. In a matter of an hour or two, they give me a signed contract to air the telecast tapes we send to their network. You can plan until your face turns blue and your brain dries out, but it won't do any good. It takes the Holy Spirit to get through that door."

In summing up with a small part of what I was able to catch of the heart of this Holy Spirit-driven man, I can only quote the words that he gave me: "Every day that we are here (at JSM) it is just God because we really don't deserve to be here. But, I feel if you are faithful in what you are doing at the moment for God — use what He has given you by His grace at the moment in the way He wants you to — He will open the door in what he wants you to do next, without you having to connive, maneuver, or anything. God will meet you each step of the way."

There you have it — a glimpse into the heartbeat of this man sent from God.

"And He said unto me, My grace is sufficient for thee: for my strength is made perfect in weakness. Most gladly therefore will I rather glory in my infirmities, that the power of Christ may rest upon me " (II Cor. 12:9).

CHAPTER 1

20° 20' 54" S
57° 33' 7" E

THE PLANE THAT FELL OUT OF THE SKY

"To preach the gospel in the regions beyond you, and not to boast in another man's line of things made ready to our hand."

— II Corinthians 10:16

THE PLANE THAT FELL OUT OF THE SKY

20° 20' 54" S | 57° 33' 7" E

AS THE AIR MAURITIUS Boeing 737–200 jet aircraft had just closed its side front and rear doors, the announcement came over the static-filled PA system, "Ladies and gentlemen, please take your seats. Fasten your seat belts and prepare for takeoff." Here I was, herded onboard this aircraft with approximately 100 other passengers, with hopes of traveling from the beautiful country of Mauritius — located in the Indian Ocean — to Johannesburg, South Africa. It was a flight of just under 2,000 miles that should take only four and a half hours. For the last three days, I had spent most of my time with a very extraordinary man of God, Pastor Lindsay N. Blackburn. He was the superintendent of what was now a very large group of churches, with literally thousands of believers over the entirety of this large, French-speaking island nation.

After a rather long connecting flight from Hong Kong in the Far East, I arrived in Mauritius where this godly brother took me directly to one of the churches to preach the gospel of Jesus Christ.

Upon finishing this first service, with several people giving their hearts to the Lord and it being toward evening, I thought maybe we would be going to the hotel so that I could check in and get a good night's rest before going to the Mauritius Broadcasting Corporation (MBC). I was to go to the MBC television network headquarters' offices the next day to offer the French Jimmy Swaggart gospel telecast to be included in this fine network's programming.

However, to my surprise, Brother Blackburn said, "We have just enough time to reach another church that starts their next two-hour service at 8 o'clock tonight."

I had just finished preaching at the church we had just left. It had been packed out with hundreds of people in attendance, so I asked, "Who will be preaching at this church we are going to now?"

"You are," was Brother Blackburn's reply. "Then we will go to another church that finishes its last service of the day from 10 p.m. to midnight."

After I paused to think a minute, I then asked, "Aren't these strange times to have services? Is it a holiday of some kind?"

"No," he said. "All of our churches across the island start their first services each morning at 6 a.m. and continue having services every two hours throughout the entire day until midnight each night, seven days a week. Every service has an entirely different congregation. The believers bring their unsaved friends and neighbors to each service. In every church and every service all day and night through, we have people coming to the Lord and getting saved."

THE MAN WHO LIVES CLOSER
TO HEAVEN THAN TO EARTH

At each church where we went, before I would preach, Brother Blackburn would introduce me as, "The man who lives closer to heaven than to earth." He would then chuckle as he explained to the congregation, "He travels over 50,000 miles each month all over the world for the cause of Christ, and has for many years now, going into over 150 countries of the world. The reason: To put the Jimmy Swaggart gospel telecast on the nationwide television networks of these countries. Many hundreds of thousands of people have come to the Lord as a result of Brother Swaggart's Spirit-anointed preaching of the gospel of Jesus Christ."

Then Brother Blackburn would chuckle out loud again and explain, "Brother Woolsey literally lives up in the sky in airplanes most of the time, closer to heaven than we do down here on earth." Evidently, each congregation he would introduce me to before I would preach would get a kick out of his description because they would roar with laughter.

We had a glorious service until midnight, with the presence of the Holy Spirit working and moving in hearts and lives and dozens of new people accepting Christ as their Saviour and Lord. Brother Blackburn was telling the truth. The whole three days and nights I was with him, we did go to a different, packed out church every two hours (except for the two hours we spent at the MBC Television government-owned network) and preached the gospel, with new people getting saved in every service around the clock! I would preach just the simple message of "Jesus Christ and Him crucified" at each meeting where we went, just as I had always preached in Spanish years before as a missionary with my family in Peru, South America. Then I was preaching three and four times every day for six months in one place, a year in another, or two and a half years in still another city — as long as it took in each place until a church would be established. This continued throughout our 11 years in Peru.

Now then, I had come to the conclusion that this precious brother in Christ, Pastor Blackburn, also took Christ's Great Commission seriously:

"Go ye into all the world and preach the gospel to every creature."

He has a burning desire — the same that Brother and Sister Swaggart, Donnie and Gabriel Swaggart, others called of God, and I have — to reach as many souls for Christ as possible in the short time we have left before the Lord's return, or before we go by way of the grave to be with Him.

I have always felt that I would be in the last generation that will be alive on earth when the Lord raptures His church. Whether it plays out that way or not, of course, is up to the Lord. However, ever since I accepted Him as my Saviour and Lord, God has put an intense desire in my heart to win as many people to Christ as possible in this one final opportunity He has given us in this last generation before He comes. If we do not get it done by the grace of God, then it won't get done.

Now, at midnight, Brother Blackburn drove me to his house to eat supper with his wife and family and then dropped me off at the hotel in Port Louis, the capital of Mauritius, so I could get a few hours' rest before another big day.

THE POLITICAL LEADERS ARE AFRAID OF ME
↑

On the way to the MBC television network the next day, Brother Blackburn explained to me, "The MBC TV network is owned and operated by the government. Most all of the people working for the government are Hindus. The political leaders are afraid of me because we have won so many Hindus to the Lord Jesus Christ. They feel threatened because we have so many thousands of followers that could vote someone like me, a Christian, into office; but, of course, that is not our purpose. So, be careful with the way you speak with these people because they already have put up barriers in their minds concerning having a Christian telecast in their programming, which they have never had — not even one — in the past."

We had just driven up to the front of the MBC television office building. "Thank you so much, Brother Blackburn, for this information. Let us ask the Lord to give us His wisdom in our appointment with these people," I replied. Thereupon, we prayed together before exiting the car.

WE ARE HINDUS HERE IN MAURITIUS

Indeed, the executive director's first words were, "Don't you know that we are Hindus here in Mauritius?" My reply was, "This telecast really does not have much to do with religion but with a person, Jesus Christ. Everywhere this telecast has been included in the programming of a TV network, it has become the most viewed program of that network. In other words, it becomes the highest rated program of all secular or religious programming. It appeals to all people, no matter what their background is." I then gave them examples of other countries where it had been aired weekly on French-speaking TV networks. After viewing the Jimmy Swaggart telecast French audition VHS tape I brought for the meeting, they were delighted and exclaimed, "This is better production content than anything else we have in our current programs!"

They finished our meeting by agreeing to take the next steps in their programming protocol to pass the audition program to their different departments for approval and then advise us as to the outcome. I told Brother Blackburn upon leaving the MBC headquarters' premises: "I would have preferred a signed contract to begin sending them the telecasts each week for airing, but I guess we have to go through their protocol and trust the Lord for a good outcome."

"This is further than anyone has been able to go in the past toward the airing of a gospel program over the Mauritius Television Network. They would not even give us an appointment before," Brother Blackburn replied energetically.

Early the next morning, Brother Blackburn took me to the airport for the flight I was to take on to Johannesburg, South Africa. After thanking him for all of his kindness while in his beautiful country of Mauritius, I went through the security formalities and boarded the crowded plane.

TAKEOFF WAS SMOOTH AS WE CLIMBED TO 30,000 FEET

As I sat back in an aisle seat, I glanced at the second hand on my watch as the huge jet engines revved up to begin takeoff. I had had the privilege of traveling more than 65,000 air miles every month for Jimmy Swaggart Ministries for several years, and every time before takeoff, I would open my little pocket Bible and read from Psalm 121:

"I will lift up mine eyes unto the hills, from whence cometh my help. My help cometh from the LORD, which made heaven and earth. He will not suffer thy foot to be moved: He that keepeth thee will not slumber. Behold, he that keepeth Israel shall neither slumber nor sleep. The LORD is thy keeper: the LORD is thy shade upon thy right hand. The sun shall not smite thee by day, nor the moon by night. The LORD shall preserve thee from all evil: He shall preserve thy soul. The Lord shall preserve thy going out and coming in from this time forth, and even forevermore."

Then I would pray and sit back and enjoy the ride while reading my Bible or dictating answers to the hundreds of letters we received at the ministry each day. I would carry these letters with me on each trip to answer them while traveling.

The takeoff was smooth as we started the climb to 30,000 feet. Since it was morning, the stewardess began to serve breakfast. Everything seemed to be doing fine until we started leveling out at 30,000 feet, heading west toward the continent of Africa. En route, we were to also fly over Madagascar on the way to Johannesburg.

THE AIRPLANE'S ENGINES HAD STOPPED!

After about one hour into the flight, as I was looking out the side window, all of a sudden, the horizontal level of the blue outline of the Indian Ocean below tipped vertical! The airplane's engines had stopped! We were plummeting nose first toward the earth 30,000 feet below! There was no word over the PA system from the pilot! The plane had lurched up a moment and then turned straight downward.

WE WERE FALLING OUT OF THE SKY

We were falling out of the sky in a straight downward free fall. All the food trays went flying into the air, sending the food splattering onto the ceiling, while at the same time, the ceiling emergency air-mask compartments opened up and dropped down oxygen masks in front of each of us. Passengers began to scream and cry out while grasping onto the arms of their seats or the seats in front of them as we vertically plunged toward the Indian Ocean, dropping out of the sky.

SO, THIS IS THE WAY IT ENDS, LORD?

Strange, I just sat back in my chair, with the seat belt cutting across my mid-section, and pressed my head back against the headrest while glancing out the window on my right. I said calmly, "So, this is the way it ends, Lord?" I thought, "Well, I have trusted you, Lord, this far and if this is the way you've chosen to take me to be with You, I accept it, but there are still so many nations and people that still do not have the gospel of Jesus Christ. Lord, I would like to live awhile longer to try to reach all of them in every nation with the gospel. Please have mercy on us now!"

As we continued on our collision course with earth, the plane seemed to be gaining velocity as the deep blue waters of the Indian Ocean came up closer to us. Still, there was no word from the captain. You could hear the passengers moaning and sobbing; others were screaming out, "I don't want to die!"

The plane continued on its free fall, rushing straight down to meet destiny. I knew now that just seconds separated the passengers and me from sure death to be entombed in the chilly, ice-cold waters of this vast Indian Ocean.

Was this the end?

I had always heard that people with a near-death experience had seen their lives flash before them. All of a sudden, my life did begin to flash before me — it was as though time briefly stood still as the replay of the following chapters of my life flashed through my mind's eye before possible impact ....

"But as it is written, Eye hath not seen, nor ear heard, neither have entered into the heart of man, the things which God hath prepared for them that love him" (I Cor. 2:9).

More about Jesus would I know,
More of His grace to others show;
More of His saving fullness see,
More of His love who died for me.

More, more about Jesus,
More, more about Jesus;
More of His saving fullness see,
More of His love who died for me.

More about Jesus let me learn,
More of His holy will discern;
Spirit of God my teacher be,
Showing the things of Christ to me.

More about Jesus; in His Word,
Holding communion with my Lord;
Hearing His voice in every line,
Making each faithful saying mine.

More about Jesus; on His throne,
Riches in glory all His own;
More of His kingdom's sure increase;
More of His coming, Prince of Peace.

I've a yearning in my heart that cannot be denied,
It's a longing that has never yet been satisfied.
I want the world to know the One who loves them so,
Like a flame burning deep inside.

To be used of God, to sing, to speak, to pray;
To be used of God to show someone the way.
I long so much to feel the touch of His consuming fire;
To be used of God is my desire.

When I think about the shortness of my earthly years,
I remember all the wasted days, the wasted tears.
I long to preach the Word to those who've never heard
Of the One who can dispel all fears.

To be used of God, to sing, to speak, to pray;
To be used of God to show someone the way.
I long so much to feel the touch of His consuming fire;
To be used of God is my desire.

CHAPTER 2

4° 19' 54" S
15° 18' 50" E

6° 22' 0" N
2° 25' 59" E

ONLY GOD

"Wherefore He is able also to save them to the uttermost that come unto God by Him, seeing He ever liveth to make intercession for them."

— Hebrews 7:25

ONLY GOD

AFTER A DAY AND night on the long flight to Africa and after going through all the immigration and customs formalities, I stood in the director's office of Zaire Television (in the country known today as The Democratic Republic of the Congo). It was a very powerful television network that covered that entire country in Africa and several other nations around it.

Inside the office, directors and producers of programming and commercials, technical personnel, and news production crews crowded around my portable, battery-powered TV monitor to watch the one-hour audition videotape of the Jimmy Swaggart French gospel telecast. All of a sudden, a wave of the Holy Spirit swept over the room. I just stood to one side, praising the Lord in my heart as excitement crackled through the small crowd. Certainly God was in this place; I felt His presence!

WOULD YOU PLEASE PRAY FOR
ALL OF US BEFORE YOU LEAVE?

It was very important for Zaire's people — a population of more than 35 million who are mostly Muslims and spiritists — to receive the opportunity to hear the gospel of Jesus Christ over this nationwide television network. Violence and unrest had plagued the north and eastern part of this nation for quite some time now. Famine and lack of food had struck many parts of the country. I had shown the tape over again and again at the director's request. When I had finished the last viewing and was pressing the rewind button on the monitor, to my surprise, I was asked, "Would you please pray for all of us before you leave?" When the director said that, I felt the power of God come over these people who manage one of the most powerful television networks in the entire continent of Africa.

A few weeks later, we received the official governmental document that accepted our program for airing on this television network. It not only covered all of Zaire, but also, either in whole or in part, the surrounding countries of the Congo, Gabon, Central African Republic, Northern Zambia, and Northern Angola. God truly unlocked this formidable door as we stepped through it into these principally Muslim and spiritist populations of Zaire. Only God could unlock this door!

From the very first French Jimmy Swaggart telecast aired nationwide, many people of Zaire gave their hearts to Jesus Christ. The missionaries called to inform us, "Hundreds of letters are pouring into the new JSM outreach office located here in Kinshasa, the capital. So many are coming to the Lord that we need your help. We need to build several new churches across the country and a large evangelistic center in the capital to accommodate these many thousands now coming to the Lord and getting saved." To this request, Brother Swaggart agreed to have JSM fund the projects. Several schools were built that also provided more than 5,000 children with a meal each day. If it had not been for these schools, thousands of children would not otherwise have been able to have an education.

WE ARE FLYING OVER A WAR ZONE
AND COULD BE FIRED UPON

From Kinshasa, the capital of Zaire, I boarded a plane that would take me to Douala, Cameroon, and on to Lagos, Nigeria, where I was to meet with the national TV network of that great country of more than 100 million people. On the way, while flying in the air space of the neighboring Republic of the Congo, the captain's voice came on the plane's PA system, "Please fasten your seat belts. We are flying over a war zone and could be fired upon." Well, that was comforting to know! I had heard of armed conflicts periodically going on between government and rebel factions in the Republic of the Congo and the Central African Republic and Zaire.

All of a sudden, in broad daylight, ground anti-aircraft artillery began firing into the sky. Through the windows we could see the streaking missile tails arching up from the vast carpet of jungle far below. Then, one of these missiles burst not too far from our plane, with the explosion impact in the air space shaking the aircraft's fuselage from one side to the other. Passengers let out shrill screams.

It was strange, but all that came to my mind was:

"Surely he shall deliver thee from the snare of the fowler, and from the noisome pestilence" (Ps. 91:3).

The captain quickly banked the plane a hard left while trying at the same time to gain altitude to be out of range from these missiles. A second missile exploded a little further from us, shaking the plane less than the first one. More shrieks and screams filled the main cabin. As we finally got out of range, the impact of exploding air missiles grew less and less, as did the sound of those blasts.

AN UNSCHEDULED MEETING

As we neared the coast of Nigeria, I noticed that visibility out of the airplane window became almost zero because of a dust storm. As the plane descended into our approach pattern, the pilot came on the speaker system and said, "We will be diverting from our landing location in Nigeria to a different one because of the harmattan dust storm coming off the Sahara Desert." In some countries in West Africa, the heavy amount of dust in the air can severely limit visibility and block the sun for several days, comparable to a heavy fog. The effect caused by the dust and sand stirred by these winds is known as the harmattan haze, which costs airlines millions of dollars in canceled flights each year. Harmattan dust storms can rise to an altitude of 3,000 feet to over 6,000 feet high and can cover entire countries at the same time. They are huge!

6° 22' 0" N | 2° 25' 59" E

DIVERTED LANDING

The plane gained altitude and flew on for another 20 or 30 minutes before descending into an approach landing pattern. Visibility was still very bad. As we lowered down toward a landing strip, I noticed we were flying over some sort of city. To my surprise, right in one of the major traffic circles below was a huge red star in concrete laid out on the ground in the form of a monument. I thought, "This must be a Marxist, communist country."

Missionaries in other parts of West Africa had told me about Benin — the Muslim, Marxist country of West Africa. I had asked them about the possibility of placing the JSM telecast on the national network in Benin, but they just laughed and told me it was impossible because of the political situation. I had attempted many times in the past to acquire a visa into Benin but was always rejected. The country was more than 70 percent Muslim and most of those Muslims practiced voodoo. In fact, the capital of Cotonou was known as the voodoo capital of Africa.

"We will be landing in the capital of Benin in a few moments," the captain announced over the plane's PA system. "But we will have to wait on the ground for clearance to go back to Lagos." As we flew over the city of Cotonou to land at the airport in Benin, I asked God to someday let me come back to this country and contact the television station. In the past, I had tried to get a visa to visit the country but was unsuccessful. How little did I know that my prayer would be answered sooner than I thought.

After waiting in the plane on the landing strip for approximately 45 minutes, we were once again in the air and on our way back toward Lagos, Nigeria. However, when we were over the Lagos International Airport, we were again diverted back to Benin due to low visibility and, after landing, channeled off the plane and into the main terminal. I could sense that Satan did not want the gospel to be aired on the Benin National Television Network. I went off to a corner of the large terminal waiting area to pray and asked God to somehow let me go to the television network headquarters before I had to leave the country.

WE DO NOT ALLOW AMERICANS TO HAVE A VISA

At the terminal, I approached the head of the immigration police and asked, "Would you be able to grant me a visa to spend the night?" The answer was, "No way; we do not allow Americans to have a visa." My request was denied. By this time, the passengers and I had been herded into another waiting room to await clearance for takeoff. Another hour went by.

Walking over to the corner of this large waiting area, I prayed, "Oh, God, you are the only One who can get me to the television station here. Please show me the way for the sake of your Son, the Lord Jesus Christ." I then waited awhile and said in a low voice, "Devil, you may try to keep me for the time being from reaching the more than 100 million people in Nigeria with the gospel, but you will still get a black eye on this trip because I am going to make it to this Marxist, communist TV station in this country of Benin!"

A CHANGE OF HEART

Immediately after that, I went over to the same head police official and asked if he would permit one of his officers to accompany me in a taxi to the television station. He could ensure that I would return for the later flight that evening to leave the country. Unbelievably, he answered, "Yes, I will be more than happy to send one of my officers with you as long as you pay the taxi fare and don't take too long. They may call to reboard in about one hour." I grabbed the portable TV monitor briefcase and, with the police officer, left the terminal. We got into the taxi, which took us right into the central parking area of the Benin government-owned nationwide television network.

FOLLOW ME

Here I was in a Muslim, Marxist, communist, French-speaking country at the national television network offices. I asked the policeman who escorted me if he wanted to go into this huge television office complex, but he shook his head no. Hundreds of people were milling around this huge network office that spread out over an entire block with many different entrances. What was I to do? I saw a small crowd of people at what I thought was one of the main entrances in the middle of the office building. I walked through them and climbed a few steps toward that entrance. All of a sudden, a neatly dressed young man came out of the entrance straight toward me and in very clear English said, "Can I help you? What do you need?"

"I would like to see the director of the television network, please," was my reply.

I handed him my calling card, and he immediately said, "Follow me."

TO MY SURPRISE, IT WAS THE
DIRECTOR GENERAL'S OFFICE!

He took me around the corner, down a hallway, through a patio, and through a door into an office. To my surprise, it was the director general's office! It all happened so fast that I didn't realize I had gone this quickly into the director general's office of Benin television. I sat on a sofa on one side of a large office room, while the young man went over to the desk of what I thought was one of the director's helpers. There was a discussion in French, and then the young man turned around and left the room.

The person sitting behind the desk was, in fact, the director himself, who looked somewhat upset but motioned for me to come over and sit down. I began to talk in English and discovered that the director could speak some English. Knowing that my spoken French was not all that understandable, even though I could read and write in the French language, I asked, "Can we not call back the young man in the suit who was just in here to interpret my English into French so we can make sure we understand the terms of a contract clearly for this telecast I will be presenting to you?"

WE DO NOT EVEN KNOW WHO THAT YOUNG MAN IN THE SUIT WAS

In broken English, the director said, "We do not even know who that young man in the suit is. Let's just continue without him."

My mouth dropped open! Who was that young man in the suit?

I talked with the director at length about the Jimmy Swaggart weekly one-hour telecast and the number of countries in which it was presently airing, including French countries in Africa. After opening the portable, battery-powered TV monitor, I began to show the audition tape of the Jamaica crusade in French. The director said, "Wait a minute." He picked up the phone and called in the director of programming. I rewound the tape and began to play it again, and they both watched with excitement. Again, the director said, "Wait a minute." I pressed the stop button while the director picked up the phone again. This time, I believe it was the technical director who joined us to see the audition tape. We began to watch the tape again.

While Brother Swaggart played the piano and sang, they began to clap in rhythm with the music and smile real big. At that moment, I felt a strong presence of the Holy Spirit flood the office. Evidently they were enjoying every minute of this gospel telecast. If I remember correctly, it was somewhere in the middle of the message that the director said, "Please stop the tape now."

I asked, "What for?"

The director replied, "Because we would like to accept your kind offer. Please start sending us the telecast tapes as soon as possible!"

About this time, the policeman who escorted me to the station headquarters was at the door motioning that we must return to the airport. I thanked the director, and then I said goodbye to all of those people. Before leaving the office, I turned and said to the director, "I would like to thank the young man in the suit who brought me here to your office, but you said no one knows who he is." The director replied, "Right, no one here knows who he is. This is the first time we had ever heard of him. I thought he was with you."

WHO WAS HE?

As I walked out of the office building, I looked intently at all of the people standing around to see if I could spot the young man who had escorted me into the director's office. I could not find him. I climbed back into the taxi, and on the way back to the airport, I wondered who this young man was who had helped get me into the director's office so quickly. Could it have been? Maybe it was!

As I was leaving the airport, I sat back and gasped with amazement. How could it be that a strong Muslim, Marxist, communist, French-speaking country not even on my itinerary be opened for the airing of this gospel telecast in just a matter of minutes? Only God could have included this country on my unscheduled itinerary, given me a police escort to the TV station, had me introduced to the director in this French-speaking country by a young man who spoke perfect English, and had the program accepted for free airtime every week covering the entire country of 8 million souls!

MARXISM-LENINISM ABANDONED

Little did I know that in the weeks that followed when the telecast was aired, there would be a man in a huge palatial office weeping as he, along with the dear people of Benin, listened to Brother Jimmy Swaggart preach the gospel of Jesus Christ for the first time in their lives. Then he bowed his head in the privacy of that office and repeated the sinner's prayer with Brother Swaggart. He gave his heart to Jesus and accepted Him as Saviour and Lord of his life. Yes, the Marxist, communist president of Benin for more than 19 years, Major Mathieu Kérékou, gave his life to Jesus and a few weeks later, stood up before the entire nation and told everyone that he was now a Christian and that he had abandoned Marxism-Leninism. In a matter of a few years, he had constitutional changes made and declared democratic elections. He lost the election in 1991 but was returned to power by the people voting him back into office as a democratically elected president in 1996. He was re-elected again in 2001.

From the airing of the first telecast and for several years to come, our JSM outreach office received thousands of phone calls and letters. Now, more than 50 percent of Benin's entire population is Christian with less than 15 percent Muslim and less than 10 percent of the population practicing voodoo.

Truly the preaching of this gospel of Jesus Christ and Him crucified is powerful to save.

"He is able also to save them to the uttermost that come unto God by Him" (Heb. 7:25).

Truly He is the Lord of the harvest. He wanted more than 8 million people of the small West African country of Benin to hear and see the glorious gospel of the Lord Jesus Christ. The Devil meant it for evil to have me land and be isolated in the airport. However, God turned it for good! Only God can do such! Look to Him alone today and live!

Once my soul was astray from the heavenly way,
I was wretched and vile as could be,
But my Saviour in love, gave me peace from above,
When He reached down His hand for me.

When the Saviour reached down for me,
When He reached down His hand for me,
I was lost and undone, without God or His Son,
When He reached down His hand for me.

I was near to despair when He came to me there,
And He showed me that I could be free,
Then He lifted my feet, gave me gladness complete,
When He reached down His hand for me.

How my heart doth rejoice when I hear His sweet voice,
And the tempest to Him I can flee,
There to lean on His arms, safe secure from all harm,
Since He reached down his hand for me.

CHAPTER 3

34° 54' 4" S
56° 9' 52" W

A NATION JOLTED BY THE GOSPEL

"The people which sat in darkness saw great light; and to them which sat in the region and shadow of death light is sprung up."

— Matthew 4:16

A NATION JOLTED BY THE GOSPEL

34° 54' 4" S | 56° 9' 52" W

URUGUAY

FOR 26 YEARS, URUGUAY had never permitted the airing of a foreign religious program over television. The small country of more than 3 million people consists largely of European ancestry — many of Russian descent. Most have been confessed atheists. Missionaries tried holding outdoor meetings, with just a handful of people showing up, and that was in the midst of much persecution, to the extent of even having stones thrown at them.

I was told that in the past, other Christian telecasts were taken to the television stations in Uruguay but were emphatically rejected. Then it happened. God began to touch different ones in television regarding our inquiry.

The wife of the director of the largest television network in the country happened to be on vacation in the nearby

country of Paraguay and watched the Jimmy Swaggart telecast there in the Spanish language. The Holy Spirit touched
her so that she returned to her native country of Uruguay so
enthused that she told her husband that he must do everything he could to see that the program was aired in Uruguay. He showed little interest in what she was saying, but
she persisted.

MIRACULOUS EVENTS

While I was on a trip to the neighboring country of
Argentina in 1985, I felt led of the Lord to include a stop-
over in Montevideo, capital of Uruguay. I called the network
headquarters and asked for one of the directors. The operator
connected me to a man who was the director in charge of programming. Perfect! (I found out later that this was the same
man whose wife had seen the Jimmy Swaggart Spanish telecast in Paraguay!) Next, I asked in Spanish, "Is it possible to
meet with you today concerning a very excellent opportunity
for your network to air a number one rated weekly program?"

The program director said, "My schedule is full today, but
I can meet with you at lunchtime at the restaurant across the
street from the network's buildings. Would you be available
to do that at about 1 p.m.?"

"Certainly," I said. "I'll be glad to meet you there for lunch.
Thank you so much. Until then."

Arriving first at the restaurant, I was seated at a table near
the middle of the dining room. In a few minutes, a rather

neatly dressed gentleman entered the restaurant and came directly to my table, asking, "Are you Jim Woolsey?"

"Yes, sir," I said. "Thank you for coming. It is such a great privilege to meet you. Please have a seat." After ordering our meals from a waiter, I began explaining that I represented STARCOM Television (the name of our media outreach) and that I had an audition program to show him on the portable monitor in my briefcase. I stated that the program I wished to show him had become the number one rated weekly telecast in many countries of the world. "It is the Jimmy Swaggart telecast," I stated.

WE ARE ATHEISTS

When he heard the name Jimmy Swaggart, he said, "Oh yes, my wife has seen that program over television when she was in Paraguay recently. However, I must tell you that it won't work here; we are atheists. You are really wasting your time." He then proceeded to explain the Russian heritage of most of his countrymen there in Uruguay.

While he was talking, I was praying, "Oh Lord, what would you have me to say that will have this man put the telecast on their network?" All of a sudden, the Holy Spirit impressed upon me what to say:

"Sir, I tell you what. I am convinced that once you put the Jimmy Swaggart gospel telecast on your nationwide network, it will become the most viewed program — the number one rated telecast over all other programs. Why don't you put it on for six weeks, and if it has not become the number one rated program, I will personally return and take it off the air myself."

A MAJOR HURDLE TO SURMOUNT

His eyes got really big, and he said, "Really? You would take it off yourself? Okay, let's do it, but we have one major hurdle to surmount."

"What is that?" I said inquisitively, thinking, "What could it be?"

"Before the program can be authorized for airing, the major hurdle is the television censorship department. This is where all past religious programs have been rejected," he explained.

"Okay, let us go ahead and sign the contract but with the stipulation that this must pass the censorship department to be able to air. In the meantime, I will start sending you the weekly telecast so that there will be no delay in airing once the program is authorized." To this, he agreed and signed the contract.

A few days after returning to the United States, I received a call from this gentleman. Miracle of miracles, the report that came back from the censorship department of this network stated that they had approved the program for airing in Uruguay! They felt it was of such good quality that they gave us the go-ahead to put it on the air — every Saturday from 4 to 5 p.m. About the same time the telecast began airing, a missionary arrived in Uruguay who helped us by opening the ministry outreach office. Later, the missionary told me that this was a major breakthrough for the advancement of the gospel in Uruguay.

OPPOSITION

Hundreds of letters began to pour into the ministry outreach office located in the capital city of Montevideo. What few churches were there began to fill up with people who had come to the Lord as a direct result of the telecast. In fact, new churches had to be established. However, after the program had aired for a little over four weeks, the Uruguayan news media, which was made up mostly of atheist writers, began to print articles of opposition in the leading periodicals and newspapers of the country.

The one magazine that enjoys the greatest circulation in the country printed an article each week, titled by the writer, "Does Faith in God Really Work?" He then began his article by saying, "Does our country really need this Jimmy Swaggart program on our television network? Listen to what he said last week." Then the writer proceeded to print the entire message that Brother Swaggart preached on Uruguayan television. At the end of the article, he merely put a question: "Now, do you believe that this faith in God that Jimmy Swaggart preaches really works?" This was done constantly for several weeks, while other media articles were stating that it was useless to have the Jimmy Swaggart program on the air since no one was watching it.

CHALLENGE

There was no question about it that the number watching the program was in the tens of thousands. The office was being flooded with the letters from people wanting to know more about Jesus as a direct result of the telecast.

The opposition was so great from the news media that the brother asked me, "What should we do? It is possible that they will take the telecast off the air!" I prayed, "Our heavenly Father, you have been so gracious in opening this door to Uruguay over television for the preaching of the gospel of Jesus Christ and providing this ideal time slot in the network's programming on Saturdays. Thank you, Lord, for all of the souls who have been saved so far as a result of this Spirit-anointed telecast. Now, you see that the enemy of our souls is furious and trying to have the gospel taken off the television airwaves. Please fight this battle for us, for we are no match for the enemy, but you are God and there is nothing too difficult for you—to save by a few or by many. There are still so many people lost and in need of the preaching of this true gospel of Jesus Christ and Him crucified that you have Brother Swaggart preaching over television in Uruguay. Please show me what to do. Thank you, Lord. Amen."

No sooner had I finished saying, "Amen," when the Lord showed me what to do.

A SHOWDOWN

"It is time for a showdown with the news media to stop the mouths of the critics once and for all," was my reply to the brethren. They were instructed to make a 90-second announcement to be placed at the end of the telecast. In it, they gave an invitation to all those who wanted the program to remain on Uruguayan television to meet in the central plaza of Montevideo the following Saturday and, as the announcement stated, "Let us just see if there is anyone watching the program."

The atheist news media critics picked up on the announcement and wrote daily in the news ridiculing the idea that someone would show up that coming Saturday in support of the program.

That Saturday, members of the media came early — atheistic writers and critics who filled their columns the previous week with doubts that anyone would even show up in downtown Montevideo in support of this telecast.

But people did show up. When the appointed time arrived, not only did the central plaza fill up with thousands of people, but tens of thousands more stretched out eight blocks long in every direction. They began to march around the central part of the capital shouting, "We believe in God; keep the Jimmy Swaggart telecast on TV." Traffic was lined up for 30 blocks in all directions. The march ended with an open-air service with hundreds of people accepting Christ as their Saviour!

URUGUAY

ENTIRE NATION JOLTED

Our office administrator wrote, "The church, as well as the rest of the Uruguayan society, has been jolted out of its sleep by Brother Swaggart's Spirit-anointed messages. The telecast is being received by all social levels—cultural, religious, and political.

"The audience is rated as having the largest viewership ever on Uruguayan television. A publicity agency communicated to us a few days ago that according to their surveys, the Jimmy Swaggart program has an audience up 74 percent, which is the highest level of viewing audience in the history of the country.

"The secretary–general of the Senate of Uruguay has visited us in our offices to congratulate us on the program and told us that several legislators are watching it.

"Two faculties of the university of our Republic told us that the messages Jimmy Swaggart preaches are being used as official topics of study in the classrooms."

WHAT HAPPENED TO THE NEWS MEDIA SKEPTICS?

And what happened to the news media skeptics? The brethren told us that different periodicals in the country became echoes of the Jimmy Swaggart program. Other newspapers and magazines published favorable articles that referred to the program as having a tremendous and beneficial influence upon the Uruguayan people. Two radio stations and the television news program also commented favorably. Even a popular folkloric group composed a parody about Jimmy Swaggart and how important this telecast was to Uruguayan society.

Our office administrator continued writing, "The result of all of this publicity is that we do not need any further promotion for building a viewing audience since I believe there is not one Uruguayan who doesn't know what the Jimmy Swaggart program is and when they can watch it each week.

"Many people that have come to know Christ through the Jimmy Swaggart telecast have been added to the churches. We have already cooperated in the foundation of two new churches, and another has been founded in the city of Piriapolis, a seaside resort, with people who are being brought to Christ by the program."

COUNTRIES WITHOUT MISSIONARIES

There are many countries around the world where it is not possible to acquire a visa for a resident missionary to work for the Lord, but the dear people of those countries are receiving the gospel of Jesus Christ and Him crucified because of the coverage of SonLife Broadcasting Network. Jimmy Swaggart is their missionary over television. Truly God is unlocking doors and has opened them wide to even the supposed closed nations of the world so that this glorious gospel message of the Lord Jesus Christ may reach every nation before He returns, thus giving everyone access to hear the greatest story ever told.

"This gospel of the kingdom shall be preached in all the world for a witness unto all nations; and then shall the end come" (Mat. 24:14).

Fear not, little flock, from the Cross to the throne,
From death into life He went for His own;
All power in earth, all power above,
Is given to Him for the flock of His love.

Only believe, only believe;
All things are possible, only believe,
Only believe, only believe;
All things are possible, only believe.

Fear not, little flock, He goeth ahead,
Your Shepherd selecteth the path you must tread;
The waters of Marah sweeten for thee,
He drank all the bitter in Gethsemane.

Fear not, little flock, whatever your lot,
He enters all rooms, the doors being shut,
He never forsakes; He never is gone,
So count on His presence in darkness and dawn.

CHAPTER 4

5° 19' 0" N
4° 1' 59" W

GOD'S MIRACLES FOR MUSLIMS

"Every place that the soul of your foot shall tread upon, that have I given unto you."

— *Joshua 1:3*

GOD'S MIRACLES FOR MUSLIMS

IN THE EARLY 1980s, God spoke to Brother Jimmy Swaggart that he should throw the full weight of the ministry God had given him behind the Great Commission of Jesus Christ to go *"into all the world, and preach the gospel to every creature"* (Mk. 16:15).

So vividly do I remember when I had my first business meeting with Brother Swaggart as the newly appointed international ministries director. My family and I had just come from the foreign field where we were missionaries and had firsthand experience of the effectiveness of the Jimmy Swaggart gospel telecast in Spanish. We had the privilege of setting up the Jimmy Swaggart Ministries outreach office there, which saw literally tens of thousands of people come to Christ and channeled into churches. Where there was no church available, we saw churches established for the new believers. I asked him the question concerning this Spirit-filled, Spirit-directed ministry: "What are our goals for the foreign mission's outreach?"

He just made a very simple, to-the-point statement: "Our goal is to take this gospel of the Lord Jesus Christ to every nation on the face of the earth."

After receiving this concise but awesome job description, I was in prayer later that day and asked God concerning the seemingly closed countries of the world—such as Muslim and communist dominated countries—that had not permitted any public proclamation of the gospel among their people. God answered my question emphatically by saying, "I will open the door of each country by using the Jimmy Swaggart telecast as the miraculous tool to open the doors of closed countries around the world so that all nations may hear." God began to do just that.

IT IS IMPOSSIBLE TO AIR A GOSPEL PROGRAM ON THIS IVORY COAST GOVERNMENT-CONTROLLED TV NETWORK

Upon arriving in Abidjan, the capital of Ivory Coast, I was informed quite matter-of-factly: "It is impossible to air a gospel program on this Ivory Coast government-controlled TV network. This West African country is primarily Muslim, with more than 65 percent of the population claiming to be so, and with another 25 percent being comprised of African indigenous religions. Christians only make up a few percent of the entire population," the missionaries advised rather decisively. They continued, "Since the government authorities are made up mostly of Muslims, they do not want any gospel on the government television network. The brethren have tried for the last five years to acquire time, but with no results. The door is closed for airing a gospel program, and besides, we have tried to acquire land on which to build churches and have been denied time after time over many years."

Nevertheless, I asked this group of missionaries and national church executives, "Will you please take me to the Ivory Coast TV headquarters? I believe God can open the door if they can just see one of our French Jimmy Swaggart telecasts." These rather hesitant but dedicated men of God responded in faith, saying, "Let's give it a try and see what God will do."

NO APPOINTMENT

Without an appointment, we went to the Ivory Coast television network offices. I was praying all the way to the offices, "Our heavenly Father, please have mercy upon the people of Ivory Coast and please let not the death of Your only begotten Son, the Lamb of God, be in vain for these dear people. Have someone take us directly to the director of this nationwide network, in Jesus Christ's precious name. Amen." After arriving at the main entrance, the receptionist had us taken directly to the fifth floor of the main building to the TV director's office! On the way, the brethren revealed to me that besides Channel 1 (the national network), there would be a new channel going on the air for just the capital city of Abidjan. They suggested that if we were able to see someone, I might request airtime on that channel (Channel 2).

OH, THAT PROGRAM!

The TV director so graciously received us into his office, and I began to share with him the highlights of the Jimmy Swaggart telecast and its outreach around the world. I felt sure that this man had never heard of the program, but before I could finish my usual introduction, the director asked to view the audition tape. As he watched and listened to the opening songs and Brother Swaggart preaching the gospel in Kingston, Jamaica, translated into the French language, all of a sudden, to the utter astonishment of us all, he blurted out, "Oh, that program!"

I said, "What do you mean, 'that program?'"

"I have just been on a vacation in Canada for three weeks prior to this and had seen the English Jimmy Swaggart telecast on Canadian television," he said. "Even though the programs were in English, and I only understand French, I got up early every morning to see the Jimmy Swaggart telecast because something about that program would grab me right on the inside." (Of course, the missionaries and national pastors with me knew that that something was the Holy Spirit.)

Then it seemed as though the TV director began trying to convince us that our telecast should be on TV in Ivory Coast. While he was talking, one of the national brethren hinted to me, "Ask for the program to be placed on Channel 2 since the nationwide Channel 1 has always been closed to gospel programming."

THE MIRACLE

I asked, "What day of the week do you prefer the program be aired over Ivory Coast television?"

"Well, of course, on Sunday mornings," was his reply.

"At what time slot?" I inquired.

"Between 10:30 a.m. and 11:30 a.m. would be the prime-time slot for this program."

"Would that be on Channel 2?"

"No, it will have to be on Channel 1 so that the whole country of Ivory Coast may see and hear this program in the French language." Then he told us, "We will begin airing the program free of charge as of Dec. 2."

As we thanked the director and left the network head-quarters' offices, we were almost leaping with excitement and joy, shouting, "Glory to God; truly this is a miracle! Thank you, Jesus!"

OUTREACH OFFICE FLOODED
WITH VIEWERS' LETTERS

From the very first telecast, letters from viewers began pouring into the outreach office that the missionaries had set up in Abidjan. So many were coming to the Lord that the missionaries requested help to build new churches, but there was a problem. They could not acquire land from the government.

Later, Brother Swaggart and the crusade team went to Ivory Coast and set up the equipment for a nationwide gospel crusade in the new national stadium in Abidjan. During the stadium crusade meetings held Nov. 6-8, 1987, more than 145,000 attended the services, and 32,500 came forward to be saved. They repeated the sinner's prayer with Brother Swaggart and invited Jesus to come into their hearts and lives.

During the weekend, the president of Ivory Coast (from 1960 to 1993), Félix Houphouët-Boigny, invited Brother and Sister Swaggart, the crusade team members, and the national leaders of the churches to his house. After a very cordial, friendly conversation with Brother Swaggart and the church leaders, President Houphouët-Boigny asked them, "What can I do to help you with your work here in Ivory Coast?"

A GREAT VICTORY

The church leaders whispered in Brother Swaggart's ear, "Ask for permission to acquire land for the building of churches and schools."

Brother Swaggart responded, "Our Ivory Coast brethren have related to me that they need government permission to acquire land for the building of churches and schools. If you could help us in this respect, it would be greatly appreciated."

The president responded without hesitation. "Consider it done! From now on, these church leaders have permission to acquire land where they may build their churches and schools across the country."

Almost in unison, the brethren, along with Brother Swaggart, responded, "Thank you so very much, Mr. President. We greatly appreciate this. May the Lord bless you is our prayer."

While walking out to the vehicle to return to the hotel before the crusade service was to begin that evening, I commented to Brother Swaggart, "For decades the church could not acquire land here in Ivory Coast. Truly, a great victory has been won here today by the Lord granting land for churches and schools!"

"Yes, He has given a great victory. I would like for our ministry to help fund the new churches, evangelistic centers, and schools. Jim, please let me know when they give us the list of projects to consider for funding," and this we did. With the help of the collaborators of Jimmy Swaggart Ministries, many churches, schools, and evangelistic centers were funded and built, not to mention the continued monthly support of the missionaries in Ivory Coast.

Now the statistics show not a few percent of the population to be Christian, but more than 45 percent of the entire Ivory Coast population to be Christian! Instead of Islam claiming 65 percent of the population, less than 25 percent claim to be Muslim, and that number is dwindling. This is a miraculous move of the Holy Spirit upon the hearts and lives of an entire West African country as a result of Brother Swaggart's Spirit-anointed preaching of the gospel of Jesus Christ and Him crucified! This is God's way and God's method of reaching the lost, for which we give Him all the glory, honor, and praise.

"For the preaching of the Cross is to them that perish fool-
ishness; but unto us which are saved it is the power of God
... For after that in the wisdom of God the world by wisdom
knew not God, it pleased God by the foolishness of preach-
ing to save them that believe" (I Cor. 1:18, 21).

Not by might, not by power,
But by my Spirit says the Lord;
Not by might and not by power,
But by my spirit says the Lord.

Sometimes fears can hide your vision,
The loss of purpose chains you down,
You think I've forgotten all you're dreaming of,
But how could I forget the one I love.

And it's not by might, not by power,
But by My spirit says the Lord;
Not by might and not by power,
But by My spirit says the Lord.

I can see your heart is tired,
And your courage has worn thin,
You wonder how long you will have to hang on,
But when My love comes in, you'll be strong again.

And it's not by might, not by power,
But by My spirit says the Lord;
Not by might and not by power,
But by My spirit says the Lord.

These mountains will be removed,
I'll build My temple in you;
And what I've promised shall be done,
These mountains will be removed;
I'll build My temple in you,
And what I've promised shall be done.

And it's not by might, not by power,
But by My spirit says the Lord;
Not by might and not by power,
But by my spirit says the Lord.

CHAPTER 5

14° 45' 52" N
17° 21' 57" W

ANOTHER MIRACLE
FOR MUSLIMS

"And when He (Jesus) was come nigh, even now at the descent of the Mount of Olives, the whole multitude of the disciples began to rejoice and praise God with a loud voice for all the mighty works that they had seen."

— Luke 19:37

ANOTHER MIRACLE FOR MUSLIMS

14° 45' 52" N | 17° 21' 57" W

IT WAS EARLY SUNDAY, Sept. 15, 1985, when I arrived in Dakar, Senegal, West Africa, and met a missionary who was flying in the same morning from the other side of the globe from Vanuatu in the Pacific Ocean. In order to connect on a flight into N'Djamena, Chad, Africa, the next day (Monday morning), we were required to have a one-day layover that particular Sunday in the capital of Senegal, a French-speaking country. This had been planned for several months before because I heard he would be coming through that part of Africa on his return to the United States. So, I invited him to go into Chad with me and then finish his homeward-bound trip, to which he accepted.

EVERYTHING IS CLOSED ON SUNDAYS

All missionaries in Senegal just happened to be on furlough this particular month, so I suggested to this missionary, "The Lord has us here on Sunday for some reason. Why don't we rent a car this morning and try to make contact with someone at Senegal's television network?"

"Are you kidding?" he asked, incredulously. "Everything is closed on Sunday in French-speaking countries. This is a government-run network, and certainly everyone is off work on Sundays. Besides that, I was talking over the phone a few months ago with one of the missionaries who lives in this country, and he stated that the government-run television network does not permit any gospel programming whatsoever, and has never permitted it."

"Well, let's try to find the television network and just drive by to see if the Lord will be good to us and have someone there," I responded.

As we got into the car, he quickly added, "I'm sure it will be a waste of time, with no one there, and they do not permit gospel over television, but it will be good to see the sights anyway."

While driving toward the section of town that had the government buildings, I was praying in my heart, "Oh Lord, please have mercy upon us today and lead us by your Spirit. I am asking you, holy Father, for a miracle. Please open this door here in Senegal for the airing of the gospel over television for these dear people, no matter that it is a Sunday and everything should be closed. In the precious name of Jesus, I ask, giving you all the glory and credit."

We drove past the president's palace and turned right, not knowing where the television network was located. After only a few short blocks, we arrived at a traffic circle that stopped right in front of the Senegalese Television Network.

THE DIRECTOR NEVER COMES ON SUNDAY

After we parked the car, I went up to the armed guards at the front door of this huge radio and television complex and began asking them for information. "Does the director of television ever come to his offices on Sunday?" was my first question.

"No, sir, the director of Senegalese television has never come to these offices on Sunday during the last 12 years that I have been here."

My next question was, "Do you have a telephone number for the director general's office?"

"No, it will not be possible for you to see anyone today since it is Sunday," he responded, somewhat tight-lipped and seemingly fed up with my questions. "It would be best that you come back tomorrow when everyone has returned to work."

As I was about to respond to the guard's last statement and explain that we would be leaving on a flight early in the morning and would not be able to return, a car drove up and parked in the director's parking space in front of the network offices.

THEIR MOUTHS DROPPED OPEN

"Who is that driving up to park now?"

The guards turned around and looked, their mouths dropped open, and they exclaimed, "This is the director general of all Senegalese communications. He never comes to the offices on Sunday."

Quickly I ran over and greeted the director as he closed the door of his car. "May we see you in your office for a few minutes?"

He graciously responded, "Sure, please follow me."

As we followed him into the television building complex, past the same guards that denied us any information before, we looked at each other with reaffirming glances. It was a miracle that we had found the television network that quickly, and it was a miracle that the director of communications for all of Senegal would be at his office on Sunday!

Inside the network headquarters, the director met an assistant and asked him to take the missionary and me to another office until he was ready to see us. I asked the missionary, "Please do not let the assistant or the director go until I can return with an audition tape."

I dashed back to the hotel, picked up the audition tape and my portable battery-powered TV monitor, and rushed back to the television headquarters. Just as I found my friend inside the massive office building, the assistant asked us to follow him into the director's office.

THE ELECTRICITY WENT OUT

Suddenly, as we were going toward the office, all of the electricity in the building—actually, in the entire city of Dakar—went out! But the director still received us into his office, and we sat down and began to talk about the Jimmy Swaggart French telecast.

The director, dressed in his Muslim garb, began to apologize for not being able to view the audition tape. I opened the brief-case containing the small battery-powered television monitor and tape player and assured him that it would be no problem, that he could still see the tape. As I punched the button to begin the pro-gram, he seemed relieved and delighted as he watched Brother Swaggart play the piano and sing in the Jamaican crusade service.

During the music portion of the program at a change between songs, I commented to him how the telecast was air-ing in more than 80 countries of the world at that time, with an estimated 86 million viewers watching the program each week.

WHERE DOES THE PROGRAM AIR IN WEST AFRICA?

When Brother Swaggart was about to finish his message, the director turned to us and asked, "Where has the French Jimmy Swaggart telecast aired first in West Africa?"

I said, "The first French program will be airing in Abidjan, Ivory Coast, on Dec. 2." Then I hurriedly added, "But if you want to be first in West Africa to air the program in French, you will have to give us an air date before Dec. 2."

FIRST TO AIR THE JIMMY SWAGGART TELECAST

The director said, "We will begin airing the Jimmy Swag-gart telecast on Nov. 17. We will be the first to air the Jimmy Swaggart telecast in West Africa!"

This, of course, meant that he had accepted the program. Another miracle had just occurred!

The director and his assistant went on to explain, "The Senegalese Television Network not only covers all of Senegal, but it reaches into Mauritania (which does not have a television network of its own), Mali, all of Gambia, Guinea-Bissau, the Cape Verde Islands, and a small portion of Guinea."

In closing, the director turned to his assistant and added, "We will air this important telecast free of charge!"

As the missionary and I left the director's office, a wave of the Holy Spirit flowed over us as we began to praise the Lord. Truly God had performed His miracles of unlocking the doors of these Muslim countries in West Africa, enabling access to a total of more than 22 million Muslim viewers to hear the glorious gospel of the Lord Jesus Christ! God had just performed the impossible! All the glory is His. What a merciful God.

"So shall they fear the name of the LORD from the west, and His glory from the rising of the sun. When the enemy shall come in like a flood, the Spirit of the LORD shall lift up a standard against him" (Isa. 59:19).

Sing them over again to me,
Wonderful words of life.
Let me more of their beauty see,
Wonderful words of life.
Words of life and beauty,
Teach me faith and duty,

Beautiful words, wonderful words,
Wonderful words of life.
Beautiful words, wonderful words,
Wonderful words of life.

Christ the blessed One gives to all,
Wonderful words of life.
Sinner, listen to the loving call,
Wonderful words of life.
All so freely given,
Wooing us to heaven,

Beautiful words, wonderful words,
Wonderful words of life.
Beautiful words, wonderful words,
Wonderful words of life.

29° 39' 8" N
91° 10' 19" E

THE FORBIDDEN CITY

"How then shall they call on Him in whom they have not believed? and how shall they believe in Him of whom they have not heard? and how shall they hear without a preacher?"

— Romans 10:14

THE FORBIDDEN CITY

29° 39' 8" N | 91° 10' 19" E

"IT WILL BE IMPOSSIBLE to air the telecast behind the Bamboo Curtain. But at least you will be able to see the conditions existing today in this closed country." These were the words I heard in a city of the Far East after being asked why I was going on this trip into Tibet, which was now under Communist China rule. However, God would not let this trip be in vain.

THE NEXT DAY

Here I was, behind the Bamboo Curtain, in a city located in the very heart of a country that is said to contain almost a quarter of the world's population. This city of Chengdu in southwest China is the jumping-off point into the Forbidden City — Lhasa, Tibet. The next day, I would be taking an early flight to the "Roof of the World." However, this particular afternoon, I had to go by myself to the airline office in the center of the city to reconfirm the air tickets to Lhasa and back to Beijing.

As I entered this airline office, I was directed to a room in the back. Inside the room, I noticed a line of people waiting. Among them was a Tibetan couple, the first I had ever seen. There they stood, dressed in their full Tibetan garb made of thick leather and heavily lined with fur. They turned around and gave me a quick smile as I walked by them to ask a man at the counter if this was the right line for confirming my flight out the following day.

After completing the flight confirmation, I found the Tibetans next to a large garage door outside. I went up to them and made motions, asking them if they had a cassette player. They smiled real big and nodded yes, so I handed them a Jimmy Swaggart music cassette. They were so pleased to receive it. I then quickly pulled out of my back pocket a portion of the Scriptures in Tibetan and opened it in front of them. The man reached over my shoulder, grabbed the portion, and began reading it intently.

About that time, the taxi driver that had been waiting for me down the street came up and tapped me on the shoulder and motioned that we should go as soon as possible. "There is a guard telling me that I can no longer park where I am," he said. "You can understand that in a city of over 8 million people, parking is at a premium."

"Alright, I'll follow you back to your taxi," I replied hastily.

As I walked away, following the driver, I turned around to see the man with the Scriptures in his hand look up and smile big at me as if to say "thank you" for the music cassette and the Tibetan portion of Scripture.

Before the taxi sped away down the crowded street, I looked back to the Tibetan couple. They were huddled around the portion of Scriptures, with the man reading aloud to the woman. Several people were standing around them, listening to the Word being read.

FLIGHT INTO THE FORBIDDEN CITY

At 4:30 a.m., a taxi took me to the airport. Upon arriving, everything looked dark and locked up. Many people were waiting for the door of the terminal to be opened. I looked for the couple to whom I had given the music cassette and the Scripture portion the previous day but could not see them.

After going through the normal processing in the terminal, we passengers found ourselves in a large crowded waiting room before boarding the plane. There they were, the Tibetan couple I had met the day before! I waved hello to them. When they looked up and recognized me, they smiled and waved back.

I moved down as close as I could get to them, which was about four benches away. As I sat there, the couple kept turning around and looking at us, whereupon the man suddenly took out the portion of yellow Tibetan Scripture and waved it and smiled, giving a nod that meant "thank you." Evidently, something had happened in their lives as a result of this portion of Scripture and the music cassette.

They finally called for our flight to be boarded. We all rushed toward the door to make the long walk out to the runway, for this was the way planes were boarded in those days. As I boarded and found our seats toward the front of the plane, I felt a tap on my shoulder. I turned around to see the Tibetan couple standing behind me in the aisle, smiling real big.

TIBETAN BELIEVES IN CHRIST

The man first pointed to his heart, then to the portion of Scripture in his pocket, then up to heaven, and then he said something in the Tibetan language. There was no doubt about it, he said, "I believe." I smiled back and pointed up to God in heaven and also said, "You believe," pointing to his heart. He nodded in the affirmative. Then they went on back in the crowded plane and sat down.

As the plane took off, I thought to myself, "Could this Tibetan man and woman who now believe in Jesus as a result of that portion of Scripture be the first believers anyone knows of in Tibet in the 1980s?" (Later, back in Hong Kong, I asked a missionary that same question, and he said it could very well be true that the Tibetan and his wife were the first believers ever heard of in Tibet in the 1980s.) Even if we would not be able to air the telecast there, the trip was worthwhile just to have seen this man and wife pointed toward the Lord Jesus Christ.

After about a two-and-a-half hour flight over the highest mountain range in the world — the Himalayas—a bus took us all into the Forbidden City. I noticed a straight-looking stick jutting up into the sky on many of the dwellings with a funny-looking aluminum X on each stick. I was told that these were TV antennas.

THE TV STATION

I arrived at the airline office in town and immediately went to confirm my return flight the next day. I was told there was no way to get back to the airport the next day, and that those of us returning only had four hours before we had to reboard the bus to go to the airport where we would spend the night in order to leave on the return flight. I was shocked. I only had four hours to find the television station and show the audition tape!

Since there is no such thing as a taxi in Lhasa, I had to carry my luggage down the hot, dusty streets at this 12,000-foot elevation. After walking more than a mile, there was not a TV station in sight. A small tourist bus was stopped on the side of the road, and I asked the guide, "Do you know where the TV station is located?"

He answered, "Hop in. We will take you within half a mile of the TV station compound."

I was dropped off and then had to hike across a small valley to where the TV station was located up on a rather tall hill. To make matters worse, it was already 1 p.m., and everything in town shut down from 12:30 to 3:30 p.m. for lunch with nothing open for business. In addition, I had no appointment. I finally found the TV compound gate entrance and a gatekeeper who could not understand what I wanted.

Once inside, I was taken from one small room to another, looking for the manager. Finally, the gatekeeper gave up and was taking me back outside. I just sat down at the gate and decided to wait for someone to help, while praying all the time in my heart, "Oh merciful Father, please have mercy on the people of Tibet. You see my time is short. Please send someone to help me and take me to the television manager. Thank you Lord, in Jesus Christ's name. Amen."

All of a sudden, a nice automobile drove up to the front gate, and a well-dressed, young Chinese man got out of the car and came up and asked, "What is it that you want here?"

"I would like to see the manager of the TV station."

He said, "Get in and I will take you to him."

He drove me right on up the hill to the manager's house, which was located in the television station compound.

"Thank you so much. You have helped considerably," were my parting words to him, whereupon the young man left, and I never saw him again.

As I sat down, I realized that the manager could not understand a word of English I spoke. So, the director called in his assistant, who could understand only a few words of English. Through much difficulty, I was able to make them understand that I had an audition tape for them to view. It was not possible to bring the portable battery-powered monitor with me on this trip because of their government restrictions at the time. They said, yes, they could view the tape. "But there will be no sound."

FIRST GOSPEL TELECAST

The TV station manager motioned for me to follow him. We left his house and went toward another building that the assistant said was for the center of operations of the TV network.

Once inside the television station's small operation's building, the audition tape was placed on their monitor. Several machines began to crank up, and the program could be seen — and heard — on the small TV set. We could hear the music and the message! The message Brother Swaggart preached was in the Chinese language, a program I had picked up from our Taiwan Chinese program that already aired there.

As these kind gentlemen viewed the program, they became more and more excited. I tried to communicate that we would be happy to provide these programs free for them to air. The manager left to make a phone call in the next room, after which he returned.

I began to write the points of the agreement that would have to be made for us to send the tapes.

First, I asked them, "What day, Saturday or Sunday, would you like to air this program?"

As the assistant read this question, the answer from the manager was, "Nightly."

"You mean Saturday night or Sunday night?"

He said, "Each and every night."

I wrote down, "What time?"

"Eight o'clock every night," he said.

"Monday through Friday?"

He said, "Monday through Friday. And Saturday and Sunday."

I wrote all of this on an agreement to leave with them, and the would-be interpreter finally understood all that I was trying to tell him.

I was curious and asked, "How is it that we could hear the sound as well as see the picture on the audition tape? Before we came, you said, 'See picture but no sound.'"

"Because," the assistant said, "we decide with phone call approval to transmit the program live at the same time over the television network's transmitting tower so people in their homes all over country can see at same time."

Just think, this was the first transmission of the gospel over television in this forsaken, forbidden land on top of the world!

As we finished and shook hands, I asked, "Where is the well-dressed young man who brought me to your house in that nice new automobile?"

"Young man?" the assistant asked. "My driver is not a young man. He is a very elderly gentleman. He has been with me many years. What young man are you referring to? All of us that work here are older gentlemen. There are no young men that work up here. Please let my driver take you back down the mountain to the gate."

Whereupon, I entered the same automobile that had taken me to the manager's house, but this driver was an elderly gentleman. I then realized what had happened — God had provided a man to direct me to the television network's manager.

But who was that man, and from where did he come? Was he a man or could it have been an ...?

As I left the TV network compound's main gate down the hill and made it back to the bus just in time to return to the airport at 4 p.m., I realized that God had performed a great miracle that day. He had done the impossible so that tens of thousands of dear people in this forgotten corner of the world could hear this glorious message of Jesus Christ that changes lives.

"For whosoever shall call upon the name of the Lord shall be saved" (Rom. 10:13). ★

He is Lord, He is Lord!
He is risen from the dead,
And He is Lord!

Every knee shall bow,
Every tongue confess,
That Jesus Christ is Lord!

CHAPTER 7

55° 45' 20" N
37° 37' 2" E

A ONE-WAY
TICKET TO SIBERIA

"The LORD has made bare his holy arm in the eyes of all the nations; and all the ends of the earth shall see the salvation of our God."

— Isaiah 52:10

CHAPTER SEVEN

A ONE-WAY TICKET TO SIBERIA

55° 45' 20" N | 37° 37' 2" E

HERE I WAS, SIX miles above the Pacific Ocean, flying home after an unexpected itinerary that was improvised by God alone. It had been only eight days since I kissed my wife good-bye at the Baton Rouge airport, and now I had to turn around in one day and fly out again.

We were both a little uneasy about the terrorist situation in Europe and the Mediterranean area at that time since this trip would take me through Europe on my way to Russia. Somehow things seemed a little bit different.

A MISSING TICKET

The flight over the Atlantic Ocean was uneventful, as was the connection at the airport in Frankfurt, Germany. After that point, however, unexpected things began to happen.

Upon examining my flight tickets as I was going into Moscow, I realized something was missing. The travel agency had overlooked the round-trip ticket from Moscow to the Russian satellite country of Mongolia that I planned on visiting in order to make contact with the television station there.

RUSSIA

Naturally, I was quite perplexed that the main portion of the ticket for this trip was left out. I immediately went to the Russian Airlines service desk and asked, "May I purchase a ticket to Ulan Bator, Mongolia?"

The airline agent responded with, "We are not able to sell you a ticket until you have the proper visa. You can acquire one at the Mongolia embassy."

After a fast taxi ride through downtown Moscow, the embassy told me that I was at the wrong place to receive such a visa and would have to go to their consulate, which was located near the Russian TASS News Center.

Once there, the consulate official in charge of visas stated, "It will be impossible to issue you a visa. You have not gone through the proper channels. However, I can issue you a transit visa if you do not spend the night in our country."

"Anything will do," I said. "Please give me the transit visa."

HERE IS YOUR ONE-WAY TICKET TO SIBERIA

I returned to the airline service desk with the transit visa. Upon presenting it, I was told by a clerk, "Here is your one-way ticket to Siberia. From there you can go to your destination."

I hurriedly pleaded, "But isn't there some way I can purchase a round-trip ticket that will get me back to Moscow?"

The airline agent stated emphatically, "No. There is no way we can sell you a round-trip ticket."

I said, "Lord, maybe I should wait to make this trip until everything is just right regarding a visa and airline tickets."

All of a sudden, the Spirit of God spoke, "Circumstances will never be just right in this world to do the will of God. It's either go now with this one-way ticket or not at all."

I was so stunned by the quick answer from the Lord that I turned around quickly and asked the airline agent if I could purchase the return air ticket once I arrived at my destination. The agent assured me that I could (which later proved to be so untrue).

Here I was, getting ready to board the Aeroflot plane with a one-way ticket to Siberia and then on to the Soviet satellite country of Mongolia, with a visa that would not permit me to spend any time in that country once I arrived there.

But the Scripture verse that came to my heart was this:

"All things work together for good to them that love God, to them who are the called according to His purpose" (Rom. 8:28).

I thought, "God, You will have to get me to that Mongolian television network because from all outward appearances, there is no possible way that I will be permitted to reach it."

The flight lasted all afternoon and night, and after landing in Siberia to refuel, the airplane finally reached the capital of

Mongolia where God had directed me. As we came down on our approach for landing, I could see the tops of the mountains covered with snow. What a desolate, forlorn place!

After landing, we went through visa and customs formalities, and somehow, the immigration official stamped the transit visa, which permitted me to get into the country.

The old taxi pierced through the stinging, sandy wind, and we crept down the road leading to the capital and rounded a corner. There before us was a city of more than 400,000 people who are virtually 100 percent Buddhist in name and communist in political alignment. The visibility was hampered by the dust storm that had come up after we landed, but I could make out at one end of town a huge television transmitting tower. "Please, O God, show me some way I can get to that television network with the audition tapes of the Russian Jimmy Swaggart telecast."

PROBLEMS

The taxi took me to the only hotel in town. It was, of course, government owned. I found the manager and asked him if there was a room available for me. He looked surprised because his guests usually had made arrangements through the proper government channels long before their arrival and were already pre-registered.

He said, "Give me your passport."

I quickly pulled out my passport and handed it to him. When he saw the transit visa, he said, "There is something irregular about your being here. How did you get this visa?"

"The consulate in Moscow issued it, but I would certainly like a room please," I explained.

He checked with the front desk, came back, and said, "We have a room for you, which includes meals. A government guide with a car will tour you each day you are here. However, we will have to check with our Foreign Ministry office to see if you will be allowed to stay in our country."

I asked if I could purchase a return ticket to Moscow for that coming Saturday. After about an hour, word came that they could not sell me a return airplane ticket and that I would have to leave on a train to Beijing, China, Friday at noon.

It was Wednesday afternoon, and I still had to go to the Chinese consulate to get a visa for this unexpected trip, go to the Foreign Ministry office to work out the formalities to be able to stay until Friday, try to make reservations for the flight home, and somehow get to the television station.

When the government guide showed up to take me on a so-called city tour, he asked where I wanted to go. (I found out later that the "guide" was really their KGB agent who was to keep track of me and get information out of me.) I explained that I needed to get a visa for China, regularize the transit visa I was now holding, and purchase a train ticket to be able to leave Friday at noon as I was instructed.

The "tour" turned out to be several trips to the Chinese consulate, a trip to the Foreign Ministry office, several consultations with the government travel bureau in an attempt to acquire a train ticket, and placing a long-distance telephone call from this far end of the earth to the Jimmy Swaggart Ministries headquarters in Baton Rogue, Louisiana, to arrange for picking up the flight tickets in Beijing for the return trip home.

I kept hinting to the guide as we went from one office to another that I would like to see their television station. The answer was always, "We will give the director a call to see if it will be possible to set up an appointment for tomorrow morning before you leave on the train."

THE TV STATION

The last day of my stay in the country, I was eating breakfast when the government guide came up to me and said, "I've just received a call from the television station, and it will be impossible for you to meet with them before you leave. In fact, they do not even want to see you."

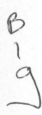

I looked the guide straight in the eye and stated, "I've not traveled halfway around the world just to hear that I can't go to the television station here. I'll go, even if I have to walk across town to get to the gate of that TV station and talk to someone!" I got up from the table and started toward the door that led outside into the street. The stunned government agent turned around and said, "Wait a minute," and left.

In 10 minutes, the answer came back that I could meet someone at the gate of the TV station and give him the audition tape. The guide warned, "The gate is heavily guarded with military personnel. So, there is no way you can go through the gate at all! It is locked. It is bitterly cold out there so put your warm overcoat on."

But, amazingly, after driving up the hillside to the front gate, a nicely dressed young man in a suit and tie came out from behind the side guardhouse, unlocked the gate, and opened it. There were no military guards anywhere to be seen. We drove right into the television station compound!

The program director met me at the bottom of the steps to the main door where our car had stopped. After entering his office, he became very excited about the program when I explained that it was in the Russian language. He viewed one of the programs. He was very gracious and asked, "How may we receive these great programs?"

Through his interpreter, I explained in Russian the way he could receive the Jimmy Swaggart Russian telecast tapes free of charge. I handed him the contract that had been translated into Russian.

He accepted both the audition tapes and the contract, and I was told that there would be no problem in our sending them the telecast tapes in the Russian language on a regular basis. He wrote down the physical address of the network headquarters and told me how they should be sent.

After thanking him for his kindness, I asked, "Where is the young gentleman dressed in a suit and tie who opened the gate for us?"

"What young gentleman in the suit? He would really need to be all bundled up in a heavy coat to be out in that cold weather. And besides, the whole compound is guarded by military personnel with machine guns."

"But we did not see any soldiers anywhere when we drove up to the gate, only this young man who unlocked the gate and let us drive through."

"Impossible," he responded adamantly. "This compound is guarded 24 hours a day by soldiers of the national army. No one except television personnel is to come and go from this television compound. You have been the only exception to this rule."

All I could think about the rest of that day was how the lock on the gate of that television station was unlocked by a man dressed in a suit and tie in such freezing cold, and the gate was opened for us to go through. I went into the television station where they said it would be impossible to gain access. Again, the only explanation was God!

"The Lord is not slack concerning his promise, as some men count slackness; but is longsuffering to us-ward, not willing that any should perish, but that all should come to repentance" (II Pet. 3:9).

Just as I am, without one plea,
But that Thy blood was shed for me,
And that Thou bidst me come to Thee,
O Lamb of God, I come, I come.

Just as I am, and waiting not
To rid my soul of one dark blot,
To Thee whose blood can cleanse each spot,
O Lamb of God, I come, I come.

Just as I am, though tossed about
With many a conflict, many a doubt,
Fightings and fears within, without,
O Lamb of God, I come, I come.

Just as I am, poor, wretched, blind;
Sight, riches, healing of the mind,
Yea, all I need in Thee to find,
O Lamb of God, I come, I come.

Just as I am, Thou wilt receive,
Wilt welcome, pardon, cleanse, relieve;
Because Thy promise I believe,
O Lamb of God, I come, I come.

Just as I am, Thy love unknown
Hath broken every barrier down;
Now, to be Thine, yea, Thine alone,
O Lamb of God, I come, I come.

CHAPTER 8

55° 45' 20" N
37° 37' 2" E

THE GOBI DESERT

"For then will I turn to the people
a pure language, that they may all
call upon the name of the LORD,
to serve Him with one consent."

— Zephaniah 3:9

THE GOBI DESERT

55° 45' 20" N | 37° 37' 2" E

AFTER SOME HOURS ON the train to Beijing, the sand dunes and the barrenness of the Gobi Desert became a monotonous view outside the window. I thanked the Lord for what He had just accomplished in unlocking this communist, Buddhist country of Mongolia for the airing of the Jimmy Swaggart gospel telecast. I kept rehearsing in my mind the events and problems of the preceding days. "Lord, why was it so difficult, and why were there so many problems?" Well, there was no answer, so I spent the next several hours wondering as the train continued its clickity-clack sound onward toward Beijing.

All of a sudden, somewhere in Inner Mongolia, the train stopped. Immigration officials got on the train and took our passports and said, "You will have to stay in the train station for three hours before you may proceed on your journey to Beijing."

Inside the train station, we were all seated together to await the reboarding of the train in three hours. I took a seat on a bench toward the back wall of the makeshift train terminal. A fellow who looked like a government agent came walking around among us. When he approached me, I asked him, "What is the name of your fine city here?"

He replied in broken English, "This is the capital of Inner Mongolia, Hohhot."

"Do you have a television station here?"

"Why yes, we do," he graciously replied. "It is a very powerful network that covers all 20 million people in our country of Inner Mongolia."

I thanked him for the information, and he continued on his rounds.

FINDING THE INNER MONGOLIAN TV STATION

After awhile, I looked around and told a fellow passenger that I was going out the back door and try to find the television station here in the city and would be back by the time our three-hour wait was up and we were supposed to leave.

Since there were no taxis, I hurriedly took off walking down one of the sandy streets of the city. I went into a café on one corner and asked in English if they knew where the television station was. Of course, they could not understand me.

As I turned around and went outside, I saw a small sign that had a TV set on it. Pointing to it, I asked a woman in the café, "Where is the TV station?" She pointed up to a window in the building next door.

I went into that building, knocked on the window, and a man's face appeared, smiling really big. He motioned for me to come around to the door. As I walked into this room, I realized that it was a TV repairman's shop. I made motions portraying a large transmitting tower and tried to convey that I would like him to take me there. Finally, he understood and put everyone out of his shop, locked the door, and asked me to follow him.

All of a sudden, a very fierce sandstorm came up. We had to walk directly in the face of this strong, gritty wind. After about five long blocks of this torturous walk, the sandstorm seemed to become stronger. Finally, we rounded a corner on the edge of town, and there to my amazement was the television station with a transmitting tower standing beside it that was approximately 26 stories high. The TV repairman bade me good-bye, while pointing to the television station door.

I walked inside, and the director of the station, a Chinese man, met me and called in 10 more people whom I assumed were program directors, technical directors, and station help. Fortunately, I had grabbed the right piece of carry-on baggage when I left the train because this small briefcase contained the audition tape and a script I had had translated beforehand into the Chinese language explaining the telecast and our offer.

COMMUNICATING IN CHINESE

"Do you have a television monitor in which we could view this Chinese telecast?" I asked. Each of the 10 assistants he brought in knew a little bit of English that each of the others did not know. So, among them all, they were able to communicate my question to the director.

He said, "Oh yes, we can do it right now," and inserted the cassette tape into a large machine that had a television monitor on it there in the control room of the television network. As they watched Brother Swaggart preaching in Chinese, they remarked again and again in broken English, "Very good, very good!"

Finally he asked, through his 10 technicians, "How can we receive this good Chinese telecast to air on our Inner Mongolian network?"

I handed this kind gentleman the Chinese script, and he began to read it out loud to everyone present. I gave him another program tape, and when he came to the paragraph in the script stating that we would supply his station with free weekly and daily program tapes, he became elated. I asked him to give me the address where we should send the tapes, whereupon he kindly wrote in Chinese characters the complete address for the shipping of the tapes to the station.

We continued awhile over some of the details of our agreement and the appropriate size of the tapes we should send, after which he thanked me. As I walked out of the station, we waved good-bye. As I rushed back to the train station, I noticed that the dust storm that met me on the way had died down. I couldn't help but think that the enemy of men's souls did not want me to reach this station with the glorious gospel message that rescues people from the kingdom of darkness.

WHAT GOD WANTED

Once onboard the train again, my passport was handed back to me, and the train lurched forward on its slow three-day and three-night journey to Beijing. As we pulled out on the edge of that city, I could see hundreds of television antennas dotting the horizon, all rising from the tops of the dwellings in this Gobi Desert city. At one end, there was this giant, 26-story television antenna jutting up from the floor of the Gobi Desert.

As I looked out the train window at this lonely, desolate spot, I knew why there were so many problems on this particular trip and why there was no return ticket to Moscow and home. God wanted the message of His dear Son, Jesus Christ, to reach these people in Inner Mongolia. I probably would never have gone to this TV station because it is not even listed as existing, plus there is no airplane service.

THE LAST THRUST

God has used Jimmy Swaggart Ministries as no other ministry in the history of the Christian church to spearhead the last intensive gospel evangelism thrust of this age of grace. Doors of nations that have been locked and closed to the gospel for so many centuries were miraculously opened to the airing of this Spirit-anointed ministry, and now, by the worldwide outreach of SonLife Broadcasting Network, which proclaims the Message of the Cross of Jesus Christ 24 hours a day, seven days a week. The coverage from the many cable television systems, satellite systems, over-the-air TV stations, and the Internet now enables more than 2.5 billion people to hear about Jesus if they are anywhere near a television set, computer, or electronic device anywhere in the world.

The amazing thing is that even on the backside of the Gobi Desert in Inner Mongolia in the uttermost parts of the earth, there are thousands upon thousands of television sets tuning into the airwaves.

Truly John was right when he said:

"For God so loved the world, that He gave His only begotten Son, that whosoever believeth in Him should not perish, but have everlasting life" (Jn. 3:16).

What a wonderful, wonderful Saviour,
Who would die on the Cross for me!
Freely shedding His precious lifeblood,
That the sinner might be made free.

He was nailed to the Cross for me,
He was nailed to the Cross for me;
On the Cross crucified for me He died;

He was nailed to the Cross for me.

Thus He left His heavenly glory,
To accomplish His Father's plan;
He was born of the Virgin Mary,
Took upon Him the form of man.

He was wounded for our transgressions,
And He carried our sorrows, too;
He's the healer of ev'ry sickness,
This He came to the world to do.

So He gave His life for others
In redeeming this world from sin,
And He's gone to prepare a mansion,
That at last we may enter in.

0° 23' 24" N
9° 27' 15" E

ALL THE GLORY IS MINE

"I am the LORD: that is My name: and My glory will I not give to another."

— Isaiah 42:8

CHAPTER NINE

ALL THE GLORY IS MINE

0° 23' 24" N | 9° 27' 15" E

IT WAS A RATHER long trip on four different airplanes.
I had seen two sunsets and was finally arriving in Gabon, a
small Central African country tucked away on the west coast
of the African continent. This beautiful country of just under
1.5 million people has a powerful radio and television network. In fact, Africa One is a radio station known to have the
most powerful signal in that part of the world. The television
network also broadcasts a powerful signal over the Republic
of Gabon in the French language.

A missionary in a neighboring country had contacted me
some months prior to this particular trip and stated that he
would be able to arrange a meeting with a pastor who knew
the people at the television network. Therefore, I left all of
the arrangements up to him. That way, I would not have to
worry about the appointment, lodging, or ground transportation while in the country. I thanked the Lord that for once I
wouldn't have to sweat out the unknown. Was I ever mistaken!

THE LIBREVILLE AIRPORT

Upon arrival in the hot, stuffy Libreville airport, I began to look for the missionary. After some rather long formalities going through customs and immigration, I went out through the airport's waiting lobby and on to the parking lot. There was no missionary! After waiting another 30 minutes, I decided there was no one to meet me. I rented a car and found the nearest hotel.

Here I was in a French-speaking country where I had never been before without any contact to tell me what to do or where to go. I began to ask God, "Why?"

Then I called the missionary. He told me, "I am so sorry. When I arrived at the Libreville airport, the immigration officers discovered that I did not have the proper visa to enter Gabon. Therefore, I will not be able to be with you on this trip."

I asked him, "What is the name and telephone number of the Gabonese pastor you said we would meet here and would have the appointment set up for us at the TV network?"

With disappointment in his voice, the missionary told me, "I am so sorry, but the dear brother is out of town and, therefore, will not be able to take you to the television network."

By now it was about 10:30 p.m., and I went out to jog and pray. As I was jogging slowly down a main street that ran along the coastline of Gabon, I began to ask the Lord some questions.

WHY SO MANY DIFFICULTIES?

"My gracious heavenly Father, I know it is Your will that this Jimmy Swaggart gospel telecast be on every television network in the world. It is Your will to save to the uttermost. Your Word says that You are *'longsuffering to us-ward, not willing that any should perish, but that all should come to repentance'* (II Pet. 3:9). It is Your will, Lord, but why are there so many difficulties?"

There seemed to be no answers from the Lord until later that night. While in prayer before going to sleep, the Holy Spirit recalled a verse of Scripture to my remembrance:

"You shall not need to fight in this battle: set yourselves, stand you still, and see the salvation of the LORD with you, O Judah and Jerusalem: fear not, nor be dismayed; tomorrow go out against them: for the LORD will be with you" (II Chron. 20:17).

THE GABONESE TELEVISION NETWORK

Early the next morning, I went to the television network headquarters in this capital city of the country and began asking the people at the front gate how I might get in to see the director. I was finally led to the director's office (even though they could not understand why I wanted to see him) by a very gracious man, who called for a young man in another part of the complex to be present in our meeting.

As I showed them the French Jimmy Swaggart audition tape, they began to show excitement. After explaining that we would be willing to send them the program for airing each week, the kind gentleman was more than delighted and said, "We would like to air the program as soon as possible. However, you will need to go see the Minister of Information of the Gabonese government to get his approval." He called and made an appointment for me and told me how to get there by 11 o'clock.

THE CENTRAL MOSQUE

As I drove over to the president's palace and the large office building complex that housed the different ministries (branches) of the Gabonese government, to my surprise, there was a huge Muslim mosque directly in front of these government buildings.

As I entered the building in front of the mosque, I was escorted into the office of the Minister of Information. This kind gentleman asked me to see his public relations officer and go over the details with him.

Once I was seated in his office, he asked, point-blank, "You know we are all Muslims here, don't you?"

My simple reply was, "I have something here that I think you will like to include for your viewer's enjoyment." I quickly opened the portable TV monitor and began to show him the audition tape.

"Please stop and rewind so I can write down everything the announcer is saying," he abruptly said to me.

I responded, "You mean you would like to write down everything that is stated on this tape?"

"Yes, please, go very slowly," he said.

It was a slow, laborious process; however, once Brother Swaggart began to preach, he did not ask me to stop again. He became very interested in the message. This particular audition tape was of the Jamaica crusade. About halfway through the message, as the crowd responded again to Brother Swaggart's preaching, I leaned over and said to the man, "Powerful, isn't it?"

The man looked up and smiled really big and said, "Please call my office this afternoon at 3 o'clock sharp, and I will have an answer for you from the Minister of Information concerning whether the program can be aired on Gabonese television."

I thanked him and was escorted back to the car.

As I drove back to the hotel, I passed several hundred dear Gabonese people who were about their business up and down the sidewalks of Libreville. They looked so sad, beaten down by sin and satanic powers of darkness. Once back in my hotel room, I looked out the window and prayed, "Oh God, my merciful Father in heaven, it is up to You now. You are the only one who can unlock this door today. We do not even have a missionary resident in Gabon, but You know how much these dear people need to hear the gospel of Jesus Christ. Please, oh please, have mercy upon the people of Gabon and let the light of the gospel shine ever so brightly over their television network. I ask this in the name of Jesus Christ. Amen."

THE ANSWER

Directly at 3 o'clock that afternoon, I placed the call to the Minister of Information's office. I asked for the public relations officer and thanked him for the time he had afforded me in his office.

He said, "I have been able to talk with the Minister of Information concerning the authorization for the French Jimmy Swaggart telecast and have some good news for you. You may begin sending the telecast tapes to the television station for airing on our network. We will have the network air the program each week on Sunday afternoons prime time between 4 and 5 o'clock."

I thanked the gentleman for his help and contacted the director of the television network to inform him of the outcome and make sure that between his office and the Minister of Information's office, the airing dates were confirmed. If I understood the network correctly, there were more than 1 million viewers under the coverage area of this network.

After packing my bags, I looked out the window toward the Atlantic coastline of Gabon and thanked the Lord. I thought over the events of the past 24 hours and asked, "Lord, why did everything go wrong that could go wrong concerning the arrangements made previously to contact this station?"

ALL THE GLORY IS MINE

Like a bombshell going off near a lonely foxhole on the battlefield, I felt the Lord speak to my heart, saying, "I made it as impossible as could be so that you and everyone will know that all the glory is Mine."

A new missionary arrived in Gabon a few weeks later when the first telecast aired, and we set up an outreach office. From that first telecast, letters began to flood into the office, with each one stating that the person writing the letter had received Jesus Christ as his own personal Saviour while repeating the sinner's prayer with Brother Swaggart at the end of his message. As each weekly telecast aired, many more thousands of letters were received from people getting saved. A great move of God had begun in Gabon and continues to this day. Now, more than 80 percent of the entire population of Gabon is considered Christian!

If a missionary, the national pastor, or I had done it, we could have reported that because of our great ability, our connections with the government, or our great planning, the gospel would be preached to this strategically located African country. However, now there was no one to whom this miracle could be attributed but God.

Truly Isaiah 48:11 is true:

"For Mine own sake, even for Mine own sake, will I do it: for how should My name be polluted? and I will not give my glory unto another."

Amazing grace! How sweet the sound,
That saved a wretch like me!
I once was lost, but now am found,
Was blind, but now I see.

'Twas grace that taught my heart to fear,
And grace my fears relieved.
How precious did that grace appear,
The hour I first believed.

Through many dangers, toils, and snares,
I have already come.
'Tis grace hath brought me safe thus far,
And grace will lead me home.

The Lord has promised good to me.
His Word my hope secures.
He will my shield and portion be,
As long as life endures.

When we've been there ten thousand years,
Bright shining as the sun,
We've no less days to sing God's praise,
Than when we'd first begun.

CHAPTER 10

26° 12' 14" S
28° 2' 50" E

CLOSED TO THE AIRING OF THE GOSPEL?

"For a great door and effectual is opened unto me, and there are many adversaries."

— *I Corinthians 16:9*

CLOSED TO THE AIRING OF THE GOSPEL?

26° 12' 14" S | 28° 2' 50" E

"NO FOREIGN RELIGIOUS PROGRAMS are permitted on South African television." In 1983, this was the answer I received from each South African when I asked for information concerning how to place a Jimmy Swaggart telecast on the powerful South African Broadcasting Corporation (SABC) television network.

In fact, one prominent religious leader, who was very well known and respected by many denominations in South Africa, told me emphatically, "Jim, I wish I could tell you that Jimmy's program can be aired in our great country, but that will be impossible! SABC-TV is closed to any foreign religious programming. We are convinced that it is the gospel program South Africa needs so desperately, but after we have tried and tried over and over again to have them air it, they won't."

A DOOR SLAMMED SHUT

A former pastor who worked with Brother Swaggart had previously tried to get the program on SABC. When I asked him about the response he had received on his many trips to South Africa, he said, "Never had a door been slammed so hard in my face as at SABC-TV in Johannesburg! Something will have to change at SABC before our program goes on the air."

It was clear that God would have to intervene or this Spirit-anointed gospel program would never reach the hungry hearts that so desperately needed the message that changes lives and saves the lost.

Even though South Africa was a so-called Christian nation, there was an element in this society that did not want the one thing that would make them worthy of the name Christian — the gospel — to be proclaimed over their broadcasting network. It seemed that there were so many adverse policies and roadblocks to the airing of this program, but even the Apostle Paul said:

"For a great door and effectual is opened unto me, and there are many adversaries" (I Cor. 16:9).

I was convinced that even though all the demons of hell had all put their own locks on the door to South African broadcasting, God would make good His promise:

"Repentance and remission of sins should be preached in His name among all nations" (Lk. 24:47).

And "all nations" includes South Africa!

BOPHUTHATSWANA

Then it happened. The powerful new BOP-TV in the South African homeland of Bophuthatswana invited me to visit the capital, Mmabatho, and talk with the program director about the telecast. The coverage area of this station included most of northern South Africa and extended far enough south to reach Pretoria and part of Johannesburg.

After traveling to the television station in Mmabatho and talking with the gentleman that directed the programming, it was agreed that I would provide them with the Jimmy Swaggart telecast tapes, and BOP-TV would air the program every other Sunday afternoon from 2 to 3 p.m., *free of charge*!

When the program started airing, responses from the viewers began pouring into our outreach office in Johannesburg. The South Africans loved the telecast, and many gave their hearts to the Lord.

After airing the program on BOP-TV for about three months, our office director in Johannesburg, Kokkie Lock, called me in Baton Rouge, and stated that he was able to arrange an appointment for me with SABC. He said, "Christians are praying all over the country. This may be the moment God will perform a miracle and open this door to South Africa."

After a long flight that took all of one night and the next day, I arrived in Johannesburg.

The next day, Brother Lock and I were sent to the program director's office to discuss the possibility of airing the telecast on SABC-TV 1, which covers virtually all of South Africa. After talking at length with this kind gentleman, he said, "Please send us several copies of the Jimmy Swaggart telecast for our review, and we will get back to you with an answer concerning what we will be able to do."

THE DOOR OPENED

In just a few weeks, the director at SABC-TV 1 told me that they would like to air the telecast, beginning with one of the programs I had given them to review. It was the Mobile, Alabama, crusade, where Brother Swaggart preached the message entitled, "Suffer the Children." An SABC representative said that they would begin airing the program only once a month and monitor the response before continuing.

The beginning date came, and the program was aired. Like an avalanche, letters and phone calls began to pour into the SABC offices and our Jimmy Swaggart Ministries outreach office in Johannesburg. People of different backgrounds either called in or wrote letters — blacks, whites, and coloreds! In fact, they said the telephone lines were jammed for three days at the SABC headquarters because so many people were calling in with favorable comments concerning the program and wanting to know when the telecast would air again.

The next month, another Jimmy Swaggart telecast was aired with the same tremendous response. Then the black channel (SABC-TV 3) requested that we send the telecast tapes to them for airing every week. God was indeed performing a tremendous miracle.

CRUSADES IN SOUTH AFRICA

The people of South Africa liked Jimmy Swaggart's preaching so much that the combined churches of the entire country invited Brother Swaggart and the crusade team to come for crusades in the giant outdoor stadiums of Johannesburg, Cape Town, Port Elizabeth, Durban, and Soweto. The crusade team, plus about 60 ministry partners, spent six whole weeks in crusades across South Africa. Many, many souls came to the Lord.

When the trip began in the United States, I was asked to be in charge of the trip for the whole six weeks. That included responsibility for the team and the partners, plus coordinating all the events, transportation, meetings, hotel accommodations, meals, and tours. Our first stop after taking off from the United States and flying all night was in Madrid, Spain, with an all-day layover in order to connect to South Africa.

GUNSHOTS WENT OFF

While in Madrid, everyone was able to freshen up in the hotel and take tours of Madrid, but we had to be back at the hotel by nightfall for supper and a 10 p.m. departure from the hotel to the airport. Everyone met in the lobby of the hotel at about 9 p.m. with all of their luggage. We were to be boarded on huge passenger buses that would take us to the Madrid airport. While in the lobby, Brother Gerald Ogg, the crusade coordinator for the stateside Jimmy Swaggart crusades, had a black briefcase that he put down by one of the lobby sofas. That was where most of us, including Brother Jimmy and Sister Frances Swaggart, were seated while waiting to be boarded onto the buses after all the luggage was loaded. All of a sudden, in the midst of the jabber of everyone talking to one another, a man of slight stature in an overcoat snatched Brother Ogg's briefcase and ran toward the middle of the lobby.

"Hey, come back here!" Brother Ogg shouted. "Someone stole my briefcase!" I guess the bandit thought Brother Ogg was carrying a satchel full of money for the team. However, as we found out later, to Brother Ogg's embarrassment, he had put all his dirty clothes and underwear from the flight over in the briefcase! He did this because he had already locked his luggage, and it had been picked up earlier and had gone down to the buses for loading with the rest of our luggage.

As the bandit ran across the crowded lobby, a big concierge porter blocked the front entrance just inside the big rotating doors. The bandit, seeing that he could not escape, turned, and as he turned toward the reception counter, pulled out a small pistol and began shooting into the air.

When the gunshots went off, everyone except three people scrambled and fled to the buses outside. Brother and

Sister Swaggart immediately jumped up from one sofa, and I jumped up from another part of the lobby. We all three simultaneously turned and ran toward the noise of the shots being fired.

By that time, the would-be bandit — still holding the black briefcase — had hurdled over the front reception counter and landed on the side of one of his legs, which crumpled under him. In the split second it took Brother and Sister Swaggart and me to rush up to the counter, a concierge from the front door of the hotel had reached the bandit, yanked the gun out of his hand, picked him up off the floor, and twisted his arm behind his back. Police arrived and carried the hoodlum off.

What was amazing to me was the fact that our natural reaction was to go toward the trouble and not flee to safety outside as everyone else did. We went outside and told everyone, "All clear. Go ahead and board the buses."

The crusades were a tremendous success in South Africa, with the blessings of the Lord upon them. Brother Swaggart preached under a heavy anointing of the Holy Spirit with thousands of people responding to the altar calls. I remember that before one of the three-night crusade services in the huge Johannesburg Ellis Park Stadium, Brother Lock, our new South African outreach office director, had given me an envelope with a handkerchief in it. He had asked me to have Brother Swaggart pray over it when I brought him into the stadium for the service, as I had done each night. He said that he would take it back to a lady who was suffering from a malignant tumor that was taking her life. She was in the last stages, and he told me, "If God does not intervene, according to the doctors, she has only a few days left to live."

I knew from the book of Acts that this type of request was biblical:

"And God wrought special miracles by the hands of Paul: So that from his body were brought unto the sick handkerchiefs or aprons, and the diseases departed from them, and the evil spirits went out of them" (Acts 19:11-12).

That night, as Brother Swaggart came through the underside of this massive stadium and rounded a corner, he spotted me. He said, "Well, Jim, let's see what God will do for the dear people of South Africa tonight." I pulled out the envelope and explained the situation concerning the dying lady and asked him to pray over the handkerchief. He said, "Well, of course!" and we both laid our hands on the handkerchief. He began to pray and pray and pray. I'm telling you, the power of God was present. We finished, and someone came and said that it was past the time to start and that we needed to get out to the platform "pronto."

HEALED BY THE POWER OF GOD

It was weeks later when we were back in the office in Baton Rouge, that I received a call one day from Brother Lock in South Africa about some of the outreach office business.

At the end of the conversation, I was ready to hang up when he said, "Say, by the way Brother Woolsey, do you remember the handkerchief from the dying lady I gave you for Brother Swaggart to pray over in the crusade at Ellis Park Stadium?"

"Well, yes, I remember," I said, recalling Brother Swaggart's earnest prayer.

"Well, guess what? She was completely healed, and her health was restored! The doctors were amazed and said they had never before seen anybody recover from the last stages of that dreaded disease. It was a miracle, and the dear lady gives the glory to God and thanks Brother Swaggart for praying for her."

Well, that is the pure grace of God! Hallelujah! That's just like our God!

"Jesus Christ the same yesterday, and today, and forever" (Heb. 13:8).

THE SOUTH AFRICAN GOLD MINE

The days progressed during the six weeks of different cities where the crusades were held all over South Africa in giant stadiums. During some of the days, we had the privilege of touring some interesting places. We went to a huge game preserve with all types of African animals, and, as well, we saw different types of historical sites and buildings. One of the most interesting places was a huge gold mine. Throughout history, South Africa, of course, has been noted for its diamond and gold mines.

On this particular day, the entire group of crusade team members and tourists, plus Brother and Sister Swaggart, were visiting one of the largest gold mines in South Africa. We were all given hard hats, like the ones used on construction sites, and taken down deep into the earth by huge metal, mesh-encased elevators. The guide explained how the formations of the earth below Johannesburg had yielded tons of the valuable mineral throughout history, as well as many other interesting facts about the mine.

They brought us back out of the mine and into a rather large tin building, similar to a cavernous warehouse, and the guide had our large group line up in front of an actual gold melting furnace. Two gold smelting workers had put crude gold ore rocks into the heated kiln and were now extracting molten gold from the furnace using a large extended rod with a receptacle at one end.

"This is the way a 25-pound ingot of gold is poured and solidifies," one worker explained, as they used the long rod to pour the pure gold from the deep bowl of molten mineral. As the worker tipped the bowl to one side of the ingot mold, the hot, liquid gold rushed in and filled the tapered mold. Then they showed us how the gold solidifies into an ingot.

As the ingot cooled and hardened inside the mold, the worker challenged all of us. He said, "Alright, I am taking the ingot mold away from the now hardened gold. You will notice the large rectangular ingot's sides are tapered to an almost flat point on the top surface. Please form a line, and each person can try to pick the ingot up by the tapered sides using one hand only. If anyone can pick it up in one hand, he may take the whole ingot of gold with him; it will be his. To date, no one in the entire more than 100-year history of this gold mining-smelting operation has been able to pick up one of these ingots with one hand. Not even one of the miners who has worked here over these many years has ever been able to pick up an ingot in one hand!"

THE GOLD INGOT

Well, of course, everybody wanted to try to pick up the ingot so it would be his or hers to keep. Why not? It was worth well more than $100,000! I looked at the slanted sides of the ingot and thought, "That's impossible. The angle of the sides of the ingot does not lend itself to the grasp of a hand." I lined up last in the long line, thinking that the only one who really might have a halfway decent chance at grasping the ingot was Rick Motter. He was our man who wrestled all the heavy equipment for the crusades and put together the platform, hung the huge lights and sound grid over the platform, and prepared all of the TV camera platforms, connecting all the various cables and electrical power before a crusade began. He was the strongest person there and if anyone could pick up that ingot, he would surely be the one.

Each person in line gave it a try, including Brother Swaggart, who was third to last in this long line of more than 60 people attempting the impossible. All had failed to lift the ingot with one hand and, after their turns, were just milling around the area, watching the others grasp at but not move the ingot a fraction of an inch off the counter. Then Rick Motter stepped up, reached out and put his big bear claw type hand on the slanted sides of the ingot, and tried to lift. He grunted, but his fingers immediately slipped upwards off of the sides of the tapered ingot. A big sigh of, "Oh, too bad," went up from the crowd of people. Nobody could lift it!

As the last person in line, I thought, "How futile. No one can pick this thing up." Still, I reached out my right hand at arms length and grasped the large ingot of gold. I squeezed my grip on it and, to my own amazement, started lifting my arm in the air with the ingot between my fingers! Then, with it still extended at arm's length, I started to walk away with it in my hand because they said that whoever could pick it up between the fingers on one hand could keep it.

I heard the host foundry workers cry out, "Stop! Stop! Come back here! We cannot let you have that ingot of gold!"

Most of the people in our group immediately retorted, "But you said the person who picked up the gold ingot could have it."

"No, no, no," the host said. "We have said that for years because it was impossible for anyone to pick it up, until now. No, bring it back," he demanded.

After swinging my arm back around with the ingot still clutched between the fingers of my right hand, I gently put it back on the counter in front of the mine host and wide-eyed workers and started walking away with the rest of the group. I heard the smelter workers gasp, "These Americans, they too strong! We cannot offer ingot anymore to the public."

Thirty years later, Brother Swaggart still remembers this incident and brings it up, even over international television, to my embarrassment. How I picked up that 25-pound gold ingot, I'll never know, except that maybe the Lord decided to do it once in the history of the South African gold industry. I give Him the credit.

NAMIBIA

As the Jimmy Swaggart program aired on both TV 1 and TV 3 in South Africa, with BOP-TV still airing our program, our outreach office was inundated with letters. Then the director of South-West African television in the neighboring country of Namibia contacted our office and requested that the program be aired on their network every other week.

The response in Namibia to the Jimmy Swaggart telecast was so great that we had to set up another Jimmy Swaggart Ministries outreach office in Windhoek, the capital of South-West Africa. One day I received a call from the television network director and he said, "This is incredible. The Jimmy Swaggart telecast has become the number one rated program on television in our country with more viewers than any other programming we have, and we only air it every two weeks. It is such a blessing to our country. There have been no negative comments concerning your telecast. If you will please have enough programs sent to us for airing it each week, we will be more than happy to air it every week over our entire network. Can you do this?"

Of course, I answered yes. "We will begin immediately to send enough programs for airing weekly. We are so glad to hear that the people of Namibia are being blessed by the telecast and the messages Brother Swaggart preaches." I immediately wrote the memo to the television department where Tom Claybaugh, who for many years, in fact, for many decades, duplicated the program tapes and had them sent out to all parts of the world for airing. He began sending to Namibia enough program tapes for a program to be aired every week as requested.

One lady in Namibia wrote:

"Let me tell you a little about myself. I am married, have two children, and I am 45 years old. I was brought up in the traditional religion. (My father is an Irishman!) I professed to be a Christian. I went to church every Sunday. I knew a Sunday God. But somehow, as I got older, I felt there was something missing. This past Easter, we had a special TV show. It was a Jimmy Swaggart service. I saw and heard you for the first time in Namibia. The name of your sermon was, 'Can God Condemn You to Hell?' Jimmy Swaggart, did you get to me! I sat there spellbound. I must tell you, I cry very easily. I cry when I'm happy, when I'm sad, and when I'm cross. On Easter Sunday, I cried for God for the first time in my life. For the first time, I pictured Him on the way to the Cross as you described it and on the Cross for me. For 45 years, I've heard and read about the crucifixion, but it had been just

another story. Now, I saw it. What a waste of 45 years!
Can I make up the rest of my life for those wasted years
without a living God? Without your music, my life would
not be the same. And now, I have been shown the way to
praise and thank God with music. Yes, Jimmy Swaggart,
you got me hooked! I sit here listening to your album,
Worship, and I can feel the presence of the living God.
May God bless you, for you have brought so much joy in
my life. Now I know what it is to love God and to feel
Him loving me. How I wish I could be there among those
lovely Americans when you talk and sing to them."

SOWETO

With all the coverage of the Jimmy Swaggart gospel telecast going out over most all of southern Africa, the city of
Soweto was receiving the weekly program. The Soweto police
chief had the Johannesburg Metro Police Service, of which
their department was part, call both our outreach office in
Johannesburg and the television network to leave the following message: "The Metro Police Service of Soweto would like
you to know that we are very thankful for the Jimmy Swaggart
telecast that goes out over all of Soweto every Sunday afternoon. It is the only one to two hours during the whole week
that we policemen can sit down and do not need to patrol
because literally everyone stops everything they are doing
to watch the Jimmy Swaggart telecast. We just want you to
know that this telecast is such a great blessing here in Soweto

and has helped tremendously to reduce the crime rate. Please do continue screening (the South African and British English word for "airing" over television) this great program. It is so uplifting to our community. Thank you so much."

GOD IS USING THIS TELECAST

All across South Africa, people were able to hear the gospel of the Lord Jesus Christ as this telecast was aired, and they came to know Jesus as their Saviour. The networks told me that more than 30 million people were now able to view this ministry's program in South Africa if they so desired! Think of it. A country that was "closed" was now having the Spirit-anointed gospel beamed into every South African home with a television set, and the Jimmy Swaggart telecast was the first foreign religious program South Africa had ever permitted to be aired on their network. It was God who opened the door!

Truly we are living in the last days. The harvest is so great, but God used the Jimmy Swaggart telecast — airing on more than 2,000 television stations around the world by the mid-1980s when it also went on in South Africa — to beam the gospel, giving access to 300 million people in 143 countries to view the telecast if they so desired. Today, the SonLife Broadcasting Network, airing 24 hours a day, seven days a week, gives more than 3 billion people access to the Message of the Cross by either cable, satellite, IP TV systems, or by the Internet, if they want to tune in.

There is a wide and effectual door being opened all over the world in this generation so that millions of people may come to know Jesus Christ as their own personal Saviour.

Never before in the history of mankind has there been an opportunity like this when God has enabled His work to reach the most people ever reached at any one time with the gospel message. No door is closed too tightly for God — not even South Africa!

"And he said, Hearken ye, all Judah, and ye inhabitants of Jerusalem, and thou King Jehoshaphat, Thus saith the Lord *unto you, Be not afraid nor dismayed by reason of this great multitude; for the battle is not yours, but God's"* (II Chron. 20:15).

God can do anything, anything, anything,
God can do anything but fail,
God can do anything, anything, anything,
God can do anything but fail.

He's the alpha and omega, the beginning and the end,
He's the fairest of ten thousand to my soul,
God can do anything, anything, anything,
God can do anything but fail.

He can save, He can cleanse,
He can keep, and He will,
God can do anything but fail,
He can save, He can cleanse,
He can keep, and He will,
God can do anything but fail.

CHAPTER 11

26° 12' 14" S
28° 2' 50" E

THE GREATEST GIFT EVER

"For God so loved the world, that He gave his only begotten Son, that whosoever believeth in Him should not perish, but have everlasting life."

— John 3:16

THE GREATEST GIFT EVER

26° 12' 14" S | 28° 2' 50" E

THERE IS PROBABLY NO other country in modern times that has been so terribly ravaged by the dark plight of war as the East African nation of Uganda. The eerie shadow of death has hovered over this region, its calloused fingers touching the people there with famine, disease, drought, corruption, and carnage. War ran rampant for more than 20 years, with 200,000 or more unconfirmed deaths. So many had died that literally hundreds of dried-out skulls could be seen stacked in heaps along the roadsides.

THE FLIGHT TO UGANDA

It was 1983, and Brother and Sister Swaggart and the crusade team had just finished a series of crusades that spanned six weeks in South Africa. Instead of returning home to the States with them, I took a flight out of South Africa to Rome, Italy, to connect with a flight going back down into East Africa. I was on an all-night flight from Rome to Kampala. Every seat was taken in the old Boeing 707. The front half of the plane was converted into a cargo hold full of crates, paraphernalia, and even animals and chickens! The plane would be landing at the Entebbe Airport. That was where Ugandan President Idi Amin had been surprised by the Israeli commando raid that liberated the hostages being held against their will. It was the same airport terminal where I would be landing the following morning. I wondered how the airport looked now and how the bullet holes that had riddled the walls that fateful night had been patched.

However, my main concern on this long flight was how to approach Uganda television about airing the Jimmy Swaggart telecast so the people of this war-torn country could hear about the One who can bring peace: Jesus! There was a strong Muslim element in the Ugandan population of more than 12 million people that dominated the religious landscape. I had already been told that all broadcasting was government-controlled.

THE ENTEBBE AIRPORT

When the airplane taxied up the runway, you could see that the walls of the terminal building were still riddled with scores of bullet holes from the Israeli raid that successfully rescued the hostages. (The only Israeli soldier killed in that Operation Entebbe raid in 1976 was the future Prime Minister of Israel, Benjamin Netanyahu's older brother, Yonatan. This was where more than 100 Israeli hostages who had been hijacked by terrorists were rescued.)

Upon entering the terminal, I was told that I could not be admitted to the country for lack of the proper visa. This was quickly remedied as I was whisked into a back room to pay a small "visa fee." A broken-down taxi was my only transportation from the airport to the capital city of Kampala.

All the way into town, I noticed groups of people sitting under wiry trees, looking so destitute. What was there to smile about? Poverty was rampant. In U.S. currency terms, the minimum monthly salary for a wage earner was fixed at $1.20! The maximum monthly salary of a university professor was only $20, which was also the maximum amount a state employee could earn. Think of it, just $20 per month! A bunch of plantains — what we would call bananas and is, in fact, the staple of the Ugandan diet — cost $3. So, what did they eat? Very little!

One verse of Scripture kept coming to me as I looked at these dear people:

"The people which sat in darkness saw great light; and to them which sat in the region and shadow of death light is sprung up" (Mat. 4:16).

Upon entering downtown Kampala, I questioned the taxi driver, "Where can I stay?"

"There is only one place available, the Speaks Hostel. The main hotel is not available because it was blown out during the war," he said.

We pulled up in front of an old two-story hostel, the only one in town. I was given a room that contained only a cot, one sheet (no pillow), one hard, wooden chair, and a small table. There was no running water the whole time I was in Uganda. That night I went to the Lord in prayer knowing how impossible this whole situation was, with most of the country under Islam and the government and national television network controlled by Muslims. I did not know what to do or what to say to these government people the next day. All I could do was plead for mercy. I cried out, "Oh Holy Father, please have mercy on Uganda. In the name of Jesus Christ I come to you on behalf of these 12 million dear Ugandan people who cannot speak for themselves. Please have mercy on us. Deal with the hearts of the people in charge of the national television network. Please give me grace and favor with those who control this network. Grant me the words to speak. Only You, Lord, have the words of eternal life. Break down all resistance to the gospel of your dear Son Jesus Christ and have the audition tape of the telecast be accepted by all concerned for airing here in Uganda that all may have the opportunity to meet the Saviour who died for us. In Jesus Christ's name I ask this of You, the only One who can send the Holy Spirit now to these hardened hearts and open them for this good news to be proclaimed over television in Uganda. Thank you for hearing and opening this door. Amen."

UGANDA TELEVISION

The next morning I walked up to the Uganda television station. The first man I met was dressed in the typical full Muslim garb with the long, flowing smock and brimless hat.

He directed me to the program manager's office. This kind gentleman received me into his office and watched the audition tape. He sat there through the whole program captivated by the music and preaching.

When the program finished, I just simply turned to him and asked, "Would you like to include this high quality telecast in your weekly program schedule?"

"I would be more than happy to include the Jimmy Swaggart telecast in this network's program schedule," he said, "but we will need final approval from the respective government authority." I was told later that the head over Uganda Television (UTV) was a Muslim. Upon returning to the hotel, I called a resident missionary couple and left some of the program videotapes with them so that when the word was given, the program could air almost immediately.

Word came shortly that they would begin airing the telecast in about three months, every Sunday evening at prime time — 6 to 7 p.m.! This would be the first time, if I understood correctly, that a continuous weekly gospel telecast would be aired in Uganda!

THE RESULTS

People began watching the telecast every week, and Muslims started giving their hearts to the Lord. The missionary that was our Kampala outreach office director began receiving requests to hold gospel meetings in the homes of converted Muslims. Soon, many were coming to know Jesus as their

Saviour, not only through the telecast, but also through the meetings being held. In fact, the missionary wrote an urgent letter at one point asking all of us at the Jimmy Swaggart World Ministry headquarters to pray for him and his wife. Their lives were threatened by some of the Muslim leaders, and each time they went to one of the meeting places, they were trailed by one or more Muslims. After several months, the intimidating tactics ceased.

The missionary said, "Jimmy Swaggart and his gospel telecast have done so much good here in Uganda. When I introduce myself anywhere in the city or country as the Jimmy Swaggart Ministries representative for Uganda, whether to a government official or layperson, the doors are swung wide open. This program has speeded up missions in Uganda by decades. People from every imaginable station of life are watching the program. In fact, pressure was put on the Muslim UTV director to take the program off the air, but he could not because so many favorable letters have been pouring into UTV of how their own people had been set free of numerous bondages of drugs, tobacco, alcohol, witchcraft, and many other evil practices."

One Ugandan pastor told us how he had been a member of Idi Amin's crack troop before he was saved. He had taken part in the Entebbe hostage ordeal and had one of his legs blown off by machine-gun fire during the Israeli invasion of the airport. After Amin's departure from the country, this soldier heard the gospel and gave his heart to the Lord. God called him to preach, and he has been winning people to the Lord ever since.

But the amazing thing is this statement he made: "The Jimmy Swaggart program means so much to us Ugandans. It has practically been the only voice telling us how to have peace and find Christ as our Saviour. In fact, this program helped our people through this most recent upheaval and terrible fighting."

He went on to tell how the program helped. He said, "When the fighting around Kampala came to its worst, the television station aired the Jimmy Swaggart program over and over again to help calm the situation. In fact, during all these many, many months of heavy battles, the program was aired right on schedule each week and many times during the week. Only one time did the station lose audio transmission for five minutes, but even during those five minutes with no voice, we could still feel the presence of the Holy Spirit while watching Brother Swaggart. We want to thank him and the Lord for bringing this important gospel program to Uganda. Without it, Ugandans would have no hope. This is the greatest gift anyone could ever give Uganda because by means of this telecast, we hear the true gospel of Jesus Christ!"

Yes, this Holy Spirit-anointed ministry was like a great light penetrating into the darkest corners of the world. Today Christians now make up 85 percent of the Ugandan population with Muslims representing 12 percent of the population. That's quite a difference from before the first Jimmy Swaggart telecast was aired in Uganda in 1983. That is how powerful the gospel of Jesus Christ is when preached under the anointing of the Holy Spirit. God had made it possible for this program to be aired in 143 countries with more than 300 million viewers (a very conservative estimate based on information from the TV networks) with access to watch each week if they so desired (at the time these incredible trips took place). More than 80 million of these were Muslims! Truly, for those in *"the region and shadow of death light is sprung up!"*

Now, the greatest gift is given to the nations of the world every time these programs air live over the SonLife Broadcasting Network — Jesus, the light of the world! Truly God is a merciful God!

The enemy of man's soul has tried to put out this light. He has sent his host of demons to make a frontal assault against this gospel network, but this light will not dim until every nation in this generation hears the gospel and sees its light.

Jesus said, *"I am the light of the world: he that followeth me shall not walk in darkness, but shall have the light of life"* (Jn. 8:12).

See the bright and morning star,
Jesus, the Light of the World!
He has risen in our hearts,
Jesus, the Light of the World!

Walk in the light, beautiful light;
Come where His love and His mercy are bright.
Shine all around us by day and by night,
Jesus, the Light of the World.

He's the lamp that lights our way,
Jesus, the Light of the World!
Step by step and day by day —
Jesus, the Light of the World!

No more darkness, no more night —
Jesus, the Light of the World!
He will shine forever bright,
Jesus, the Light of the World!

6° 7' 54" N
1° 13' 22" E

YOU WILL HAVE TO GO AS A STOWAWAY

*"He that spared not His own Son,
but delivered Him up for us all."*

— *Romans 8:32*

YOU WILL HAVE TO GO AS A STOWAWAY

6° 7' 54" N | 1° 13' 22" E

UPON ARRIVING AT THE sticky, hot Lagos, Nigeria, airport terminal, I discovered that the connecting flight to Lomé, Togo, West Africa, had been canceled. An appointment had been made months before to meet with the president of the Republic of Togo the following morning. I checked the different airline counters, and there was nothing going that way. After calling the various charter companies, I found that they all had nothing available. I just had to get to Lomé for this most important meeting with the president because he was the only person in the entire country who could authorize the airing of the Jimmy Swaggart telecast on the Togo national TV network.

A STOWAWAY

One of the small charter services said that I could wait at their hangar for an incoming flight from northern Nigeria and talk with the captain about chartering the plane. When the plane finally arrived some three hours late, I approached its captain and asked if I could charter the plane to Lomé.

He said, "There is no way because the plane will be leaving in another hour for Abidjan, Ivory Coast. A businessman has booked this plane round-trip, Lagos to Abidjan, where I will pick him up and then fly him back to Lagos tonight."

I asked, "Could I please go with you, and couldn't we stop in Lomé on the way?"

He replied, "You will have to go as a stowaway because, officially, I am not to carry anyone even though the plane is empty. Once we are airborne, I will be able to make a decision concerning the stop in Lomé, Togo."

Here I was, a stowaway on a private plane without a payload, with two godless pilots taking me toward my destination! After flying for about an hour, we were nearing Lomé, Togo. I once again asked the captain if we could land there. He finally said, "No way. Lomé is not on our flight plan, and besides that, the tower will not give us clearance to land."

I said, "Well, could you do me a favor and ask the tower to call the Bible school to inform the people that I will not be able to make it in time for the appointment tomorrow with the president of Togo?"

"Fine," he said.

"By the way," I continued, "why don't you ask the tower if you can have clearance to land?"

The pilot said, "Okay, I'll give it a try."

After making contact, the captain explained the situation and had the man in the tower call the Bible school. It was

Sunday afternoon, and usually everyone would be in church. However, the business manager happened to be in the office when the phone rang. The tower explained the situation, and the African business manager said with an authoritative voice, "You let that plane land because the man onboard has an appointment with the president tomorrow morning, and no one stands up the president of Togo!"

FRUSTRATION!

The tower radioed back to a somewhat dismayed pilot who turned around in the cockpit and said, "The tower has just given us clearance to land! This has never happened before!"

When I asked him if he would land, this godless pilot pulled out a cigar, lit it, and began to puff. He looked around at me and said, "Are you a reverend?"

I said, "Yes, sir, and I do need your help desperately to keep this appointment tomorrow with the president. Will you please land?"

He looked at the fuel gauges, thought awhile, and then turned to me and said, "No, there is no way I am going to land in Lomé. It may put us off schedule in getting to Abidjan to pick up our customer."

I slumped back into a darkened corner of the empty plane and looked out the window at the lights of the great city of Lomé far below. All the prayers and preparation for this most-important meeting seemed to be in vain. I would have to wait a day or two before I could get a flight to Lomé and thus miss this appointment with the president of Togo that most likely would open the way for the airing of the Jimmy Swaggart telecast there.

Then the Holy Spirit prompted me to pray, "Oh God, my heavenly Father, hallowed be your holy name, please have mercy on us for Jesus Christ's sake. If there is any plane in Abidjan that is supposed to go to Lomé today or tonight, please hold it there until after I land so that I can board it and still arrive in Lomé tonight. In the name of Jesus Christ, I ask this for the sake of the dear people of Togo that so desperately need to hear the gospel."

MIRACLE OF MIRACLES

Upon landing around 8 p.m. in Abidjan, Ivory Coast, I noticed that there was an Air Afrique plane fully loaded and waiting for clearance to take off on the tarmac. I rushed into the terminal to ask if there was a flight to Lomé, Togo, that same night. The ground agent said, "No, there is no scheduled flight tonight." He then conducted me to a large schedule sheet in the departure hall and said, "The last flight was to leave at 2 o'clock this afternoon; however, it is still here and is to leave at 8:30, in just about 15 minutes!"

I anxiously asked, "Would there be a space available for one person on the plane?"

After radioing someone, the answer came back, "There is only one seat left!" He hurried me through the immigration check and security check and then out to the plane.

Just after I boarded and sat down, the plane jerked forward toward the end of the runway. I thought, "This is incredible! God is going to get me to that meeting with the president of Togo someway, even if all the forces of hell try to stop it! God made a way for me to come over here as a stowaway on a private aircraft and then held this plane on the ground over six hours so I could board and arrive in Lomé tonight. Thank you, Lord Jesus!"

THE MEETING WITH THE PRESIDENT

The plane arrived in Lomé very late that night and Missionary John Weidman was still waiting for me at the terminal, rejoicing that I had made it to Togo. He said to me, "This is a miracle. I don't know how you were able to make it here with your flight from Lagos being canceled, but I knew one thing — no one stands up the president of Togo when he has a confirmed appointment to meet with him." Then he continued, "We have to get up at 4 a.m. to begin the security check at the president's palace before we can be admitted for an audience."

Early the next morning, we went to the president's palace, and the security procedures, which would last 10 hours, began. Yes, they lasted 10 full hours! Finally, we were conducted to the military headquarters for one last security search and then into the presence of the gracious president of Togo, Gnassingbé Eyadéma.

I asked the president if he would be interested in seeing a demonstration tape of the Jimmy Swaggart telecast. He was most delighted, and I pulled out the portable TV monitor that I carried with me and started the tape. As he watched, he said, "Say, this is better than most programs on our television network."

We told him about the many outreaches of Jimmy Swaggart Ministries, including the 200,000-plus needy African children that were helped each day from the famine-stricken countries of Ethiopia, Sudan, Mozambique, and other places across Africa. I explained to him that we had a Christmas special we wanted to leave with him to be aired on the Togo television network, and we asked if he would authorize the airing of the telecast not only at Christmas but also on every Sunday from then on. He kindly responded, "Well, of course! We will air the Christmas special, and after that, I will get with our people in charge of television and have the weekly program set up for airing." We thanked him for his kindness.

PERSONAL APPRECIATION OF A PRESIDENT

Before we left, he said, "Wait a minute. Would you please tell Jimmy Swaggart and his partners that we here in Africa are so grateful for all of the help to relieve this terrible situation that we find ourselves in. Please let Jimmy Swaggart know that I personally appreciate what he is doing."

I thanked him for the time he had been able to afford us, and I assured him that I would relay his message to Brother Swaggart.

Reports came to us after this meeting that it would still be impossible for the French Jimmy Swaggart Christmas program to air in Togo. Several critics tried to stop any religious programs of this nature. Satan had unleashed some of his mightiest demons to stop the airing of this gospel telecast in Togo. However, God brought the president of Togo to the forefront in order to unlock and open the door so this telecast might be approved and aired in a Muslim country, and lives could be changed by the power of Jesus Christ.

Then it happened — the telecast was aired during Christmas week.

So what if I had to be detoured as a stowaway or had only a one-way ticket to Siberia.

So what if I had to climb the highest mountains to the rooftop of the earth in Tibet, go to the lowest, hottest jungle valleys of the Amazon and Burmese jungles, or endure the feverish sweat of malaria at death's door.

So what if on almost every trip, I had to suffer death-threatening migraine headaches that not only caused vomiting more than 20 times with dry heaves, but also such intense pain in my head that my eyes would go completely blind for hours.

So what if I had to almost die of pneumonia after traveling to South America, or if I had to escape a massacre of people in the room next to mine in a downtown Moscow hotel.

So what if I was given up to die by the doctor who said that the hepatitis I had contracted in my body in Mexico was too far advanced to be able to cure, or if I had to go into war-torn

Nicaragua with bullets still flying to ask the Marxist-Sandinista government if we could have a crusade there.

So what if I never would be able to own a house and call it home.

So what if I was only allowed four hours' sleep each night for more than 25 years, was in the line of fire in the Tiananmen Square massacre, had the plane in which I was flying fall out of the sky from 30,000 feet, was in 12 major earthquakes that killed hundreds of thousands of people around me, was fired upon in more than 10 countries' major revolutions, or almost drowned in the Pacific Ocean by an undertow current pulling me underwater and hurling me helpless three miles out from shore.

So what if I was threatened with death at gunpoint in the high Andes Mountains by guerrilla fighters of the Peruvian Shining Path revolution that killed 19 of the pastors that I had just trained for ministry, plus 60,000 others that were massacred throughout the country.

So what if in Bagdad, I had 12 soldiers of the elite Republican Guards of Iraq's Saddam Hussein point their machine guns at me ready to fire.

So what if I was rejected and kicked out by the self-righteous religious leaders of the Assemblies of God denomination in which I had spent 25 years putting millions of new converts into their churches and channeling more than $120 million into their missions' projects (from Jimmy Swaggart Ministries), plus substantial monthly support of more than 600 of their missionaries around the world for many, many years. This rejection was in spite of never having ever broken one of their denomination's bylaws while credentialed as a minister with them.

So what if Satan and all the hordes of hell tried to kill me not just once, but on many separate occasions, while I was trying to get this blessed gospel of Jesus Christ to the lost.

So what if I had to lose everything for the cause of Christ. It's worth it all so people of this generation can hear the glorious message of Jesus Christ and Him crucified!

When the telecast began to air in Togo (and several other countries that came online), there were more than 3,000 television stations in more than 143 countries of the world airing the telecast, making it possible for more than 300 million people to watch it each week if they so desired. By far, Jimmy Swaggart is the most watched preacher of the gospel in the world today, with people coming to the Lord as a result of each and every message! So many people got saved in Togo as a result of the telecast that Togo today is no longer considered a Muslim country but a strong Christian country with more than 30 percent of the entire population being Christian, and it's still increasing!

"He that spared not His own Son, but delivered Him up for us all, how shall He not with Him also freely give us all things?" (Rom. 8:32).

God spared nothing. He gave us His best, His only begotten Son, Jesus Christ, to die on the Cross on our

behalf! He gave *all* for you and me, and the whole world.
Can we do anything less than give ourselves completely to
Him and His cause?

Down from His glory,
Ever living story,
My God and Saviour came,
And Jesus was His name.
Born in a manger,
To His own a stranger,
A Man of Sorrows, tears and agony.

O how I love Him! How I adore Him!
My breath, my sunshine, my all in all!
The great Creator became my Saviour,
And all God's fullness dwelleth in Him.

What condescension,
Bringing us redemption;
That in the dead of night,
Not one faint hope in sight,
God, gracious, tender,
Laid aside His splendor,
Stooping to woo, to win, to save my soul.

Without reluctance,
Flesh and blood His substance
He took the form of man,
Revealed the hidden plan.
O glorious myst'ry,
Sacrifice of Calv'ry,
And now I know Thou art the great "I Am."

CHAPTER 13

17° 58' 59" N
76° 47' 60" W

NEVER SAY NEVER

"I will loose the loins of kings, to open before him the two leaved gates; and the gates shall not be shut."

— *Isaiah 45:1*

NEVER SAY NEVER

17° 58' 59" N | 76° 47' 60" W

"*NEVER* WILL JBC-TV AIR a program of this nature on our network. It is strictly prohibited to screen (air) foreign religious programs in our country!" This was the emphatic reply of one of the directors of Jamaica Broadcasting Corporation (JBC) concerning the placing of the Jimmy Swaggart telecast on their stations in 1983. When I first heard this reply from them, I said to myself, "You should never say never to God."

As far as we knew at that time (which was several years ago), our telecast was not airing anywhere in the Caribbean area, unless it happened to be picked up by some obscure satellite dish on a lonely island somewhere. From all available sources, we were told that Jamaica television had never put a foreign religious program on their airwaves since the mighty British Broadcasting Corporation (BBC) had established the station many years prior. It looked as though the "nevers" were piling up into a wall as high, or higher, than the walls of Jericho.

On the first trip I made to this beautiful Caribbean island country, I was met by Missionary Herb Adkins. Herb and his lovely wife, Vivian, were two of the most dedicated missionaries I have ever known. They related to me, "Jim, some years before this, someone came and tried to place the program on JBC-TV."

"What was the result?" I asked.

"They were given the same answer that we had been given previous to this trip," Herb said, "that Jamaica television would never air our program, and besides that, they were not even interested."

Though we were met with a cold smugness that almost defied even an attempt to place the telecast on this powerful network, we were convinced that God could make a way. We believed He could make these seemingly insurmountable walls of resistance come crumbling down so that the dear people of Jamaica would be able to hear this Spirit-anointed message of Jesus Christ.

After all, His Word says,

"Commit thy way unto the LORD; trust also in Him; and He shall bring it to pass" (Ps. 37:5).

We committed this whole matter to the Lord and asked Him to show us the way. I agreed in prayer with Brother and Sister Atkins: "Our heavenly Father, You who are holy and true, we come to You in the name of Jesus Christ. Thank You for being so gracious and kind to us by giving up Your only begotten Son on the Cross of Calvary so that whosoever will may come to You and be saved from sin and death through faith in the slain Lamb of God. Thank You for saving our souls. Please have mercy on the dear people of Jamaica. You know how the enemy of man's soul has the door to Jamaica Broadcasting Corporation's TV network closed shut with policies that do not permit a foreign gospel telecast. We know that You are using the Jimmy Swaggart telecast all over the world to reach the lost with the gospel of Jesus Christ, giving all in each country the opportunity to hear the Spirit-anointed messages You have given to Brother Swaggart. Please let not the sacrifice of Your dear Son, Jesus, be in vain for the people of Jamaica because they do not have the opportunity to hear what He has done for them at the Cross. Have mercy upon us all and open this door to Jamaican television, showing us the way by Your Spirit. Lead us and guide us into this network and move upon the hearts and lives of those in charge to change their policies and permit this program to air every week across this land of souls for which Christ died. Let the light of the gospel shine ever so brightly now in Jamaica, and we ask this all in the wonderful name of Jesus and for Your glory alone. Amen."

SHIRT-TAILING

Not too long after that first trip, in Kingston, the capital of Jamaica, Herb Adkins spoke with one of the local pastors who had just begun a television program of his own on JBC-TV. The program was sponsored by the church he pastored. He suggested to us, "Maybe Jamaica television would permit me to include portions of the Jimmy Swaggart telecast in my program on Sunday mornings."

"Why don't we give this idea a try? It just could be the Lord," was my reply.

When we (this kind pastor, Herb Adkins, and I) approached JBC-TV with this idea of "shirt-tailing" on this Jamaican brother's telecast, there was some hesitancy on the part of the man in charge of the station. We were convinced that if the people of Jamaica and JBC-TV could at least see the program a few times, they would understand why it was so powerfully well-liked.

Finally, the television network gave us a somewhat wavering reply, saying that we could try shirt-tailing the program on the other man's telecast every other week for a few months. After that, a final decision would be made concerning a time slot of our own.

AN AVALANCHE OF LETTERS

This kind Jamaican pastor began including long portions of our telecast in with his program on Sundays. Herb called me just a few weeks after the telecast had aired in this manner and said that both JBC-TV and his office were receiving an avalanche of letters from viewers who were very pleased with the program and asked that it continue on Jamaica television. JBC-TV's switchboards were jammed with phone calls all the next day after every time the telecast was aired, with Jamaicans calling, wanting to know when the telecast would be on again. The walls were beginning to tumble down!

PLEASE SIGN HERE

Then it happened. Herb called and asked me to make an emergency trip to Jamaica because JBC-TV had requested that we go to their office in Kingston and discuss a one-hour time slot of our own for the Jimmy Swaggart Ministry telecast. Of course, I hurriedly made arrangements for the trip, and we met with the people in charge of allotting programming time on the network. Right before entering the office where we would negotiate a contract for the program, I was told that the man with whom I would be speaking was the same person who had told our ministry several years before, "Never will we air this type of program on our network!"

As we began to talk about the telecast, the gentleman in charge said, "I do not understand it. We never thought in the past that a foreign religious program would be so well-liked here in Jamaica. In fact, we had banned such programs from our programming schedule. Never could we foresee a response as large and favorable as this telecast has had on our airwaves. Most all of the responses are favorable. In fact, we have drawn up this contract. Would you please sign here?"

The man handed me a pen to sign on the dotted line to authorize the airing of this ministry's telecast from 8 to 9 a.m. every Sunday morning. At that moment, the full impact of what had just occurred hit me. As I signed the contract, something in my spirit said, "Never say never to God!" He had just worked a tremendous miracle by changing the entire policy of JBC-TV in order for this one foreign gospel telecast to be aired.

God's promise is true:

"I will loose the loins of kings, to open before him the two leaved gates; and the gates shall not be shut" (Isa. 45:1).

The enemy tried to close the gates of Jamaica to the broadcasting of the gospel, but God promised, *"the gates shall not be shut!"*

The number of letters coming into our local office in Jamaica began to increase. People were coming to know Jesus as their own personal Saviour.

Read the following testimony of one such person who gave his heart to the Lord:

"On Saturday, Feb. 22, 1986, at about 8 a.m., I sat in the recreation room of the police station and watched your broadcast on television, and I was touched by the Spirit-filled conclusion of your message. I always remember these few words you spoke, 'You are not here by accident, neither are you watching the broadcast by accident, but it was ordained by God for you to be here.' I meditated on those words for a few minutes, and then I heard the tender voice of Jesus saying, *'Come home, my child, you've been too long gone.'* In an instant, I felt the Spirit of God move within my body, and I gave my life to Christ. I began to sing along with you, 'Lord, I'm coming home.' I know that my name is written down in glory. I am praying for your broadcast, and I want you to pray for me. Jimmy, I love you, but most of all, I now love God and His Son, Jesus Christ."

One lady wrote to the office, asking the following question:

"Brother Swaggart, I appreciate so very much your telecast each Sunday morning here in Jamaica, especially the program entitled, *There Is a River*. I did not understand everything that was said since I have just given my heart to the Lord Jesus Christ. I am a new Christian. However, the other day, I was washing the dishes and was thinking about Jesus. I began to pray out loud, and strange words began to come out of my mouth. I just continued praising the Lord in this strange language. Brother Swaggart, is it all right to pray this way?

Yes, people were getting saved and being baptized in the Holy Spirit as a direct result of the telecast. Many more testimonies such as this had come into the Jimmy Swaggart Ministries outreach office in Jamaica—people praising God for all He had done in their lives, for the bondages of sin having been broken by the power of God, and for the help they had received as a result of the telecast.

THE CRUSADE

After several months, the telecast began making a large impact upon the entire country of Jamaica. Letters coming into the Jamaica outreach office were full of questions asking when Brother Swaggart would come for a countrywide crusade. The churches then sent me an official invitation for a Jimmy Swaggart crusade to be held in Kingston. Arrangements were made, and a date was set. The National Stadium holds 35,000 people. However, when the Sunday night service was held, the stadium was completely packed. When the seats filled, crowds of people stood down on the field and around the track. More than 45,000 people attended that crusade service.

We found out later that this was the largest crowd ever gathered in the history of Jamaica in the National Stadium. Think of it! The largest crowd in the history of the country, and it was for a gospel crusade — people who gathered to hear more about Jesus! (I believe that every stadium ever built on the face of the earth is there precisely for the preaching of the gospel.)

The following year, when the newspaper with national coverage printed the outstanding events of the previous year, they started the article by stating that this ministry's crusade and telecast did more good for the country of Jamaica that year than any other single event.

In country after country, God is making a way where there is seemingly no way at all for the gospel to be broadcast via television. God is unlocking the lock and opening door after door, giving people the opportunity to see and hear the true gospel of our Lord Jesus Christ.

Country after country is opening to the gospel of the Lord Jesus Christ, and whether they are Buddhists, Muslims, communists, Shintoists, spiritists, or whatever, people are learning to "never say never to God," for He can do anything. He saves to the uttermost!

Truly the harvest is great, and we have a great God who is the Lord of the harvest. Men try to put up walls of doubt, trying to stop the advance of the gospel of Jesus Christ, but God is fulfilling His Word that:

"From the rising of the sun even unto the going down of the same My name shall be great among the Gentiles; and in every place incense shall be offered unto My name, and a pure offering: for My name shall be great among the heathen, saith the LORD of Hosts" (Mal. 1:11).

I've a yearning in my heart
That cannot be denied;
It's a longing that has never
Yet been satisfied.
I want the world to know
The One who loves them so;
Like a flame it's burning deep inside.

To be used of God, to sing, to speak, to pray;
To be used of God to show someone the way.

I long so much to feel the touch
Of His consuming fire;
To be used of God is my desire.

When I think about the shortness
Of my earthly years,
I remember all the wasted days,
The wasted tears.
I long to preach the Word
To those who've never heard
Of the One who can dispel all fears.

What can wash away my sin?
Nothing but the blood of Jesus;
What can make me whole again?
Nothing but the blood of Jesus.

Oh! precious is the flow
That makes me white as snow;
No other fount I know,
Nothing but the blood of Jesus.

For my pardon, this I see,
Nothing but the blood of Jesus;

For my cleansing this my plea,
Nothing but the blood of Jesus.

Nothing can for sin atone,
Nothing but the blood of Jesus;
Naught of good that I have done,
Nothing but the blood of Jesus.

This is all my hope and peace,
Nothing but the blood of Jesus;
This is all my righteousness,
Nothing but the blood of Jesus.

Now by this I'll overcome —
Nothing but the blood of Jesus,
Now by this I'll reach my home —
Nothing but the blood of Jesus.

Glory! Glory! This I sing —
Nothing but the blood of Jesus,
All my praise for this I bring —
Nothing but the blood of Jesus.

3° 45' 0" N
8° 46' 59" E

JESUS IS THE WAY-MAKER

"Behold, I will do a new thing; now it shall spring forth; shall ye not know it? I will even make a way in the wilderness, and rivers in the desert."

— *Isaiah 43:19*

JESUS IS THE WAY-MAKER

3° 45' 0" N | 8° 46' 59" E

HOW SHOULD I DESCRIBE Equatorial Guinea? It sounds like some far-off, exotic place, doesn't it? Believe me, as beautiful as this small African country may be, it is not included in your everyday travel brochures as one most frequented by tourists.

Why?

There was a period in its history when the iron claw of communism almost devastated this Spanish-speaking nation. When the communists left, Equatorial Guinea's economy was literally bankrupt after pulling out from under communist rule that lasted more than a decade.

OUR RESPONSIBILITY

Equatorial Guinea was seemingly forgotten by the rest of the world, but God had not forgotten this needy land at the middle of the western end of the African continent. Why was I going to such a hopeless place, to that steaming hot, malaria-infested, tropical jungle? God wanted that generation of dear Equatorial Guineans to know His Son, Jesus Christ.

"That they may know from the rising of the sun, and from the west, that there is none beside Me. I am the LORD, *and there is none else"* (Isa. 45:6).

"He that hath the Son has life; and he that hath not the Son of God hath not life" (I Jn. 5:12).

We may not be held responsible for the past generations of a nation at the end of the earth, but we are held responsible for letting this generation know that "Jesus saves, and His blood washes whiter than snow."

"Look unto Me, and be ye saved, all the ends of the earth: for I am God, and there is none else" (Isa. 45:22).

"All the ends of the earth" includes Equatorial Guinea! That's why God is thrusting the Jimmy Swaggart television ministry out over all the earth — that this generation of more than 7 billion people might come to know the Lord Jesus Christ and be saved.

ONE IMPOSSIBILITY AFTER ANOTHER

Even before arriving, it was not possible to acquire a missionary contact. There might have been a missionary working in this country in the past, but from all available sources, there was no missionary to meet me and help put the telecast on Equatorial Guinea television. On top of that, it was impossible to get a hotel reservation before going there because the telex or telephone would not connect to or answer back from this country. Upon arriving in the capital of Malabo, I found out why: there were no hotels and no working telecommunications systems to the outside world.

After being dropped off in the middle of town, I discovered there were no taxis to speak of, so I began walking, looking for a place of lodging. When I asked one man on the street where I might find another hotel, he laughed and said, "Hotel?"

"Yes, a hotel," I said. "I have just arrived and need a room."

The man said, "There are no hotels in Malabo. The one that was operating had to close down because of the destruction it suffered, but maybe the caretaker will lend you a bed to sleep on."

After he gave me directions on how to get to this old hotel, I picked up my luggage and set out on foot. I walked about two miles, only to discover that, indeed, the place was closed and would not accept another guest. The caretaker referred me to an apartment building downtown.

Again, I started my long trek on foot. After lugging the suitcase back downtown, I found that every apartment was taken; not one room was left.

Here I was in a strange country with no missionary to help, no communications, no hotel room, no transportation but my own two feet, and no food to speak of. The only food for sale at the open-air market was a few battered bananas, moldy oranges, and what looked like strips of dried chicken meat, if you can imagine such a thing.

DESPAIR

I went down a side street and found a tree, under which I stood as the sun set. Looking around, I noticed that many of the buildings had been blown up when the communists left. The streets were all torn up with deep trenches because when the previous government left, they took all the city water and sewerage plan maps with them. So, as a result, when work had to be done to fix a broken pipe embedded deep underground, the workmen had to dig a zigzag trench more than six feet deep to find the damaged pipeline.

At that moment, I felt almost completely overwhelmed and destitute. There would be no flight out of this place for three more days! It looked as though the enemy of men's souls was making it more impossible than ever, but I knew one thing: God told me to come to this forgotten place and try to put this Spirit-anointed gospel telecast on the air because these dear people were just as important to Him as those in more developed countries. (In fact, maybe they were even more important since they did not have the opportunity we do to hear the gospel every day.)

I cried out in prayer: "My heavenly Father, hallowed be Your holy, holy name. Please show me the way. I need Your help. Please have mercy upon these people and upon me. Let not the death of Your only begotten Son on the Cross be in vain for Equatorial Guinea. They must hear the good news. Please provide me with a place to stay and show me how to get to the TV station tomorrow. I ask this for the sake of Your glory in Jesus' name. Amen."

No sooner had I said, "Amen," than He impressed upon my spirit: "Go back to the manager of that small apartment building and tell him you could not find a room for the night, and he will tell you what to do."

To make a long story short, the manager of the apartment building said there was one room on the third floor that was occupied by a Frenchman who would be gone for three days, and if I would not touch his things, I could stay in that room.

AT DEATH'S DOOR

At least I had a bed for the night—three nights, in fact. However, the windows had no screens on them, and I soon discovered, as I tried to go to sleep, that several mosquito squadrons were on a night dive-bombing run, and I was the target! Little did I know that these mosquitoes that almost ate me alive each night were malaria carriers. I even found a drugstore in town, but the pharmacist just laughed at me when I asked him for some malaria tablets.

"What?" the pharmacist said, laughing. "We don't carry hardly any medicines, much less malaria tablets, because we can't get them shipped to our country in the quantities we need. Sorry."

As a result, 10 days after leaving Equatorial Guinea and returning home, I came down with a very serious, life-threatening disease. The hospital where I was had never had such a case before. It happened while I was driving my family across Texas. We had not taken any time off together for more than three years. We were on our way to New Mexico to see relatives on my wife's side of the family. While I was driving in the western part of Texas, all of a sudden, I got very nauseated, started sweating, and had to stop the car to throw up on the side of the road. I felt so very fatigued that I had to have my wife, Jean, drive the rest of the way into New Mexico and to the town that was our destination. I thought I had come down with the flu, but the next morning after arriving late into the night, I realized that a sweating fever had set in, and I was deathly sick.

At the doctor's office, I was trembling so badly with chills and had such a terrible headache that the doctor immediately put me in the hospital. As he was running lab tests on my blood, the doctor would come in and out of the examination room where I was seated and just shake his head and say, "Well, we can't figure it out yet. I'll be back in a minute." Each time he came back into the room, he would say the same thing, "Well, we can't figure it out yet."

While I was waiting, I began to think back on the trip to Equatorial Guinea from where I had just returned some 10 days before. I remembered the hot, tropical, jungle-like climate and the mosquitoes that ate me up each night. Then I remembered the missions' director for Southeast Asia. A few months before, he had visited Baton Rouge. He told Brother and Sister Swaggart and me about the time he came down with malaria in the jungles of Southeast Asia, and how every once in awhile, he would have a return bout of the malaria with chills, fever, nausea, vomiting, and headaches. Many times, he would have to stop off in the middle of a trip to recover. He said that some strains of malaria follow a person the rest of his life.

The doctor came back from the lab a third time, again shaking his head and saying, "We still are not able to figure it out." If I remember correctly, he added, "Your white blood cell count is 3,000 white blood cells to only one red blood cell. This is critical and very abnormal."

I explained to the doctor how I had been in Equatorial Guinea, Africa, just 10 days prior and bitten by mosquitoes. "Could it be malaria?" I asked.

The doctor went back to the lab again and in a little while, came back and said, "I should have known. I served in Vietnam as a medic, but here in the desert of New Mexico, we have never had a registered case of malaria. It is definitely malaria, but you have an acute case in the last stages, and I will have to put you in a hospital room."

Well, I had to share a hospital room with another patient. During the night, the fever and chills became very bad, and my body was trembling uncontrollably. In fact, it was trembling so much that the metal-framed hospital bed I was in was making a terrible rattling noise from the shakes, not to mention the death rattle in my throat. It was so loud that the other patient in the room heard it. He called the nurses and said, with desperation in his voice, "Please get me out of here and put me in another room. I don't want to be in a room with a dead man!"

That was encouraging, to say the least! As I lay there alone in the dark early morning hours with my body shaking uncontrollably and with a death rattle in my throat, I cried out to God, "Oh holy Father, I come to You in the name of Your dear Son, Jesus Christ. As You know, I'm dying. You've been so good to me and so merciful. In Your grace, You have carried me around the world into so many countries and opened so many closed doors, putting the Jimmy Swaggart telecast on in so many nations, and saving so many hundreds of thousands of souls, but there are still so many nations without the gospel. Please, oh God, have mercy on me for Jesus Christ's sake and heal me. I'll go where You want me to go, I'll say what You want me to say, and I will do what You want me to do if You will just spare me a little longer. I ask this of You in the name of Jesus. Amen."

No sooner had I said, "Amen," than the trembling began to subside, and the death rattle in my throat stopped. The next morning, I was released from the hospital, and within a week, my blood cell count was back to normal.

God had healed me, but better yet, the doctor told me when he finally released me, "Fortunately, Jim, the strain of malaria you had is the fourth strain, which does not keep recurring periodically the rest of your life."

Hallelujah! To God be all the glory! He healed me!

You might ask, "Was it worth it? Was it worth it to hazard your life for the cause of Christ and go through all that torment and pain?"

Yes, yes, yes, it was! A million times, yes!

You see, I believe the devil tried to kill me in Equatorial Guinea to stop the advance of the gospel. Please understand, I don't believe that I am the only one who could have gotten the job done, but at that moment, in that nation, God had sent me to carry out a specific task. If I had not gotten it done, it would have gone undone, and souls would have eternally perished.

So, it was worth the long, hot walk uphill each day in Malabo to the TV station because after watching the audition tape, the kind manager and his staff had the government's Minister of Education, Culture, and Communications sign the contract to air the Jimmy Swaggart telecast each Sunday. Praise God! All was not lost!

A RUSSIAN SPY?

On the second afternoon in Malabo, I was on my way up to the TV station again when a big, burly, blond-haired man came walking down the street right toward me. I remembered that just that same morning, quite by accident, I had walked over to a building in the center of town that had photos of school children on the windows and walls. I noticed that the captions underneath mentioned places inside what was then known as the Soviet Union.

I stepped back into the street, looked up, and to my surprise, I was standing right in front of the Russian embassy building under the red hammer-and-sickle flag! All the surveillance cameras were pointed right at me from every corner of the building. I only did what anyone would do when he is in the wrong place at the wrong time — I turned as fast as I could and took off in the opposite direction.

Surely the man walking toward me now had to be one of the Russian spies working in their embassy. He approached me and greeted me in Spanish saying, "What are you doing in a place like Equatorial Guinea?

I said, "I am on my way to the TV station to talk about a Spanish gospel telecast we are offering them." I then quickly added, "Do you have a cassette player?"

"Yes," was his reply.

I quickly snatched a music tape out of the bag I was carrying, along with a cassette of one of Brother Swaggart's messages in Spanish entitled, "What Shall the End Be?" Handing both to him, I said, "Here's a gift for your listening enjoyment. What do you do in this country?"

He said, "I'm with the Soviet diplomatic mission," and happily accepted the tapes from me. "Adios!"

I can just see all those Russians back at the top-secret embassy huddled around a tape player, listening to the gospel!

WAS IT REALLY WORTH IT?

After the telecast aired, the first response letter we received in our offices was from a leading rock 'n' roll singer in Equatorial Guinea. He said that he had just given his heart to the Lord while watching the telecast and that Jesus had changed his life and saved his soul. So, yes, it was more than worth it!

Today, people in this far-off country at the end of the earth can hear about Jesus because of the uncompromised gospel that God has called Jimmy Swaggart to preach—the Message of the Cross. Today, instead of the nation of Equatorial Guinea being the greater part Muslim as it was when I first arrived there, it is now 82 percent Christian and only 2 percent Muslim, with no communists to speak of!

SO MANY MORE

There are so many more all over the world waiting in darkness for the only message that saves the lost and sanctifies the believer — the message of the gospel of Jesus Christ and Him crucified! This ministry is attempting, as no other in the history of the church, to reach as many people as possible by airing this Message of the Cross. Many have written that their souls are saved, bondages are broken, and their lives are changed through the power of God as a direct result of watching the television programming now airing on the Son-Life Broadcasting Network around the world.

God can make a way where there is seemingly no way because He is the way-maker!

He makes good His promise:

"Behold, I will do a new thing ... Shall ye not know it? I will even make a way in the wilderness, and rivers in the desert" (Isa. 43:19).

Let's keep going through the way that God opens wide, and we will reach this entire generation with the gospel! That way is the Cross of Jesus Christ!

Jesus said, *"I am the way, the truth, and the life: no man cometh unto the Father, but by Me"* (Jn. 14:6).

Sometimes the day seems long,
Our trials hard to bear.
We're tempted to complain,
To murmur and despair.
But Christ will soon appear
To catch his bride away!
All tears forever over
In God's eternal day!

It will be worth it all
When we see Jesus!
Life's trials will seem so small
When we see Christ.
One glimpse of his dear face,
All sorrow will erase.
So, bravely run the race
Till we see Christ.

At times the sky seems dark,
With not a ray of light;
We're tossed and driven on,
No human help in sight.
But there is One in heaven,
Who knows our deepest care;
Let Jesus solve your problems,
Just go to him in prayer.

Life's day will soon be o'er,
All storms forever past;
We'll cross the great divide
To glory, safe at last!
We'll share the joys of heaven:
A harp, a home, a crown;
The tempter will be banished,
We'll lay our burdens down.

My heart can sing when I pause to remember,
A heartache here is but a stepping stone;
Along a trail that's winding always upward,
This troubled world is not my final home.

But until then my heart will go on singing,
Until then with joy I'll carry on,
Until the day my eyes behold the city,
Until the day God calls me home.

The things of earth will dim and lose their value
If we recall they're borrowed for awhile;
And things of earth that cause the heart to tremble,
Remembered there will only bring a smile.

But until then my heart will go on singing,
Until then with joy I'll carry on,
Until the day my eyes behold the city,
Until the day God calls me home.

This weary world with all its toil and struggle,
May take its toll of misery and strife;
The soul of man is like a waiting falcon;
When it's released, it's destined for the skies.

But until then my heart will go on singing,
Until then with joy I'll carry on,
Until the day my eyes behold the city,
Until the day God calls me home.

CHAPTER 15

13° 43' 40" N
100° 31' 26" E

BUDDHA IS DEAD

"Moreover ye see and hear, that not alone at Ephesus, but almost throughout all Asia, this Paul hath persuaded and turned away much people, saying that they be no gods, which are made with hands."

— Acts 19:26

BUDDHA IS DEAD

13° 43' 40" N | 100° 31' 26" E

"WHY DO YOU PRAY to Buddha?" I asked the government guide who had just conducted me through a Buddhist temple in the country of Mongolia. We were now outside in front of some rather large prayer wheels that had scribbled prayer requests pasted to them.

The guide was quick to answer my question. "We pray to Buddha because he is God."

"But Buddha is dead," I insisted. "Nowhere in his writings did he say he was God."

"Yes," he said, "but we make him God!"

MAN HAS MADE HIS OWN GODS

Sad to say, down through the ages, man has made his own gods. The psalmist described these gods:

"Their idols are silver and gold, the work of men's hands.

They have mouths, but they speak not: eyes have they, but they see not:

They have ears, but they hear not: noses have they, but they smell not:

They have hands, but they handle not: feet have they, but they walk not: neither speak they through their throat.

They that make them are like unto them; so is everyone that trusteth in them" (Ps. 115:4-8).

In conversing with another Buddhist, I was asked, "What makes your Christian religion any different from Buddhism or any of the others?"

My answer surprised him.

I said, "Even the so-called Christian religion has its works of men's hands — their icons, statues, crucifixes, amulets, and false ways of the 'motivation gospel, greed gospel, purpose-driven gospel, G-12 gospel, seeker-sensitive gospel, self proclaimed prophets-apostles gospel, and a hundred other so-called gospels,' all set up in the hearts of devotees — worshiping the invention of men's corrupted minds and not the only one true God.

"Actually, Christianity, in the pure definition, is not a religion. Yes, you heard me right. It is not a religion at all. It is a relationship with a person, the divine person — Jesus Christ. He died on a cruel Cross for our sins, was buried and rose again from the dead the third day, and ascended into heaven to be seated at the right hand of God, having completely defeated sin, the world, the flesh, and the devil, and *He lives!* Whosoever will call on Him can have God's pardon for being a sinner and can be saved from eternal perdition. As well, they can be freely given eternal life by faith alone in this finished work that Christ Jesus accomplished there on the Cross by paying our sin debt in full before a thrice-holy God. This was done with His own precious, innocent, spotless, and undefiled life's blood that was poured out there for you and for me."

THAILAND

A similar Buddhist country to Mongolia, as it regards traditional religious belief, is the southeast nation of Thailand, or the Siam of history. At the time of the trip I'm about to describe, Thailand was a beautiful country of more than 53 million people. It had more than 24,000 Buddhist temples overrunning the landscapes of its cities. Ninety-six percent of its population claimed to be Buddhist, while a mere three-tenths of 1 percent claimed Christianity. The remainder of the people adhered to either the Muslim or tribal religions.

THEY TOLD ME IT WOULD BE IMPOSSIBLE

The first time I had the privilege of being in Thailand, I was told, "It will be impossible for the Jimmy Swaggart telecast to be aired in this country because it is one of the strongest Buddhist nations in the world. In fact, the capital city of Bangkok is the central headquarters of the World Fellow-ship of Buddhists."

I said, "God called us to try to put this gospel telecast on in every nation of the world. We will at least try, and we believe God will unlock the lock and open the door. The Holy Spirit can do what no man can do, and He will lead us each step of the way."

In the 16-mile stretch of road from the Bangkok Don Muang International Airport to town, I counted about 20 Buddhist temples. They were all over the place!

Unfortunately, during this first contact with the television station, no one was available, and the best I could do was leave an audition videotape for the TV management's consideration.

Months went by, and we still had not received an answer. Finally, we heard, but the news was not good. The audition tape was given back with a note that said that at that time, Thai TV could not include our telecast in their program schedule. We tried another station and got just about the same answer. It looked as though the Devil had bolted this door closed and was leaning up against the other side of it to make sure the door to Thailand would not open to the gospel.

MAYBE WE COULD GO THROUGH THE BACK DOOR

Missionary Ron Maddux, Thailand's director for Jimmy Swaggart Ministries, had been producing gospel radio pro-grams in the Thai language for several years, with the support of this ministry. Ron and his lovely wife, Penny, are two of the godliest and most dedicated missionaries that you could ever hope to meet. They had been preaching and establishing new churches all over Thailand, several of which JSM helped to build. In fact, Ron preached to more than 250,000 people in outdoor crusades every year.

In talking with Ron on one occasion about the possibility of airing this ministry's telecast, he suggested that maybe we could begin by going "through the back door."

"What do you mean, 'through the back door?'" I asked.

He said, "Well, it could be that if we can get one of the local TV stations up-country to air the telecast, then it will be easier to contact other stations to air the program."

Although nothing is very easy in Thailand, we agreed that God could, in this way, give us a foothold to expand to new stations — and eventually to the capital of Bangkok.

THE FIRST STATION

Then it happened. After much prayer, both in Thailand and in North America, God opened up one of the TV stations. One of the up-country TV stations accepted the program and said they would air it each week.

As the first programs began to air, people watching the telecast were touched by the Holy Spirit and began writing to our outreach office in Bangkok. The letters started pouring in daily with requests for the teaching booklets, Bibles, and home study Bible courses.

Several months later, in another up-country city, the telecast was accepted and began to air. One by one, God was toppling down the walls of resistance. First one station and then another was added until 10 TV stations were airing the program in the Thai language, including one in the capital of Bangkok. One of the stations in the northern Thai city of Khon Kaen had a coverage area that included the neighboring country of Laos. In fact, they told us that the Laotian people preferred to watch this Thai TV station even more than the Laos National TV Network.

COVERAGE IN ONE YEAR!

Just a few days later, Ron Maddux called to say that the last three TV stations in Thailand had started airing this ministry's gospel telecast as of the first of that year. This meant that in just one year's time — almost to the day — God made a way for this gospel program to be put on all 13 major TV stations throughout Thailand, giving total coverage of the entire country of 53 million people! Not only did the telecast cover the whole of Thailand and Laos, but it also spilled over somewhat into eastern and northern Burma and northern Malaysia.

Missionary Ray Trask, former president of the Jimmy Swaggart Bible College and the last missionary to leave Burma in 1966 (when all missionaries were expelled by the Burmese government), said that while he was at Louisiana State University attending a debate between Brother Swaggart and a Muslim leader, he met a Burmese man in the audience who was visiting the United States. The man told Brother Trask,

"I watch Jimmy Swaggart's telecast in Burma from a TV station in Thailand that reaches into my country. I don't miss a program; I see them all!"

God made good His promise:

"The LORD hath made bare His holy arm in the eyes of all the nations; and all the ends of the earth shall see the salvation of our God" (Isa. 52:10).

SOME OF THE RESULTS

The JSM office in Bangkok was flooded with mail from people who responded to the telecast by giving their hearts to the Lord. One lady in northern Burma wrote to our office and told how she was so depressed after a failed suicide attempt:

"I had made up my mind to get on my motorbike and drive it right out in front of a bus on the busiest street in town. As I was going out the door of my house, the TV was on and I saw 'that man' singing at a piano. I returned and sat down to listen, not being able to understand the English, but I felt a peace come over me on the inside. Then he began to speak in the Thai language, and for the first time, I heard about Jesus Christ. I then prayed with Brother Swaggart and asked Jesus to come into my heart. I am a changed person now and want to thank you so much for this telecast that helped save my life and introduced me to Jesus!"

Another man wrote in, thanking us for the telecast:

"I was an executioner for 25 years in a prison in southern Thailand. All those years, it was my occupation to kill people; I feared death itself greatly. Besides this intense fear that had gripped my life for so many years, I felt so guilty all the time. Then your telecast started coming over my television from the Had Yai TV station. For the first time, I heard about Jesus and how He had defeated death and fear. I accepted Christ during the telecast. Now I no longer fear death, and a great peace has come into my life because of Jesus!"

FOLLOW-UP

Hundreds more testimonies similar to these came into the Thailand JSM outreach office, but space does not permit more to be printed here. Let me say, though, that every letter that came into our office (and at the time, there were 64 of these international JSM offices around the world) was followed up in several ways. This was to ensure that these people continued serving the Lord and attending church. In Thailand, each person who wrote was sent a free gospel booklet in the Thai language, a Bible study course, and a JSM magazine.

When there was a considerable response from a certain area of the country that had no church, our office in Bangkok would send out invitations to those who had written from that area and invite them and their friends to an outdoor follow-up rally. Ron then took a team of national evangelists and preached nightly to crowds that averaged about 2,500 people, the majority of whom attended as a direct result of the television and radio programs.

From these meetings, a church was formed, land was purchased, and a building was built. This was evangelism on a new level because of the Holy Spirit anointing on the Jimmy Swaggart television ministry.

More than 20 new churches across Thailand were started in this way.

"And I say also unto thee, That thou art Peter, and upon this rock I will build my church; and the gates of hell shall not prevail against it" (Mat. 16:18).

A MIGHTY TOOL OF EVANGELISM

This gospel outreach of SonLife Broadcasting Network (SBN) is speeding up world evangelization by more than one generation. There's really no way to describe completely how much this ministry's telecast meant to Thailand, and now over SBN, to so many, many countries of the world. Actually, the telecast was the only gospel program on Thai television over the greater part of this Buddhist nation for many years. Our Thailand outreach office director described in these words what the telecast meant to missions and the dear Thai people:

"The Jimmy Swaggart telecast gives us a means to do what otherwise would be impossible. If we were to personally witness to each person in Thailand, taking 10 minutes per person, it would take us 949 years to tell them about Jesus and the salvation message in a one-on-one situation. However, with this gospel telecast on ThaiTV, we can reach the whole country of over 50 million people, giving them access to hear, if they so desire, during the time it takes to broadcast the program. Television is one of the greatest tools of evangelism — if not the greatest — enabling us to reach the largest number of people possible in the shortest time. We just thank God for this telecast in Thailand, making possible a great harvest of souls."

OBSTACLES COMING DOWN

Someone asked me the other day, "Do you really think Jimmy Swaggart can preach the gospel over television in every nation of the world?"

I replied, "I believe God can do anything, and He is bigger than any of man's puny obstacles, walls, and closed doors! I have seen His Holy Spirit do more in five minutes than years of man's efforts that never accomplish anything worthwhile. He is in control. If we will keep on believing Him, He has ways of working in the stubborn hearts of man that we could never think of, and God will make a way!"

Think of this:

- The obstacles the Devil has placed in the path of the gospel are being broken down.

- The doors that have been locked are opening to the proclamation of this glorious gospel of Jesus Christ and Him crucified.
- The false gods of man's imagination are nothing compared to the only true God who can do anything against impossible odds.
- While the Devil was blocking the front door to Thailand, the Holy Spirit came through the back door and flooded the country with the gospel!
- As never before, God is moving by his Spirit across the whole earth, enabling this Spirit-anointed Message of the Cross to go forth around the entirety of the world.

It is happening just as He said it would:

"For that which had not been told them shall they see; and that which they had not heard shall they consider ... I am the first, and I am the last; and beside Me there is no God" (Isa. 52:15; 44:6).

Buddha is dead! Christ is alive!

I serve a risen Saviour
He's in the world today.

I know that He is living,
Whatever men may say.
I see His hand of mercy;
I hear His voice of cheer;
And just the time I need Him
He's always near.

He lives, He lives, Christ Jesus lives today!
He walks with me and talks with me along life's narrow way.
He lives, He lives, salvation to impart!
You ask me how I know He lives?
He lives within my heart.

In all the world around me
I see His loving care,
And though my heart grows weary,
I never will despair;
I know that He is leading,
Through all the stormy blast;
The day of His appearing
Will come at last.

Rejoice, rejoice, O Christian,
Lift up your voice and sing
Eternal hallelujahs
To Jesus Christ the King!
The hope of all who seek Him,
The help of all who find,
None other is so loving,
So good and kind.

CHAPTER 16

14° 36' 47" N
90° 32' 7" W

AGAINST ALL ODDS

"But as for you, you thought evil against me; but God meant it unto good, to bring to pass, as it is this day, to save much people alive."

— *Genesis 50:20*

AGAINST ALL ODDS

14° 36' 47" N | 90° 32' 7" W

"WE ARE VERY SORRY, but your program this Sunday will be the last one we can air," said the Guatemalan TV station manager, hesitantly, over the telephone. "It will not be possible for you to continue the Jimmy Swaggart telecast on our network."

When I heard this in 1982, my heart sank. At that time, my wife and I, along with our four children, were resident missionaries in Guatemala and had the privilege of establishing the Jimmy Swaggart Ministries outreach office in that huge capital city called Guatemala City.

It was a time in Guatemala when a terrible civil war raged for more than 20 years. Fear and despair had ruled the nation. Every morning, just in the capital city alone, more than 300 dead bodies were picked up off of the streets. These were people whom the rebels, trying to intimidate the population, had killed by shooting innocent people at random. Just one block from the house where we lived, in front of the national university, the insurgents blew up a popular fried chicken restaurant called Pollo Campero.

WAR BROUGHT TO AN END

That was the terrible situation of the whole nation of Guatemala when my family and I moved to the capital of Guatemala after serving as missionaries in South America for some 14 years. The house where we lived was located in Zone 12 of Guatemala City, the capital of the country, right in front of the University of San Carlos. The long Guatemalan civil war lasted from 1962 to 1982. We had arrived in 1981 and were asked by Jimmy Swaggart Ministries to put the ministry's Spanish gospel telecast on a national television network and to establish and operate the JSM Guatemalan outreach office. I accepted, knowing that it was God who had called us to such an hour as this.

We had helped another counseling-type TV ministry establish an office in a downtown office high-rise building, but the response was meager at best, with an average of only one letter per day, if that many, coming into that office. I located a small 12-by-12-foot office space for JSM in the twin towers Sheraton Hotel office complex building. (One tower high-rise was the hotel, and the other tower was the office complex building where companies leased office space for their businesses in downtown Guatemala City.) I was not prepared for the tremendous response, actually, the avalanche of responses from the viewers who watched the very first airing of the telecast.

There were 100 letters the very first day and every day for the first week alone!

The second week, there were 250 letters per day every day that week!

By just the third week, we were receiving more than 500 letters per day — 3,000 letters per week from Guatemalans writing into the Jimmy Swaggart Ministries outreach office address that was placed on the air at the end of the weekly telecast.

Those letters were from people saying that they had prayed with Brother Swaggart and had received the Lord as their Saviour for the first time in their lives. They wanted a Bible portion sent to them and wanted to know where they could attend a church that preached "this same gospel message Brother Swaggart preaches."

PUTTING 3,000 NEW BORN-AGAIN PEOPLE INTO CHURCHES

Very quickly it became evident that the existing churches were not big enough for such a large harvest of souls coming to the Lord. People were getting saved in areas of the city and across the country where there were no churches to put them. All of a sudden, new churches had to be formed, and pastors, many of them lay pastors who had to also work a secular job, started pastoring the new churches that were springing up.

About the third week that the JSM outreach office was in existence, I remember having to get up the nerve to call the JSM headquarters in Baton Rouge, to say that I had miscalculated the small monthly office budget. I related that my wife and a Guatemalan sister who served as secretaries were not enough personnel to confront the avalanche of letters coming into the office. I told them that we needed to add another office helper and expand the office space to the next adjoining room that connected to the small room where we were already located. Of course, JSM responded, and we added another person and the next office room.

Then, the next month, I had to call JSM headquarters again to ask for more help to add another person and add another room. The letters were stacking up, and the office space would not accommodate all the equipment, literature, etc. that was needed to keep up with the response coming directly into the office from so many thousands of television viewers. Finally, we had to rent the whole floor of multiple office spaces to confront the tremendous response to the telecast. A harvest of souls of unparalleled proportions was taking place in Guatemala as a direct result of the Spanish Jimmy Swaggart telecast.

THE SUPREME COURT

The Jimmy Swaggart Spanish telecast was reaching into all levels of Guatemalan society from the lowliest hovel to the highest political, government offices of the land. I remember one morning while briefly at my small desk in the downtown JSM outreach office, the telephone rang.

I answered, "Hello, this is Jimmy Swaggart Ministries. This is Missionary Jim Woolsey. Can I help you?"

"Hello, this is the director of the Guatemalan Supreme Court. We have over 600 employees, including the appointed Supreme Court judges, and we have all been viewing the Jimmy Swaggart telecast on the weekends. Would you be able to send us enough weekly video programs of the telecast so that we can all watch them together each day during our one-hour lunch break?"

"Why, yes," I said. "We will be able to send those over to you on a regular basis."

After the director of the Supreme Court gave me the address at the Supreme Court complex where the tapes could be delivered, he added, "We are using our lunchtime each day now to have a devotional with Brother Swaggart while listening to his preaching."

Approximately a month later, when the daily Jimmy Swaggart teaching program, *A Study in the Word*, began to air in Spanish, the same Supreme Court director called, asking for copies of the daily half-hour teaching programs for the 600 employees' devotional time at lunch, which, of course, we sent over to him. What an impact the telecast was having all over Guatemala!

PENTECOSTAL CHRISTIAN INSTALLED AS PRESIDENT OF GUATEMALA

Then it happened. The government changed and installed a Pentecostal Christian man and former general in the armed forces as the president of Guatemala. Rios Montt, the new president, began to lead the country to peace.

I believe that he was the greatest president Guatemala ever had to serve in that high office, and there has not been one as great and good for the country after him. I remember that he renounced, first of all, the presidential salary. He said that he was a servant of the people and would only operate on the expense budget of the official meeting and travel expenses of the office. He stated that he would not receive the personal large salary a president receives and would still live in his small two-bedroom house in Guatemala City. (Just as an aside, years later, in 2010, I was in Guatemala, and a driver of the rent-a-car told me that he had served as a chauffeur to the previous president of the country. The president the chauffeur worked for received a larger salary than the money earned by the president of the United States.) So, you see, President Rios Montt was not in it for the money as most other presidents were.

INSURGENTS LAY DOWN THEIR ARMS

President Rios Montt invited another missionary, Brother Walter Haydus, and me to the president's palace to speak with him. He was such a congenial, likable man. Of course, we had already seen him on TV talking to the Guatemalan people out of his heart. Actually, he would teach them over television in his nationwide addresses. The people loved him. He began a program of amnesty for the insurgents that was called, "Eighty percent beans and twenty percent bullets." He would supply the insurgent rebels with 80 percent beans (food supplies) and 20 percent ammunition. That was

unheard of, but the number of dead bodies found each morning in the streets began to decrease from an average of 300
per day down to none! Then he offered amnesty to the rebels, saying that if they would turn in their weapons, he would
pardon them and assimilate them back into their hometowns
and give them employment. More than 60,000 hardened
insurgents lay down their weapons and were reinstated back
into their communities and families with a full government
pardon and a job! Peace came to Guatemala at last!

EX-GUERRILLA SOLDIER SHOWED
UP IN THE CARPORT OF OUR HOUSE

One morning during the days of amnesty, while tens of
thousands of rebels were turning in their weapons to the government, I was going out the door of the house where we lived
by the university, and there stood before me a young man.
You could tell that he had been hardened physically from
being in many battles.

He said, "Sir, please forgive me for coming onto your
property, but I do not have anywhere else to turn. They told
me a missionary lived here. I am one of the rebel soldiers who
has surrendered and turned my weapons over to the Guatemalan government. President Rios Montt has given me the
official pardon and has a job waiting for me when I get back to
my home pueblo of Puerto Barrios. My family that I have not
seen in over five years is waiting for me. My problem is that I
do not have the bus fare to return home. Can you help me?"

My mind raced quickly to Puerto Barrios, which is on the exact opposite end of the country, about 300 kilometers (186 miles) northeast of Guatemala City, facing the Gulf of Mexico and located in the Gulf of Honduras. My family and I had been invited to visit this town several weeks before, so I knew very well where his hometown was.

"Well, yes, of course, I will help you," I said. "Congratulations on your amnesty pardon and being reinstated back into your family! I imagine they are very happy about this."

"Yes, they want to know when I will arrive back," he said, "but I could not tell them that I did not have enough money for the bus fare."

CAN GOD FORGIVE ME?

I decided to ask him straight out, "Are you in the family of God? Do you know Jesus Christ as your own personal Saviour?"

"Oh, I want to, but God cannot forgive me," he said. "I have done some terrible things in the war, killing many innocent people. Can He forgive a person like me?"

Repeating his question, I said, "Can He? That is exactly why He died on the Cross. It was for you. Yes, He can forgive you."

I pulled out a Spanish Bible that I carried in the car and asked him to sit down with me on the little 2-foot high wall that ringed the carport area. I began by showing him the answer in God's Word and then listened as he read aloud to me, in Spanish, the following verses:

"For God so loved the world, that He gave his only begotten Son, that whosoever believeth in Him should not perish, but have everlasting life.

"For God sent not His Son into the world to condemn the world; but that the world through Him might be saved" (Jn. 3:16-17).

After explaining with several other Scriptures how Christ came to save us sinners by dying on our behalf as the only perfect sin offering accepted by a thrice-holy God, we then read Isaiah, Chapter 53, together:

"Who hath believed our report? and to whom is the arm of the LORD *revealed?*

For He shall grow up before Him as a tender plant, and as a root out of a dry ground: He hath no form nor comeliness; and when we shall see Him, there is no beauty that we should desire Him.

He is despised and rejected of men; a Man of Sorrows, and acquainted with grief: and we hid as it were our faces from Him; He was despised, and we esteemed Him not.

Surely He hath borne our griefs, and carried our sorrows: yet we did esteem Him stricken, smitten of God, and afflicted.

But He was wounded for our transgressions, He was bruised for our iniquities: the chastisement of our peace was upon Him; and with His stripes we are healed.

All we like sheep have gone astray; we have turned every one to his own way; and the LORD *hath laid on Him the iniquity of us all.*

He was oppressed, and He was afflicted, yet He opened not His mouth: He is brought as a lamb to the slaughter, and as a sheep before her shearers is dumb, so He openeth not his mouth.

He was taken from prison and from judgment: and who shall declare His generation? for He was cut off out of the land of the living: for the transgression of My people was He stricken.

And He made His grave with the wicked, and with the rich in His death; because He had done no violence, neither was any deceit in His mouth.

Yet it pleased the LORD *to bruise Him; He hath put Him to grief: when Thou shalt make His soul an offering for sin, He shall see His seed, He shall prolong His days, and the pleasure of the* LORD *shall prosper in His hand.*

He shall see of the travail of His soul, and shall be satisfied: by His knowledge shall My righteous servant justify many; for He shall bear their iniquities.

Therefore will I divide Him a portion with the great, and He shall divide the spoil with the strong; because He hath poured out His soul unto death: and He was numbered with the transgressors; and He bare the sin of many, and made intercession for the transgressors" (Isa. 53:1-12).

"You mean He did all of that for me?" he asked.

"Yes, He did it all for you. All you have to do is invite him into your heart and life now by faith. Bow your head and repeat after me." I led him in the sinner's prayer, and he repeated it with tears flowing down his cheeks. When He finished, he looked up at me and said, "Thank you, thank you so much. Now with Jesus in my heart, I will not be returning to my family and pueblo as the same old sorry, hateful creature I was but as a new man in Christ! I am truly pardoned now!"

"Yes, hallelujah!" I gave him the Bible we had been reading, some bus fare, money for food, and the times and days to watch the Jimmy Swaggart telecasts. As we parted ways, I thanked God for saving this ex-guerrilla's soul and for all the wonderful things God was doing in this war-torn country through the Jimmy Swaggart telecast and through President Rios Montt's policies. God had truly used these two men of God to bring peace to Guatemala! Of course, Satan did not take it lying down, this great work that God was doing in restoring an entire country to God through the power of the Cross.

SATAN CONTINUED TRYING TO BLOCK THE GOSPEL

After I had received the phone call from the TV network saying that we were off the air for good, I immediately went to the station in the mile-high capital of Guatemala City to speak personally with the manager to see if there was any way we could continue. The response to this weekly gospel telecast had grown to such an extent that nearly 3,000 letters per week were coming into the JSM Guatemala outreach office. Many of those letters related how people had been touched and had given their hearts to the Lord while watching this program. We had been channeling the thousands of new believers into churches all over the country. Where there were no churches, we were establishing new ones so these many people could continue growing in the knowledge and grace of the Lord.

Byron Barbosa, a viewer from Guatemala City, wrote:

"There is such joy in my heart that I just have to write you and tell you what God has done. I have seen your programs on TV, and I love to hear the messages that the Holy Spirit gives you to impart to His people, and that are also for those who are not Christians yet. I had been telling my family about the wonderful TV program that I had seen for the first time. I was so anxious to hear another one of your programs.

On Sunday when it was time for the program to come on, I went through the house, telling everyone to come and watch. My brother was watching another program, so I changed the channel and told him to watch this new program. He said, "Okay," and all of my brothers and my father who were in the house watched with me. When you finished your message, my father, brothers, and I were all sobbing because we had received blessings from God while listening to your preaching. That Sunday night, I invited my father to go to church with me. He accepted the invitation and went with me. He gave his heart to the Lord that night. God broke his heart through your message that afternoon. May God bless you, and I remain your brother in Christ."

So many had been blessed that it did not seem right that the enemy should be able to take the program off the air. A whole generation could possibly be lost if this telecast did not continue. The situation had become a battle between life and death.

I pleaded with the manager, "Is there any way we can continue?"

"No, I am sorry, but the board of this network decided this would be your last program," he said. "As much as I personally would like to see it continue, there is nothing I can do."

THE POPE'S VISIT

This particular network covered about two-thirds of Guatemala. The week after the last telecast was aired, the main TV station's offices were bombarded with telephone calls from irate viewers who protested the station's action in taking our program off. After three days of so many phone calls jamming the station's central switchboard, the manager called to let me know about all of these people calling. He said, "I wish I could do something to get the program back on, but my hands are tied."

He finally admitted "unofficially" that during the pope's recent visit to Guatemala, the wife of the TV network's owner was the special escort to all of the functions on the papal tour.

She went to her husband and complained about our telecast, saying, "We are Roman Catholic. How can we permit this evangelist's program to continue on our network when we are the special hosts for the pope's tour? We cannot let this program continue on our network."

So she had her husband go to the TV station board and cancel the contract for our telecast.

It did not seem right that the enemy of men's souls could use one woman to take the number one rated telecast off the air, all in the name of religion. Christians began to pray. One thing is certain — it is God's will that this gospel be proclaimed on television in every nation of the world.

"And this gospel of the kingdom shall be preached in all the world for a witness unto all nations; and then shall the end come" (Mat. 24:14).

Satan's evil plan is to silence the proclamation of the gospel and to hinder it any way he can because he knows that all who believe in Jesus are liberated from his dark kingdom, just as God's Word states:

"Who hath delivered us from the power of darkness, and hath translated us into the kingdom of His dear Son" (Col. 1:13).

WOULD EVIL PREVAIL?

You see, every time God opens the door of a nation to have this Spirit-anointed ministry aired, it is a miracle. We give God the glory and praise for every TV station that has aired this gospel telecast. However, every time the program begins on a new foreign TV station, the battle also begins. Quite literally, all hell breaks loose! The battle lines are drawn. Powerful forces of darkness begin to work, trying to take this program off the air, thus damning souls to hell. If it weren't for God's power, it would not be possible to be on any station in the world with this glorious gospel message that saves the lost from sin and death.

When in prayer, I asked God, "My Father in heaven, hallowed be Your holy name. You have done great things for us here in Guatemala, for which we are truly thankful and give You all of the glory, honor, and credit. You see how the enemy has come in and tried to stop Your work of the Holy Spirit in bringing Guatemalans to our blessed Lord Christ Jesus. Please have mercy on us now and on the people of Guatemala. Please move on hearts. Please lead me by Your Spirit and show me what to do and what to say."

The next morning, I felt led of the Spirit to go to the largest TV network in Guatemala and try to have the program put on the air. This particular network covers virtually all of Guatemala's 7.5 million people.

After checking around to find out with whom to arrange an appointment, I was told in no uncertain terms: "You know you are going against all odds. This network, even though it is the best in Guatemala and has the largest viewership, is under strong Catholic control and has never permitted any foreign program to be aired on its stations. It will be a miracle if they even give you an appointment."

The first few visits to this powerful TV network's offices were quite discouraging, but each time, the Lord would say, "Keep going back."

Finally, after more than five attempts, the station management called a meeting with all of the board members present. We negotiated price, time slot, and dates back and forth during three more meetings. Still, there was no word as to whether the network's owners had accepted the program.

VICTORY

The phone rang. The person on the other end was the TV network's director. He called to give me the final decision: "You're on! Come and sign the contract. We've never done anything like this before, but somehow, everyone involved has approved the contract. Not only that, but our affiliate network will also air your daily programs."

What a victory! Not only was the ministry's weekly Spanish telecast now on the best network in Guatemala that covers the whole country plus spilling over into El Salvador, Mexico, Belize, and Honduras, but the daily Spanish *A Study in the Word* programs were also added and put on the air. What the enemy meant for evil, God turned to good. It reminds me of words spoken a long time ago:

"But as for you, ye thought evil against me; but God meant it unto good, to bring to pass, as it is this day, to save much people alive" (Gen. 50:20).

After the telecast began airing on this large network, the number of response letters grew from 500 per day to more than 1,500 per day — more than 8,000 letters per week! People were coming to the Lord literally by the thousands. The people began asking when Brother and Sister Swaggart and the team would come for a nationwide crusade. An official invitation was sent from the combined evangelical churches of Guatemala, requesting that Brother and Sister Swaggart come to Guatemala to hold a crusade. They kindly accepted.

DONNIE SWAGGART INSTALLED CRUSADE IN THE NATIONAL STADIUM

We were able to acquire the large National Stadium located in Guatemala City. When Brother Donnie Swaggart and the television crew, singers, and musicians arrived, they began to install the platform and equipment for the crusade to be televised worldwide. This was no small undertaking. Brother Donnie worked tirelessly directing the massive installation of the necessary equipment, which took several days to complete before a crusade could begin. Later, I watched Brother Donnie in the many subsequent overseas crusades in various countries of the world work tirelessly each day on the ground before the crusade services began. His job was to ensure that everything was in place and operational so that there would be no glitches during the live televised and recorded crusade services. They would be seen around the world and would enable millions of people — not only in America, but also in nations all over the face of the earth — to share in the blessings these crusades would bring to the hosting country. (The story of what God did in the many other crusades around the world will have to be told in another book at a later date.)

On the first day of the crusade, before the service took place, I had the privilege of interpreting for Pastor Donnie when he addressed a large gathering of the pastors and their wives, along with the leaders of the work of the Lord in Guatemala. Brother Donnie preached in a large meeting auditorium and wow, what a message of encouragement he delivered that day! Everyone was primed and ready with anticipation for the start of the first crusade service that night in the huge soccer stadium.

The entire National Stadium was packed to capacity with the dear Guatemalan people seeking God at each service. There were more than a total of 152,500 people in attendance during the three days of meetings. The Sunday meeting drew so many that 10,000 people had to be turned away outside because the stadium was filled to maximum capacity. We were told later that this was the largest gathering for a gospel event in the National Stadium in the history of the country.

Brother and Sister Walter Haydus, missionaries for more than 38 years of their lives in the harvest fields of the Caribbean and Central America, stated: "If it were not for Jimmy Swaggart's ministry in Guatemala, we would never have experienced this harvest of such great magnitude. Without your help, we would still be so far behind."

IVORY COAST: THE ENEMY TRIED AGAIN

I want you to know that Guatemala was not an isolated case. The enemy does not like the true gospel of Jesus Christ and wants to stop it, therefore, let us revisit Ivory Coast for a minute. There was another instance of God going against all odds. In that great West African country, the dear missionaries had tried everything they could to have the program aired each week, but to no avail.

An Ivory Coast missionary described it this way: "The first broadcast was televised on Christmas Day, and that was to launch the weekly programs, but there were no further broadcasts for three months. Then, in April, the weekly program began airing each Sunday morning. Six weeks later, the telecast was abruptly discontinued and replaced by an aerobics show. We called the station and were told that there had been opposition from some religious leaders who said that such a program would 'drive people crazy.'"

On the other hand, hundreds of letters began pouring in to the Ivory Coast television station, demanding that the telecast continue. We were later told that the telephone switchboards of the network were jammed with calls for three days straight.

Not knowing what to do, the program director presented the conflict to his superiors. There are unconfirmed reports that this went all the way to the president of the republic (prime minister), who issued an order to the TV station to put the telecast back on the air. The JSM one-hour program went back on every Sunday morning all over the country, for which we thanked the Lord.

UPLIFTING NEWS

No matter how great the odds are against the gospel and evangelization, God is greater!

We are told that in Guatemala today, more than 45 percent of the population is made up of born-again believers! We would like to think God has used this ministry's telecast as a great part in this harvest. As missionaries to Guatemala at the time, we can attest to this fact because we personally channeled hundreds of thousands of new believers into the churches of Guatemala through the JSM outreach office.

As well, we had new churches built where there were none to accommodate the great numbers of people who came to Christ as a direct result of Jimmy Swaggart Ministries. This is the real story of what the Holy Spirit accomplished and continues to do through Jimmy and Frances Swaggart's ministry to a lost and dying world. I am so thankful as a missionary to Guatemala that the Jimmy Swaggart telecast was able to go to Guatemala because it changed the lives of millions of people forever!

A missions leader of one of the largest numbers of missionaries on the field in Latin America called the other day to say, "Does Brother Swaggart know that an intensive survey was made of all churches in Latin America, which took over a year to collect all of the data? Among the questions asked of believers in each country was, 'How did you come to the Lord and get saved?' Over 85 percent of all believers throughout Latin America responded, 'It was through the Jimmy Swaggart telecast that I received Christ as my own personal Saviour.' The survey concluded that 85 percent of all born-again believers in Latin America came to the Lord as a result of Jimmy Swaggart Ministries."

God is performing a work unknown in the history of missions to reach a lost world with the gospel, for the time is short.

"For He will finish the work, and cut it short in righteousness: because a short work will the Lord *make upon the earth"* (Rom. 9:28).

To God be all the glory!

There are things as we travel this earth's shifting sands,
That transcend all the reason of man,
But the things that matter the most in this world,
They can never be held in our hand.

I believe in a hill called Mount Calvary,
I believe whatever the cost,
And when time has surrendered and earth is no more,
I'll still cling to that old rugged Cross.

I believe that the Christ who was slain on the Cross,
Has the power to change lives today,
For He changed me completely, a new life is mine,
That is why by the Cross I will stay.

I believe that this life with its great mysteries,
Surely someday will come to an end,
But faith will conquer the darkness and death,
And will lead me at last to my friend.

I believe in a hill called Mount Calvary,
I believe whatever the cost,
And when time has surrendered and earth is no more,
I'll still cling to that old rugged Cross.

CHAPTER 17

25° 1' 58" N
121° 33' 55" E

THIS IS A REAL HALLELUJAH

"Open to me the gates of righteousness: I will go into them, and I will praise the LORD."

— *Psalm 118:19*

THIS IS A REAL HALLELUJAH

25° 1′ 58″ N | 121° 33′ 55″ E

"Your program will not work here because the Chinese people do not relate to Americans, much less to a North American preacher."

This was the first thing the missionary told me, in no uncertain terms, as he drove me from the airport to downtown Taipei, Taiwan. I had just come off a flight that took some 38 hours straight, including connections, to arrive and hear this statement of unbelief.

He continued, "If Jimmy Swaggart goes on television here, the people will not understand the terms he uses in his preaching. The only way to reach the Taiwanese people is with Taiwanese people in their own language."

"Yes, that is one way," I agreed, "but another way to reach even more Taiwanese is with this ministry's gospel telecast. The same thing had been stated in country after country before our telecast was aired."

I gave him an example. "For instance, in Japan they told us that the stoic Japanese people are not emotional and, therefore, would not display any emotional response. However, when the programs began airing, the missionaries immediately received calls from Japanese pastors, with each stating something like this: 'We do not understand it, but as we watch the program, our hearts are touched by what Brother Swaggart says. Tears stream down our cheeks as we hear about Jesus and His wonderful love for us.'"

Still sensing the missionary's unbelief, I continued.

"The Japanese television network switchboard was jammed three days straight with Japanese calling, wanting to know when they could see another Jimmy Swaggart program. Even the network's board of directors confessed that they viewed the first telecast together in their boardroom. As the Holy Spirit touched their hearts, the shoulders of grown Japanese men began to heave, and they began to weep, with tears running down their cheeks while listening to Brother Swaggart preach."

Of course, we know it was the Holy Spirit cutting through hardened shells of culture, tradition, and sin to reach each viewer's heart. That was what made this telecast so different — the preaching was for the heart, not so much for the head.

FRUSTRATION

Even though I tried to explain to this dear missionary brother the impact this Spirit-anointed telecast had had upon the hearts and lives of viewers, even those in nations seemingly resistant to the gospel, his response was still: "I just cannot believe it. Even though it may have happened in other countries, it cannot happen here. The Taiwan Chinese are different from other countries."

I asked the doubting missionary, "Could we at least give it a try? I know you do not believe that this program will work here in Taiwan, but I believe you are wrong. Let's at least give the Holy Spirit a chance by trying to place this program on a television network here in Taiwan and then let the results speak for themselves."

He responded reluctantly. "Okay, we will try our best, but just remember, this North American program will have little influence upon the Taiwanese."

FALSE GODS

As we drove through the streets of downtown Taipei, I noticed that along the sidewalks were smoking pots with small posters or pictures standing behind them.

"What are these people doing?" I asked.

He explained, "The Chinese people purchase worthless paper money called 'god money' to burn in these containers. In this way, they worship the many gods they serve and also reverence their long-departed ancestors that have gone into the other life. They believe that as a result of burning this paper money to their ancestors, they will receive prosperity and blessing upon their businesses and families."

As we rounded another corner on this Chinese New Year's Day, we came head-on into a long "parade of dragons." There were hundreds of people dressed up with dragon heads covering them, chanting in loud voices. Firecrackers and loud music blared as they trampled down the center of the street in this religious ritual. I was told later that when they put on these dragon heads, they believe they become gods and, at the same time, act on behalf of the many other gods they serve.

My heart ached as I thought not only of the many millions of people in Taiwan that are lost in the darkness of a religious lie, but of the billions around the world that are lost in serving false gods.

Only our God can save the lost! Speaking of Jesus, the writer of Hebrews declared:

"He is able also to save them to the uttermost that come unto God by Him" (Heb. 7:25).

Can God actually use the telecast and now the SonLife Broadcasting Network to break through these insurmountable cultural and religious barriers? I know beyond the shadow of a doubt that He can. I am convinced that if this SBN programming can be put on the powerful TV and cable networks of any country, the Holy Spirit will use it to bring in the greatest harvest of souls that has ever been known in a country's history.

MORE OBSTACLES

After meeting with a television agent in Taipei, we found out that the major network in Taiwan was controlled by a Roman Catholic priest and that the agent through whom we would have to negotiate was a devout Buddhist. These would be two enormous obstacles we would have to overcome in order to get the program aired. You see, Satan does not want this gospel programming to air in any country. He knows it will liberate people of any nation from his iniquitous kingdom of darkness. He uses every means available to try to stop the proclamation of the gospel, but our God is greater than the Devil and all of his devices, demons, and despots put together! Jesus has actually already defeated every one of them in the Cross! There are no more demons to defeat.

"It pleased God by the foolishness of preaching to save them that believe" (I Cor. 1:21).

Since there wasn't enough time for an appointment with either the Buddhist or the Roman Catholic priest during this particular trip, I asked the missionary to set up some appointments to show the audition tape at a later date.

Several weeks afterward, I received an exciting telephone call from the missionary in Taipei. He said, "I cannot believe it! I started showing the Jimmy Swaggart audition tape to the Buddhist agent and several other people. I actually saw how much the telecast affected them and how much they liked it. This program really does cause an impact upon those who view it!" He asked me to come back to meet with them.

DO YOU KNOW ANYONE?

After another long trip, I was meeting with the Buddhist when he blatantly told me, "It will be impossible to get on any of the television networks here in Taiwan because you have to know someone related to these networks to acquire a time slot. Do you know anyone?"

I said, "I know God, and I know you. Hallelujah! I think that is enough."

The Buddhist looked at me in utter dismay and said, "Yes, I said you have to know someone, but God? And what does 'hallelujah' mean? I have never heard that before."

Of course, I explained to him, "Christians use the term *hallelujah*, meaning *'praise the Lord,'* when they feel God is in something, is about to do something, or has done something impossible."

The Buddhist said good-bye and stated, "The only thing I can promise you is to at least try to see if there might be a time slot available on Sundays for the program."

Although he gave us very little hope, I continued on to my next destination.

A REAL HALLELUJAH!

A few weeks later, the missionary received a telephone call from the Buddhist, who was very excited and didn't know how to begin to relate the good news. Trying to describe something out of the ordinary that had happened, he blurted out, "Pastor, this is a real hallelujah!

The missionary asked, "What is it?"

"It's hard to believe," the Buddhist said, "but there will be a time slot available from 10 to 11 o'clock on Sunday mornings for the Jimmy Swaggart telecast! He continued, saying, "A Catholic priest will have to sign the authorization for this particular nationwide network so the program can be aired."

About one week later, the Buddhist called again and said, "This is another real hallelujah! The Catholic priest has just signed the authorization for this telecast to be aired. Can you bring me the telecast tapes as soon as possible?"

THE RESULTS

After the telecast went on the air in Taiwan, reaching more than 19 million people in this Far East country, the response was truly phenomenal.

In fact, the response to the weekly program was so great that the ministry's daily program, *A Study in the Word*, also began airing all over Taiwan because of what the network called, "by popular demand."

This gospel of Jesus Christ is for everyone! Truly this is a real hallelujah!

"He staggered not at the promise of God through unbelief; but was strong in faith, giving glory to God" (Rom. 4:20).

Hallelujah, what a thought!
Jesus full salvation brought,
Victory, victory;
Let the pow'rs of sin assail,
Heaven's grace can never fail,
Victory, victory.

Victory, yes, victory.
Hallelujah! I am free,
Jesus gives me victory;
Glory, glory! hallelujah!
He is all in all to me.

I am trusting in the Lord,
I am standing on His Word,
Victory, victory;

I have peace and joy within,
Since my life is free from sin,
Victory, victory.

Shout your freedom everywhere,
His eternal peace declare,
Victory, victory,
Let us sing it here below,

In the face of every foe,
Victory, victory.

We will sing it on that shore,
When this fleeting life is o'er,
Victory, victory;

Sing it here, ye ransomed throng,
Start the everlasting song:
Victory, victory.

CHAPTER 18

24° 51' 41" N
67° 0' 35" E

THE GIANT OF KARACHI

*"All flesh shall know that I the Lord
am thy Saviour and thy Redeemer."*

— Isaiah 49:26

THE GIANT OF KARACHI

24° 51' 41" N | 67° 0' 35" E

AFTER FLYING ALL NIGHT from Beijing, China, to Karachi, Pakistan (a long and tiring 8-hour flight across Asia), I found myself in the midst of an almost 100 percent Muslim country. After checking into the downtown hotel, I picked up an English language newspaper with the blaring headlines, "All Pakistani TV stations have been closed to visitors, and security has been doubled until further notice." The leaders of the country had taken these added precautions to ensure the security of their national communication in the face of on-going fighting of insurgents trying to overthrow the government.

I prayed, "Oh, merciful heavenly Father, what do we do now? I have come halfway around the world only to find that the television network is closed. What shall I do, Lord?" After praying, I felt impressed of the Lord that I should at least try to get into the TV station and speak to the program director concerning the possibility of airing the Jimmy Swaggart telecast.

A CLOSED TV STATION

After a rough taxi ride through downtown Karachi, I arrived at the control gate of the TV station at about 8:30 in the morning. Sure enough, guards stood at the entrance gate and door of this main TV center for Pakistan. I went into the security office at the main gate and asked, "May I please see the program director?"

The man in charge replied, "You have come too early, but maybe if you come back at 10 o'clock, you can see someone, but I can't guarantee it."

I used the next hour and a half to confirm my airline ticket on to Frankfurt, Germany, for a departure flight that same night.

A GIANT ENTRANCE

At about 10 a.m., I returned to the television station and asked the head of security in the same office at the main gate, "May I see the program director now?"

He started shuffling the papers on his desk and making some lame excuses. "Well, he is very busy at the moment; I think he is in a meeting."

Once again I asked the man, "Please take me to the program director." While I was saying this to him, I heard the door open behind me and the shuffle of feet.

Just as I finished my plea to the military guard, I heard a deep voice behind me say, "Come, I take you!"

When I turned around, I was looking stomach-level at the belt buckle of a giant of a man—undoubtedly the largest man I had ever seen in my life! Now, at 6 feet 2inches tall, I am not a short man. Still, I found myself lifting my eyes higher and higher up at this man who was towering over me; he seemed to be over nine feet tall!

"Follow me!" he commanded.

What do you do when a huge giant tells you to follow him? Of course, you follow him.

THEY PUT THEIR GUNS DOWN

As I walked with this man into the main door of the television station, the guards all stepped back and put their weapons to one side, laying them down on nearby tables. I don't know who this man was; he could have been employed by the TV station, or he could have been someone off the street, I really don't know. However, as I walked alongside him, I felt a strong sense of security — this man could go into any office of this building complex he wanted without anyone questioning him.

We walked down several halls together on the way to the office of the director general of the Karachi television station. This giant of a man opened the door, walked right through the secretary's office, opened another door to the director general, and motioned me inside and to take a seat. I was barely able to mutter a "thank you" when he turned and left.

Here I thought I was going to see a program director, but God sent a giant to open the door of the director general's private office on the very same day the government had taken security measures and had closed the television center of Pakistan to all visitors!

Who was that very large man? I don't know, but one thing I do know: I felt the presence of the Lord as I walked with him and even as I waited in the director's office.

WE WATCHED THE TAPE

The director general and I began to talk, and I pulled out of my briefcase one of the audition video tapes of the Jimmy Swaggart telecast that I had with me and asked, "Do you have a video tape player and TV monitor available on which we can view this? I think you will enjoy this program. It is the number one rated program in many of the countries where it airs on their nationwide television networks."

He took the tape out of my hand and turned around to a huge wall of high-tech electronic equipment behind him. He shoved the professional video cassette tape of the Jimmy Swaggart program into a complex, multi-slotted player designed for this purpose.

When we were about a quarter of the way through the videotape, he said, "Please, let me stop the tape for a moment and call my technical director and program director in here to see this great program."

These other directors brought in their assistants, and the room became quite crowded with people watching the telecast tape. After the first tape was finished, the director general asked, "Do you have any more tapes?"

"Yes, of course," I replied, pulling another program tape out and handing it to him.

A TELEPHONE CALL TO THE TOP

While we were watching the second program, the director general picked up the telephone and called the head of communications in the capital city of Islamabad. They talked in the Urdu language for quite some time. Then he handed me the telephone, saying, "Here, the director of all television in Pakistan would like to speak with you."

This man in charge of the five government-owned TV centers located throughout all of Pakistan said to me, "My director general of the Karachi television center says that the program you are marketing is quite good and I agree. It is very good. I saw it at the same time you all were viewing it."

"How were you able to do that from so far away?" I asked.

"I had my Karachi director air it nationwide from the equipment in his office that he used to play your program video tape. His equipment is wired to have that capability," he said. "What kind of arrangement can we make to have this program aired over our nationwide Pakistani network?"

He was delighted when I offered him 13 programs free of charge. After a lengthy conversation, he invited me to meet with him again in three months to discuss a continued contract. While we were talking, the director of Karachi TV was having the physical shipping address and telephone numbers written down so we could send these first tapes to the network.

GOD AGAIN PERFORMED THE IMPOSSIBLE

After the customary cup of tea, the Karachi director general and all of his associates bade me farewell. As I was going out the door of his office, I turned around and asked them, "Who was the kind, giant of a man who led me all the way here to your office? Does the giant work for the Pakistani television network?"

"Giant? What giant? We did not see anyone with you and besides, there isn't a giant on the premises," was their reply.

As I walked back out of the television network's multi-story office building, I looked for my friend, "the giant," but he was nowhere to be found. As I went out the guarded front gate, I stopped a minute and looked back at the television network complex and gratefully said, "God, You have done the impossible again. You unlocked the lock by sending a giant to escort me through the front door of a TV network barricaded by military in an Islamic country. Thank you so much! I give You the glory for fulfilling Your Word!"

This was a beginning for Pakistan — a crack in the door that was closed so long. God's promise is that:

"All flesh shall know that I the LORD *am thy Saviour and thy Redeemer"* (Isa. 49:26).

"And this gospel of the kingdom shall be preached in all the world for a witness unto all nations; and then shall the end come" (Mat. 24:14).

GOD WANTS THIS MESSAGE PREACHED IN THE ENTIRE WORLD

Why? Because there are more than 100 million dear Pakistanis who need Jesus as their Saviour. In fact, this entire world of more than 7 billion people needs to know Him. Only 13 programs aired for 13 weeks at that time; they could not continue because of a military coup that changed the government. But at least for a moment, all Pakistan television viewers of that particular generation had the privilege of hearing the glorious gospel of Jesus Christ.

"For whosoever shall call upon the name of the Lord shall be saved.
"How then shall they call on Him in whom they have not believed? and how shall they believe in Him of whom they have not heard? and how shall they hear without a preacher?
"And how shall they preach, except they be sent? as it is written, How beautiful are the feet of them that preach the gospel of peace, and bring glad tidings of good things" (Rom. 10:13-15).

Just who was the giant of Karachi?

In shady, green pastures, so rich and so sweet,
God leads His dear children along;
Where the water's cool flow bathes the weary one's feet,
God leads His dear children along.

Some through the waters, some through the flood,
Some through the fire, but all through the blood;
Some through great sorrow, but God gives a song,
In the night season and all the day long.

Sometimes on the mount where the sun shines so bright,
God leads His dear children along;
Sometimes in the valley, in darkest of night,
God leads His dear children along.

Though sorrows befall us and evils oppose,
God leads His dear children along;
Through grace we can conquer, defeat all our foes,
God leads His dear children along.

Away from the mire, and away from the clay,
God leads His dear children along;
Away up in glory, eternity's day,
God leads His dear children along.

Sometimes I feel discouraged and I think my work's in vain,
I'm tempted oft to murmur, to grumble and complain,
Oh, but then I think of Jesus and what He's done for me,
And then I cry, oh, Rock of Ages, hide Thou me.

Oh, Rock of Ages, hide Thou me,
There is no other refuge can save, Lord, but Thee,
And through this dark world I've wandered far, far from Thee,
But then I cry, oh, Rock of Ages, hide Thou me.

Oh, Rock of Ages, hide Thou me,
There is no other refuge can save, Lord, but Thee,
Through this dark world I've wandered far, far from Thee,
But then I cried, oh, Rock of Ages, hide Thou Me.

Oh but then I cried, oh, Rock of Ages, hide Thou Me.

24° 51' 41" N
67° 0' 35" E

LOOK TO JESUS

"But mine eyes are unto Thee, O
*G*OD *the Lord: in Thee is my*
trust; leave not my soul destitute."

— *Psalm 141:8*

LOOK TO JESUS

24° 51' 41" N | 67° 0' 35" E

"YOUR FLIGHT INTO ANGOLA has been canceled. There will not be another flight until Friday, and we cannot confirm that one," was the announcement given to me by the airline office.

There I was in the very heart of Africa in Lusaka, Zambia, and it looked as if months of preparation to go into the war-torn country of Angola would be wasted.

This was on a Wednesday, and I would have to wait until Friday to go into Angola, with the possibility of that flight also being canceled. Going in on Friday also meant that I would have to meet with the people at the Angolan television network on Saturday — if they would be in. This particular journey was getting more complicated all the time.

Should I just forget about Angola and change the itinerary?

The Holy Spirit impressed upon my heart, "There will not be a better opportunity. There are more than 9 million people in Angola who need the gospel *now*. If you wait, I will make a way."

NO APPOINTMENT

A telephone call into Angola was not possible, so I contacted our Baton Rouge office to see if they could get word to the missionary to see if it would be possible to arrange an appointment for Saturday. The answer came back that an appointment had been arranged.

Sure enough, Friday evening I was on a plane going into the capital city of Luanda. Upon arrival, I was met by some of the most dedicated missionaries I know, as well as the leaders of the Angolan Assemblies of God.

As we drove away from the airport toward the Bible school that Jimmy Swaggart Ministries had helped build in a new section of this large capital city, I told the brethren, "Thank God it is at least possible to meet with the network director tomorrow even though it will be Saturday."

"You are to meet with the TV director tomorrow?" one of the missionaries asked. "Your office called from the States, telling us that *they* made an appointment for tomorrow. Is this true?"

"Oh, my!" I exclaimed. "They told me that *you* had set up the appointment here in Angola." At some point in the translation, there had been a mix-up, and no appointment had been set up.

Making matters worse, the missionary told me, "The audition tapes you sent me about seven months ago were returned to me with a note saying that they could not use them on the network."

An impossible situation was getting worse by the minute!

"Can we at least call the station tonight and get the telephone number of the director to see if we could meet with someone tomorrow?" I asked.

The missionaries denied my request, saying, "It would not do much good, and no one knows the telephone number of the station anyway." It seemed that everyone had given up on the idea that our telecast could be aired on Angolan TV.

These brethren were some of the kindest, godliest men I had ever met, but you have to understand that in most Marxist countries, the opportunity to air a gospel program looks rather forbidding — even next to impossible. This is because of the many restrictions that can exist regarding religious activity, and the freedom to preach is greatly curtailed or prohibited.

AN IMPOSSIBLE SITUATION

As we drove on toward the new Angolan Bible school, we passed one of the large Cuban military bases. Earlier, when my plane had landed, I had noticed that huge Soviet airplanes were unloading many tanks. Out of curiosity I asked, "Have they been delivering tanks to Angola for awhile now?"

With some concern in their voices, they told me that for several weeks, a steady stream of Soviet tanker airplanes had been landing and unloading scores of these tanks and weapons of warfare.

War continued to rage daily in this place.

One missionary told me, "On the average, every four minutes, a child dies in Angola. Tropical diseases, such as cholera, are on the increase in various parts of the country. Just yesterday, I helped a poor man and his wife bury their 2-year-old daughter. I counted 40 fresh graves where children had been buried only the day before."

My heart was broken when I knelt to pray sometime after midnight. It seemed that the Devil had gained the upper hand in this beautiful country and now wanted to destroy these dear people with war, starvation, and disease.

I could almost feel the weight of a million worlds bearing down, with every demon of hell screaming, "See, you're wasting your time. You've come more than 15,000 miles to no avail. No one will be at the station tomorrow. You are a fool to even think the telecast can be aired on Angolan television in Portuguese!"

I began to pray, "My merciful Father in heaven, oh Lord, what are we to do now?"

LOOK TO ME

The answer came so clearly to my heart: "Look to Me!" I knew that was all that was needed. Micah the prophet said it like this:

"Therefore I will look unto the LORD; I will wait for the God of my salvation: my God will hear me" (Mic. 7:7).

When the powers of hell have closed all doors, and it seems there is no way out, look to Him! He is the only answer in every situation!

I knew after that time in prayer that this impossible turn of events was the opportunity for which God was waiting to let the Holy Spirit have His way where there was seemingly no way at all. Oh, what a mighty God we serve!

GUNSHOTS WENT OFF

The next morning, I awoke with a start. Gunshots were blasting from a machine gun on the hill behind the Bible school. Somewhat startled, I said to the missionary, "Somebody is shooting a gun near here!"

"Don't worry about it," he said. "Some Cuban soldier is probably just shooting a round into the air to scare thieves away." I could not know if he was saying this to be kind, but I did know that I didn't want my wife's husband to be hit by a stray bullet!

When we arrived at the station, to everyone's amazement, the director was in his office. He watched one of the audition tapes in Portuguese on the portable unit I carried with me. You could feel the Holy Spirit in the room. You could also see that the director was engrossed in the program. Then in the message Brother Swaggart said, "Don't look to America for help! Don't look to religion for help! Don't look to Islam, Buddhism, or socialism! There is only One who can solve your sin problem—that's Jesus! Look to Him! Because Jesus is God! Jesus is God! Jesus is God!"

TOO DIRECT

After viewing the tape, I explained to the director, "The telecast is reaching more than 300 million people in about one-third of the world each week. This Portuguese Jimmy Swaggart program covers all of Brazil and is on TV in Portugal. On more than 3,400 TV stations on all continents of this globe, people are pointed to Jesus as the only Saviour who can set man free from sin and change the human heart, and it's because of His death on the Cross of Calvary."

"The policy of our network does not permit such religious programming," the director said. "It is too direct. We are a secular society."

"With all due respect, it is more than a mere religious program," I countered. "We are not talking about a religion but a relationship. We are talking about a person — Jesus Christ. These telecasts deal with the heart of man. The messages in these programs give hope and change lives."

I went on to tell him how, when Brother Swaggart was in the Soviet Union, he was interviewed on local Soviet television and asked what he felt was the USSR officials' concept of Christians.

I said, "If I remember correctly, Brother Swaggart responded with, 'All the Soviet officials I have met feel that true Christians make the best Soviet citizens. True Christians do not lie, steal, or drink. They are punctual on the job, work the hardest, and are faithful to their families and to the betterment of Soviet society. Even in the Portuguese-speaking Marxist country of Mozambique where our telecast is aired, the government has written, thanking us for the tele-cast and stating that it gives their people hope.'"

I could see that the Holy Spirit was touching the director's heart.

He said, "As much as we would want to put your program on, it is too direct. We are not allowed to put someone on our network who talks directly to the people."

"Well, maybe you can try our half-hour daily telecast for 26 weeks and then put the weekly one-hour program on thereafter," I suggested.

He viewed some segments of the dailies with music and said, "Very well, we will take 26 weeks of the half-hour program, but only one per week."

After leaving the station, the brethren with me burst out, "Didn't you feel the presence of the Holy Spirit in there? It was so evident!"

Later we showed the audition tape to the executive brethren of the Angolan work, and they praised the Lord, exclaiming, "This is the kind of preaching we need here in Angola!"

LOOK TO JESUS

As the brethren drove me to the airport, they stopped at the downtown Luanda Evangelistic Center where a youth rally was in progress, with thousands of Angolan youth present. They had asked me to preach. As I preached the only gospel that changes hearts and gives hope to the impoverished soul, I said, "Look to Jesus! He will bring you through!"

As the psalmist said so aptly long ago,

"But mine eyes are unto Thee, O GOD the Lord: in Thee is my trust; leave not my soul destitute" (Ps. 141:8).

We did not have to wait 26 weeks to see if the weekly telecast could be aired. It was only after airing a few half-hour programs of *A Study in the Word* that the director called, saying, "This is amazing! So many people like the Jimmy Swaggart telecast that our switchboards are jammed for two to three days all day long, with people calling and asking, 'When can we see another Jimmy Swaggart program?' Even Cuban soldiers have called, asking the same thing."

"So," the director continued, "our Angolan executive television board has decided to ask you to send the weekly one-hour Portuguese telecast and the daily half-hour *A Study in the Word* programs so we can air them every day of the week. Are you able to do that?"

"Of course," I said. "We will be more than happy to send these to you on a continuing basis." As a result, many Angolans came to the Lord in a great harvest of souls!

This message is so important that God says,

"Look unto Me, and be ye saved, all the ends of the earth: for I am God, and there is none else" (Isa. 45:22).

Look to Him alone and what He did for you at the Cross!

O soul, are you weary and troubled?
No light in the darkness you see?
There's light for a look at the Saviour,
And life more abundant and free!

Turn your eyes upon Jesus,
Look full in His wonderful face,
And the things of earth will grow strangely dim,
In the light of His glory and grace.

Through death into life everlasting
He passed, and we follow Him there;
O'er us sin no more hath dominion —
For more than conqu'rors we are!

His Word shall not fail you — He promised;
Believe Him, and all will be well:
Then go to a world that is dying,
His perfect salvation to tell!

CHAPTER 20

64° 10' 30" N
51° 44' 20" W

64° 10' 30" N
51° 44' 20" W

THE MOST
IMPORTANT THING

"For I am not ashamed of the gospel of Christ: for it is the power of God unto salvation to every one that believeth."

— Romans 1:16

THE MOST IMPORTANT THING

64° 10' 30" N | 51° 44' 20" W

AFTER BEING CAUGHT IN a snowstorm an entire day and night on the southern tip of Greenland, we finally boarded the small plane that would take us to the capital city of Nuuk. We were trying to get to the TV station headquarters on this largest island in the world. Our JSM Iceland office director, Gunnar Thorsteinsson, one of the godliest men I know, was traveling with me from Reykjavik. Thank God, the snow had stopped long enough for the plane to take off.

No sooner had we arrived in Nuuk than we made our way over to the KNR Greenlandic television network station. As we walked down the street, Gunnar pointed out, "Did you notice that almost everyone we have passed on the street is drunk? They tell me that Greenland has the highest drinking rate in the world and the highest number of broken jawbones. Entire towns stay drunk for days. Also, this nation has the highest venereal disease rate in the world. It seems that the people have no hope. They have nothing to live for."

We were escorted into the TV building, but the network director was in the studio interviewing political candidates on a live program. It seemed that their main platform for running in the upcoming election was a promise that "no government officials would be allowed in the parliamentary sessions if drunk." Since the interview would last another hour or two, we were asked to return at 10 p.m. This did not pose a problem as the sun did not set at that particular time of the year in Greenland until after midnight.

After a bite to eat at a hotel nearby, we returned to the station and wandered into the studio where the interview had been held. Everyone had left by then, and we were asked to wait for the director's return, which would be in a few minutes.

The thing that startled us was that almost the entire floor of the studio was covered with empty beer bottles and glasses. Apparently, after the live interview, the participants had celebrated with a full-scale beer bust. I wondered, "How many in America do the same after media interviews, pop and rock music shows, or even newscasts?"

When the director arrived, we went into his office. Shelves were lined with books and pamphlets from Russia. He watched an audition tape of our program with us, and since he could speak English, he said, "The video quality is excellent, but since we are still under Danish broadcasting policies, it will be impossible to air a religious program."

My heart sank. We talked for awhile, but we weren't getting anywhere. It looked hopeless.

GREENLAND'S ONLY HOPE

Then I said, "Sir, this is more than just a religious program. This is the most important thing in all of the world. It is the gospel of Jesus Christ — the only thing that can give Greenland hope and set your dear people free from the bondages of sin."

I spotted a Greenlandic newspaper near his desk and picked it up. "What does this headline say?"

He translated, "Aids Will Destroy Greenlandic Society In A Short Time."

Still holding the newspaper I said, "Sir, do you mean to tell me that your network will not air the only thing that will restrain this menace of sin and save your beautiful country from extinction? Do you mean to tell me that you would prefer that your dear Greenlanders die of AIDS and venereal disease and go to hell than to have the gospel that saves men's souls and changes their lives preached over your airwaves? Sir, this gospel telecast is your country's only hope! This is the most important program you will ever have on TV in Greenland because of the gospel it brings to your people!"

The director coughed, sputtered a little, and then reluctantly said, "All right! But your program will probably start out on Monday nights at 11 o'clock, and it has to be in our Greenlandic language."

"Fine, any time will do to start, but you will see that it will become the most liked and most viewed program on your network. And we are more than happy to prepare it in your language," I said, elated.

Now, you may be thinking, "Why be so abrupt and to the point? What you said seems too hard!"

I'll tell you why—because men and women are lost, and Jesus is the only answer! The preaching of the gospel is the most important thing in the world. When Philip went down to Samaria, he preached Jesus (Acts 8:4-40).

Philip didn't sit around strategizing or forming committees on how to evangelize the world; he went and preached Jesus, being led of the Holy Spirit.

15° 25' 0" S | 28° 16' 59" E

NOT THE ONLY TIME

This is not the only time I have had to get down to basics when negotiating with a station. The beautiful country of Zambia in the heart of Africa was a country not only dominated by Islam and communism when I first arrived there, but also by Satanism. In Zambia, after having a phenomenal effect on the viewers, our program — the only gospel program on the air at that time — was taken off the air because too many of Satan's captives were liberated by the power of the Holy Spirit.

After a long and tiring flight from another part of the world, I landed once again in Lusaka, the capital of Zambia, and went directly to the television headquarters. Several reasons were given for canceling the program, such as the reorganization of Zambia Broadcasting Services (ZTV) and the need for fairness to other religious groups. Of course, these were no excuses at all for taking the most important thing in the world — the preaching of the gospel — off the air.

In fact, I am of the firm belief that God permitted every television station and every cable and satellite system in the world to be built so that they could broadcast the gospel of Jesus Christ. Every station is there for the express purpose of taking the Spirit-anointed gospel to the greatest number of people in the shortest amount of time. Just about everything else that goes out over the airwaves is a total and complete waste of time.

While talking with the powers that be at ZTV in the capital of Lusaka, I could tell by the excuses given to us that we were not getting anywhere.

While the executives agreed that the Jimmy Swaggart program was "very well-liked by the Zambian people and was probably the most watched program on Sunday evening prime time," they would still not be able to air it until sometime toward the end of the year when everything was reorganized.

A LIFE-AND-DEATH SITUATION

At that moment, the Holy Spirit's presence filled the room. At His leading I said to those executives, "May I tell you how we look at the airing of this program? This is a life-and-death situation. During the last three months that the program has been off the air, how many Zambians have died without hearing the gospel that saves their souls from an eternal hell? You see, gentlemen, to us this gospel makes the difference in whether your people make it to heaven or not. The longer your network keeps it off the air, the more Zambians there will be who could die and, as a result, could be lost for all eternity. Now, I'm sure you do not want that responsibility when you stand before God in eternity. This preaching of the gospel is the most important thing there is. Can you possibly start airing the program again this weekend?"

These kind ZTV gentlemen were not prepared for such a spiritually shaking statement. There was a long gasp and then, "What? This weekend? This weekend will not be possible because the schedule is already made out, but beginning next month, we will include the program in our TV schedule."

Glory! Only God can change men's hardened hearts and minds so that this gospel may be preached among all nations.

THE MOST IMPORTANT MESSAGE

Consider this: the most important message in the whole world, the gospel of Jesus Christ, goes beyond all human thresholds and covers most of the world by means of television.

This is unheard of in the annals of television broadcasting. It is only God who can propel this gospel out beyond the Iron Curtain, the Bamboo Curtain, and all the religious curtains.

The Apostle Paul put it like this:

"For I am not ashamed of the gospel of Christ: for it is the power of God unto salvation to every one that believeth" (Rom. 1:16).

While others are strategizing, forming committee after committee on evangelism, and holding their seminars, this ministry is actually getting the job done — we are evangelizing the world. At the time of the journey into Greenland and Zambia in the 1980s, because of the telecast, in any given month, more than 100,000 letters came into our international outreach offices. These letters were from people who wrote saying that they had come to the Lord as a direct result of this ministry's efforts. Nowhere in the Bible do we find anything about the "strategies of the apostles." There are, however, many stories relating to the "acts of the apostles."

You can resolve, strategize, and write your *whereases* until the proverbial doomsday, but unless you act now, the Holy Spirit cannot do a thing to reach the lost with this glorious message of Jesus Christ.

The only method God knows and uses to evangelize the world is the preaching of the gospel. All other methods are a pure waste of time, money, and, most importantly, lives.

THE HEART OF THE MATTER

The gospel is the only answer to man's every problem, whether the problem involves an individual, a family, groups, a community, a nation, or the world.

The true gospel addresses itself right to the root of the problem — the heart of man. This is why the world is in such a mess. Political, educational, and social solutions invented by man only treat the symptoms; they do not treat the cause, which is sin in the heart. The gospel deals with the heart and is the only solution for the sin problem.

I had the distinct privilege of traveling roughly 65,000 miles each month all over the world. I've seen many different countries, cultures, societies, and peoples. One thing I've found to be the same in every culture, nation, and dialect in the world, including in my own country, is this: the human heart.

Thank God, Jesus came to take away all sin by means of His death on the Cross! Oh, what a glorious message that we can be set free through faith in Him and what He did on the Cross.

DOES IT REALLY WORK?

Susan had tried to take her own life. She worked in a bank in downtown Lusaka. Everything was going wrong. She tried to end it all with half a bottle of Valium pills, but her husband caught her just in time and took them away. Later that same night, she got a rope, but again, her husband found her in time to keep her from hanging herself. The next day while walking down a main street during the noon hour, she saw a Jimmy Swaggart program on TV. The program was being played on someone's VCR machine, and while she was viewing it out of curiosity, Brother Swaggart pointed his finger at her and said, "You have tried to take your life with pills and then a rope, but if you will give your life to Jesus, He will set you free and change your entire life." It startled her.

Susan said, "I went home and immediately knelt down and asked the Lord to forgive me for what I had done. He came into my life and changed me into a new person."

For Susan in far-away Zambia, it worked!

ONE HUNDRED PRISONERS ACCEPTED CHRIST

This telecast was viewed by the inmates of a Barcelona, Spain, prison, and about 100 of them accepted the Lord and were changed by the power of the gospel.

For those 100 prisoners, it worked! Their hearts were transformed.

DELIVERED AFTER 27 YEARS

A man from Japan, Tatsuji by name, sent this letter to our office:

"I am so thankful to the Lord. On a Saturday in October, I came home after driving my taxi all day. As usual, I poured a glass of sake (Japanese wine) and, while holding it in my left hand, I turned on the TV. On one channel, a man was singing and playing the piano. Without paying much attention, I began listening to him.

Suddenly the TV camera got a close-up shot of some individuals in the audience. At that moment, I felt something in my heart. Each face was so serious and awesome, unlike any other program. I felt there was something important in this program, and I watched intently, feeling as though something unknown was touching me. Something preciously hidden in the depth of my heart was pulled out to the surface by Reverend Swaggart. I felt that I had found something that I had been seeking for a long time.

When I came to myself, I found that I had drained my glass of sake into the sink. I had been drinking sake for 27 years and 10 years earlier, I had been hospitalized because of cirrhosis of the liver, but I could not quit. However, after I heard Brother Swaggart's message, I prayed with him and invited Jesus Christ to come into my heart. Immediately the desire for drinking sake completely disappeared.

After listening to your program, I called your office in Tokyo, and they introduced me to an Akashi Assemblies of God church. Now I am filled with unspeakable joy and happiness. God's words are the light of my pathways. I am saved, and now I am living a life of praise and prayer, looking to the Lord. I would like to live a life of truth by the help of the Holy Spirit. I have been born again by the blood of Jesus Christ. I am saved from my sin, hallelujah!"

For this dear Japanese man, Tatsuji, it worked! Jesus set him free from sin and alcohol.

Today, Zambia is no longer a communist country but has a democracy. In its 1996 constitution, Zambia was officially called a Christian nation. Now, less than only 1 percent of the entire population is Muslim, while more than 95 percent of the population is Christian! The country elected a president that is of Pentecostal belief. This is the power of the gospel of Jesus Christ! By the way, Satanism and its practices have been outlawed.

HOW ABOUT YOU?

How about you, dear reader? This is the most important question you will ever address in your lifetime. God is writing the last chapter of the church, Acts 29, if you will, through us — you and me.

Will the Lord say that we had good resolutions, good strategies, and good intentions, but did not carry out the command to *"Go ye into all the world, and preach the gospel to every creature"*? Or in that great day, will God proudly say, "These I have truly used to carry out the 'acts of the Holy Spirit' to reach a lost generation with the gospel of Jesus Christ"?

Let's do all we can to carry this glorious gospel of Jesus Christ and Him crucified —the most important thing in the world — to every person on this planet! Jimmy Swaggart Ministries is endeavoring to do just that, by the grace of God.

"Go ye into all the world, and preach the gospel to every creature" (Mk. 16:15).

There's a call comes ringing o'er the restless wave,
"Send the light! Send the light!"
There are souls to rescue, there are souls to save,
Send the light! Send the light!

Send the light, the blessed gospel light;
Let it shine from shore to shore!
Send the light, the blessed gospel light;
Let it shine forevermore!

We have heard the Macedonian call today,
"Send the light! Send the light!"
And a golden off'ring at the Cross we lay,
Send the light! Send the light!

Let us pray that grace may everywhere abound,
"Send the light! Send the light!"
And a Christlike spirit everywhere be found,
Send the light! Send the light!

Let us not grow weary in the work of love,
"Send the light! Send the light!"
Let us gather jewels for a crown above,
Send the light! Send the light!

41° 54' 10" N
12° 29' 46" E

WALKING THROUGH
THE WALLS

"Confirming the souls of the disciples, and exhorting them to continue in the faith, and that we must through much tribulation enter into the kingdom of God."

— *Acts 14:22*

CHAPTER TWENTY-ONE

WALKING THROUGH THE WALLS

41° 54' 10" N | 12° 29' 46" E

IT WAS A HOT summer day in Rome, Italy. The taxi in which I was riding stopped at a traffic light in front of a building that looked like it could have once been a prison. Tourists were lining up to go inside. I thought, "Why would people want to see such a building?" Then the light changed, and the taxi sped away to our destination — the Albanian consulate.

AN IMPOSSIBLE TASK?

When you think of a country closed to the gospel, most people will tell you that the tiny Mediterranean country of Albania is the most impenetrable nation on the face of the earth. We are told that it was ruled by one of the purest forms of communism in existence during the 1980s.

And yet, I was on my way there for that very purpose.

Why? Because Jesus said,

"And this gospel of the kingdom shall be preached in all the world for a witness unto all nations; and then shall the end come" (Mat. 24:14).

The Holy Spirit is not limited by closed doors. God has called this ministry to preach the gospel in every nation. This means that we must at least try to air the Jimmy Swaggart telecast in every nation that will permit it. But, Albania?

As the taxicab stopped in front of the consulate gate, the driver said, "You will have to go to the intercom and try to talk your way into the building." After pleading for several minutes, I heard a click at the gate, and a voice told me to approach the building.

An individual met me at the front door and asked, "Where are you from and what do you want?"

I said, "I am an American, and I need your help to obtain a visa to visit the capital of Albania."

He told me, rather curtly, "We do not allow any Americans to visit our country!"

"My only desire is to visit their TV network," I said, "and leave some top-quality programming with them on a free trial basis."

This angered him even more. He said, "I am sorry, but our country is closed to you, so the best thing you can do is leave."

I thanked the man and left.

On the way back to my hotel, I was praying, and it seemed as if the Devil was laughing out loud, saying, "You are a fool to have even tried to get into Albania, much less put that program on television. You are wasting your time!"

I was beginning to feel that another attempt would be useless, and that we should write Albania off as a closed door. Even so, I asked God what the next step should be. Then, all of a sudden, the taxi came to a jerking halt in the heavy late afternoon traffic around Rome.

I looked out the window, and again we were in front of that prison-like building with bars on the windows. The traffic jam gave me time to read some of the signs and nomenclature on this mysterious building.

THEN IT DAWNED ON ME

According to history, this was the building used to imprison the Apostle Paul before his death. He was not simply cast into a prison cell with bars on the windows; we know that he was put in a cell beneath a cell. There was no light and only a trapdoor in the ceiling, through which guards dropped some bits of food. Imagine the stench, the darkness, and the loneliness.

This man, touched by God on the Damascus Road so long ago, preached the gospel all over the then-known world and wound up in the depths of this horrible building.

But did Paul give up? Did he acknowledge any closed doors to the gospel of Jesus Christ and Him crucified? No!

Even in this horrible place, he preached to the soldiers and prisoners above him.

The Holy Spirit impressed upon my heart to return to the Albanian consulate the next morning. In no uncertain terms, He told me, "Go back, and I will open the door."

The next morning I was back at the gate of the Albanian consulate building talking on the intercom. This time, I was met by a rather cordial gentleman who led me into a room and asked what my business was. I began to talk about the television program and asked if there was some way I could send the tapes to the Albanian television station in the capital city. He asked me to wait a minute and went upstairs to get the consul general. While I was waiting, the individual I had talked with the day before came through the hallway and looked in. Very sternly he said, "What are you doing here again? I thought I told you to leave!"

Rather hurriedly, I explained that I just wanted to talk to someone about the telecast we were offering to Albanian television. Fortunately for me, about that time, the consul general walked into the room and closed the door behind him, leaving the stern-looking man to go on his way.

This gentleman in charge of the consulate was a very kind and gracious man. After we talked awhile about our program offer, I asked him, "Which language do you recommend for our program so that the Albanian television station can use it? Would the Italian Jimmy Swaggart program be the best to air?"

He said, "No, we are receiving programming in the French language, which has worked out very well. Do you have a program in French?"

"Yes we do," I said, "and we have, in fact, been airing our program in the French language for quite some time now in France, parts of Europe, Africa, and the Caribbean."

"I'm delighted to hear that," he said, and began to write out the address and the instructions for sending the tapes.

God was true to His word. He opened this seemingly closed door so the gospel could be sent into Albania.

The amazing thing about all of this is that out of the first 50 programs sent into Albania, not one of them was rejected by the television network. It is my belief that these gospel telecasts paved the way for Albania to shed the iron claw of communism and become the thriving democracy that it is today with freedom to preach the gospel.

Many countries are still officially "closed," but Jesus continues to walk through the walls around "closed countries," and enables the only message that can change hearts and lives and save the lost, reaching unto the uttermost.

WE CLOSE DOORS WITH MAN-MADE OBSTACLES

Many times we Christians close doors in our minds with our doubt and unbelief, education and psychology, and foolishness and froth. Many, even in missions, close doors with their cross-cultural studies, saying, "It cannot be done that way! It is not relevant."

In fact, most cross-cultural studies, including church growth materials, seminars, and seminaries, have possibly done more to close doors to the advance of the gospel than any other single thing. These people who conduct these studies are just demonstrating their unbelief.

What do I mean?

I mean that Christians, even some in missionary work, do not attempt to reach certain lost people because our great learning has convinced us that the gospel will offend these nations because we are supposedly "too American."

THE MESSAGE OF THE GOSPEL
TRANSCENDS CULTURE

That is no excuse. The gospel of Jesus Christ is non-negotiable. It is the same for every culture and every nation. The message of the life, death, burial, and resurrection of Jesus Christ — preached under a powerful anointing of the Holy Spirit — is the message for all men everywhere, irrespective of their nationality, education, cultural backgrounds, or idiosyncrasies. Jesus Christ's death on the Cross made the way and is the means for *"whosoever will"* to come and be delivered from their sinful "culture" and be saved!

Our problem as Christians is that in our attempt to adapt the gospel to each culture, we have watered it down to where it is not the message Christ commanded us to preach. It is only as sin is exposed through the preaching of the Cross and the answer to sin is proclaimed — that "Jesus saves and His blood washes whiter than snow" — that sinners respond and give their hearts and lives to the Lord Jesus Christ.

This ministry's programming now covers most of the world on powerful cable and satellite television networks, not to mention the many over-the-air TV stations. This attests to the fact that there is only one gospel message, and it does not need to be adapted to any race, color, or culture. It alone is heaven's culture for the believer's everyday life and living, which is found only in the Cross of Jesus Christ and the power of the Holy Spirit that flows to those who maintain his or her faith in Christ and the Cross alone.

When we say such things as, "It's never been done like this before," or, "These people will not relate to an American preaching the gospel," we fall victim to the lies of Satan. Such statements are nothing short of excuses given by the masses of Christian laymen, preachers, or missionaries who are not fulfilling the Great Commission.

Every time we close a door to the lost, we hurt the work of the Holy Spirit. I wish the people who say, "It can't be done," would just give the Holy Spirit the opportunity to get it done through those of us who do believe.

Jesus even warned,

"Say not ye, There are yet four months, and then cometh harvest? behold, I say unto you, Lift up your eyes, and look on the fields; for they are white already to harvest" (Jn. 4:35).

In other words, the Holy Spirit is saying to 21st century Christians: "Now is the time of harvest! Go into all the world!" That means every single nation, tribe, village, and hamlet on the face of this earth.

That is why this ministry keeps trying to get SonLife Broadcasting Network into countries even where it looks hopeless. That is why, in the past, this ministry's weekly telecast was lip-sync translated into 16 different languages and subtitled into 39 other languages. I believe God will walk through the doors to help us reach the lost if we will give Him the opportunity.

The Apostle Paul was taken out of that dark dungeon cell and led down a path toward the Mediterranean Sea to a spot where he would die. As he laid his head on the chopping block for his faithful witness to the gospel of Jesus Christ, I can hear him say:

"For I reckon that the sufferings of this present time are not worthy to be compared with the glory which shall be revealed in us" (Rom. 8:18).

The doors are open! The walls are falling! Let's walk through them! And as Brother Swaggart says, "Man can build a wall around a country, but he can't build a roof. Therefore, they can't block the gospel from being preached over television."

My passport says the journey is still continuing!

Sometimes the day seems long,
Our trials hard to bear.
We're tempted to complain,
To murmur and despair.
But Christ will soon appear
To catch his bride away!
All tears forever over,
In God's eternal day!

It will be worth it all
When we see Jesus!
Life's trials will seem so small
When we see Christ.
One glimpse of His dear face,
All sorrow will erase.
So, bravely run the race,
Till we see Christ.

At times the sky seems dark,
With not a ray of light;
We're tossed and driven on,
No human help in sight.

But there is One in heaven,
Who knows our deepest care;
Let Jesus solve your problems,
Just go to Him in prayer.

Life's day will soon be o'er,
All storms forever past;
We'll cross the great divide
To glory, safe at last!
We'll share the joys of heaven:
A harp, a home, a crown;
The tempter will be banished,
We'll lay our burdens down.

21° 8' 9" S
175° 11' 54" W

LET THE ISLES SEE

"Preach the word; be instant in season, out of season; reprove, rebuke, exhort with all longsuffering and doctrine."

— II Timothy 4:2

CHAPTER TWENTY-TWO

LET THE ISLES SEE

21° 8' 9" S | 175° 11' 54" W

GOD HAS GIVEN US a mandate to *"go ye into all the world, and preach the gospel to every creature"* (Mk. 16:15). This great commission given to every follower of Jesus Christ means literally that we must carry the gospel of Jesus Christ unto the ends of the earth — from the densest interior of the world's most congested city to the farthest islands of the sea.

All of us are able to "go" in two ways: One way is to help send the gospel message to the uttermost parts of the earth by supporting those who are called to announce the good news over television, radio, and Internet technology. We do this with our prayers and our finances and by joining our faith with those who are called to full-time ministry. Thus, we enter into the same call of the apostle and prophet and reap the benefits and blessings of that call into which they have entered. The other way is for the believer with a call on his or her life to actually journey as a missionary to help bring in the harvest. So, every believer has a part, but all "go" by fulfilling their call of God faithfully, while depending on His grace to carry out that call. Of course, the call is to preach the gospel of Jesus Christ and Him crucified unto the uttermost parts of the earth.

This mandate is not negotiable; we have no choice. It is the command of the Lord of Lords to have His wonderful redemption story taken to every person in this generation. More and more, God is using television to achieve this end. There are few nations today that do not have television broadcasting capabilities, and those few without local access have the opportunity to view television programs from satellite coverage or the Internet.

Think of it: this technology literally covers the entire earth.

THE MARKETPLACE

If we do not avail ourselves of this most effective tool to proclaim the gospel, then we not only will have failed to obey our Lord's command, but we will also have failed an entire generation!

The early church *"went forth, and preached everywhere, the Lord working with them, and confirming the word with signs following"* (Mk. 16:20).

A strategic meeting place for the early church was the city marketplace. Each day, great multitudes would congregate and mill about in search of food and clothing and to hear the latest news from travelers coming from all directions. The marketplace was the center of daily interests and activities. Virtually the entire population frequented the marketplace and the water well.

I am convinced that the most prominent marketplace in society today is the television set. There is no other marketplace in today's world where so many people congregate at any one given time than the television marketplace.

Many times, it may seem that we stress the importance of the television ministry to such an extent that it seems we exclude all others and believe this is the only means God is using to reach the world with the gospel.

Of course, God-called missionaries and pastors are called to specific locales or regions to help bring in the harvest before Jesus returns for His church. (Unfortunately, there are very, very few of these truly called of God, and even fewer who actually preach the true gospel of Jesus Christ and Him crucified.)

Yes, God uses all available means — including radio, the printed page, and a host of other tools — to reach the lost. But television, I feel, is the most effective tool that is available for reaching this entire generation with the gospel.

No one can be genuinely saved without hearing the true gospel of Jesus Christ and Him crucified in some way. So, the responsibility is even greater upon us — Brother and Sister Swaggart and you and me — to make sure this true gospel is made available to every nation and every person on the face of the earth. If we do not get it done by God's grace, then it won't get done, and millions of souls will be lost for all eternity.

ACCELERATING THE MISSIONS THRUST

While on a trip the other day, missionaries told me that this particular television ministry has been used of God to speed up the worldwide proclamation of the gospel as no other single means in the history of the church. All of God's people can participate if they obey the Lord, making it the largest, concerted, unified effort ever known to reach an entire generation for Christ. It is the work of the Holy Spirit, and we give God the glory!

The foreign crusades attest to this. In the countries where these nationwide meetings were held, leaders and members of almost all—if not all—churches and denominations cooperated in the planning, coordinating, and follow-up in order to bring in the harvest of souls. The distribution of The Expositor's Study Bible (authored by Brother Swaggart) also attests to this concerted effort of the Holy Spirit. Pastors and leaders of almost all of the church and denomination affiliations in each country joined — and are joining — together to make sure that each and every one of the thousands of pastors and workers throughout each country received and will receive their own free copy of this amazing study Bible. These Bibles are made available through the free-will gifts of those who participate in the television Bible-thons. It is a phenomenon in itself to have so many people of different backgrounds and originations come together in one united effort to reach the lost.

In one particular Central American country, the large evangelical mission that weekly denounced "tongue talkers" — as they called Pentecostals — over their powerful radio station was, in fact, one of the first to volunteer to help when our crusade coordinating committees were formed. It was the first time in the history of that country that all denominations and churches were represented in a common cause. Today, The Expositor's Study Bible distribution is coordinated and accepted by every church affiliation in each country, with very few, if any, not participating in this Jimmy Swaggart Ministries' outreach.

How did this happen?

It was largely the result of this ministry's program being on television in that country! The same can be said about country after country all over the world. The Holy Spirit is using the mighty tool of television as the last major thrust to reach this generation with the only message that changes the heart of man.

Even the remote islands of the sea have access to television. As a result of our telecast being aired over this all-important tool of TV, many dear people at the ends of the earth are able to see the salvation of the Lord.

WHERE TIME BEGINS

After a two-week trip that took me around the world through Europe, India, the Far East, and Australia, with ministry business stops in each, I arrived in the beautiful South Pacific nation of Tonga. This nation is composed of a string of islands with Nuku'alofa as the capital city. When I landed, missionaries Terry and Theresa Hanna told me, "You are now in the country where time begins. Since the international dateline runs north and south just east of here, Tonga is the closest nation to the dateline, and each day starts on the clock right here."

It was largely through the Hanna's efforts that the Jimmy Swaggart telecast had recently been placed on Tongan television, accepted on a provisional basis. They had asked me to come to meet with the authorities to see if the program could be aired on a more permanent basis. They told me that the program had become so popular that even the bartenders in the cocktail lounges would play the music on their sound systems.

The Tongan people are a most congenial people. I had the privilege of speaking in the main church in the capital city. I'm telling you, Tongan music is out of this world!

THE KING

Following the service, I was standing out in the courtyard when an entourage of vehicles sped down the street in front of the church. I asked, "What were all of those big black limousines and Suburbans about?"

Brother Hanna said, "That is the king of Tonga. I am told that he has a habit of going over to his relatives' house each week about this time to watch the Jimmy Swaggart program with them. They tell me he enjoys it immensely. He is one of the last ruling monarchs in the world today."

The next day we had the privilege of visiting the prime minister in his home to see if the continued airing of the weekly telecast would still be acceptable. When we arrived, there was a group of Tongans singing some familiar hymns and choruses about the Saviour. I knew I was in the right place.

The prime minister expressed his appreciation for the program and said he watched it often. He liked the music, but he especially liked the preaching. He said, in essence, "This is what our people need. We need to hear the truth preached. Please tell Brother Swaggart that the program means so much to us here in Tonga. His message uplifts and inspires us. Please keep sending the programs to our country."

After returning home, I received word that not only was the telecast officially accepted for airing, but that it would also be aired twice each week! Later, our program, *A Study in the Word*, was also broadcast daily over Tongan television.

So many all over the world are touched by the programming. Even people from island nations who do not have TV stations are watching the program by carrying copies of the program to their own countries so that others can see it on home players or even over the Internet.

A MAN FROM FIJI

One man from Fiji, for instance, said he was on a business trip through Tonga and went to his hotel room and turned on the television set. He said, "There I was, far from my island home and thinking I would entertain myself by watching TV.

Your program came on, and I had never seen anything like it. As I watched, something happened inside me. The words were so powerful that I was praying by the end of the program and asking God to forgive my many sins. I gave my life to Jesus Christ, and I returned to Fiji a new man. Thank you for your program! Even though Fiji does not have a TV station (at that time), we are able to see the program with videotapes in our homes. Your program means so much to all of us on the islands. Please keep on preaching the truth that changes men's hearts."

The tremendous results that we're seeing of souls coming to the Lord Jesus Christ are due to the heavy anointing of the Holy Spirit. It is more than just religion or a format, a show or music, or a presentation or a speech. It is the almighty Word of God, anointed by the Holy Spirit, that cuts through the cultural, religious, social, or political barriers to reach the very heart of man.

This ministry needs your help! God is opening doors so fast all over the world that it is all we can do to stretch every dollar to be able to walk through these unheard-of opportunities to take the gospel to countries that previously have been closed to evangelism.

Every week, in this one ministry alone, the gospel message is transmitted over satellites that cover almost the entire world. People have the privilege to access and see and feel the Holy Spirit in action. The tragedy is that there are still so many who do not have this privilege.

If you and I pray, give, and go, then even the isles of the sea *"and all the ends of the earth shall see the salvation of our God"* (Isa. 52:10).

Magnify the Lord with me!
Blessed Lamb of Calvary!
For His grace so rich and free,
Magnify the Lord with me!
Magnify the Lord with me!
Blessed Lamb of Calvary!
Jesus gives me liberty, so
Magnify the Lord with me!

I will bless the Lord at all times,
His praise shall always be in my mouth,
My soul shall make its boast in the Lord,
The humble shall hear it and rejoice.

O magnify the Lord with me!
O magnify the Lord with me!
And let us exalt His name together!
Magnify the Lord with me!

O fear the Lord you His saints,
To those who fear Him there is no want,
The eyes of the Lord are toward the righteous,
His ears are open to their cry,
Ascribe to the Lord O mighty ones,
Ascribe to the Lord glory and strength,

Ascribe to the Lord the glory due His name,
Worship the Lord in holiness.

O magnify the Lord with me!
O magnify the Lord with me!
And let us exalt His name together!
Magnify the Lord, magnify the Lord!
Magnify the Lord with me!
Magnify the Lord, magnify the Lord!
Magnify the Lord with me!

CHAPTER 23

15° 25' 0" S
28° 16' 59" E

ONLY GOD CAN

*"Yea, though I walk through the valley
of the shadow of death, I will fear no
evil: for Thou art with me; Thy rod
and Thy staff they comfort me."*

— *Psalm 23:4*

ONLY GOD CAN

15° 25' 0" S | 28° 16' 59" E

"ZAMBIA IS A SOCIALIST country, and television is state-controlled," the young pharmacist said as we awaited a flight to leave the hot, sultry Maputo, Mozambique, airport. At the time, Mozambique was at the height of a gruesome civil war, with the powers of communism trying to take over the country. Thousands were fleeing their war-torn country to neighboring Zimbabwe. Brother Swaggart, a small TV crew, and I had flown in from our refugee camp in neighboring Zimbabwe to see the need firsthand. The country was almost totally devastated.

In talking with this pharmacist, I learned that he was from Zambia, in the very heartland of Africa. He continued, "There will be no chance at all that you can acquire airtime in my country. It's closed. Communism already rules the entire country of Zambia."

Every time someone tells me, "It can't be done," I think back to the vision of the harvest God gave Brother Swaggart on July 1, 1985. Brother Swaggart had gone out to a secluded place near his house on the edge of town to pray. He usually walked in those days as he prayed, seeking God's guidance. This particular day, he had parked by a railroad track and had begun to walk down the track and pray as there were no residences or houses in the area. (Today the area is filled with houses and is no longer secluded.) As he was walking down the track, all of a sudden, the Lord gave him a vision of a vast field filled with cotton as far as the eye could see. Off in the distance were cotton picking machines moving down the rows of cotton. To the east, there were dark, menacing storm clouds with jagged lightning bolts coming out of them. The huge, dark, ominous storm clouds were moving toward the extensive cotton fields that were heavy laden with large bolls of cotton on each plant. The Lord spoke to Brother Swaggart, saying, " I have called you to reach the entire world with the gospel. The storm is coming when it will be too late to harvest, but I will hold back the storm so that the harvest may be brought in before it is too late. Don't fail Me."

About one month later in August, a word came from the Lord during a service at Family Worship Center in Baton Rouge, saying, "I will put the key in the lock and unlock the door, but it is up to you to walk through the door.")

When this gentleman from Zambia told me in no uncertain terms that the doors of Zambia were closed, I prayed in my heart, "Lord, put the key in the lock of Zambia television and make it possible for us to walk through the door someday."

You see, when someone says to me, "There is no way it can be done," he does not realize it, but he has just sounded a battle cry within my own heart that responds, "We can't, but our God can! He will make a way."

At the time that God gave that vision to Brother Swaggart, his ministry's telecast had whole or partial coverage in some 75 countries of the world. After that, God extended that coverage into some 65 more countries, making a total of 140 nations of the world receiving this Holy Spirit-anointed programming. Think of it — 65 more countries, mostly Muslim, communist, or Buddhist in belief, and the majority was supposedly closed to airing the gospel.

How did the doors open? God fulfilled His Word as Brother and Sister Swaggart, the team, and the partners of the ministry stepped out in faith to reach the unreachable with the gospel of Jesus Christ. You see, our God can and did!

BLACK MAMBA SNAKE

We had traveled from Zimbabwe into Mozambique. Just as an aside, while in Zimbabwe, we visited the large refugee camp that Jimmy Swaggart Ministries was funding substantially with food, clothing, medical supplies, and medical personnel. The camp director, a very amiable black-African brother from Chicago invited us into his living quarters to answer any questions we might have. We had just seen a huge tractor-trailer of meat delivered to the camp. It would come every week to drop off these tons of beef for the thousands of people in the camp. JSM had been funding all of this for more than two years. I was quite impressed as this was no small operation. Thousands of refugees fleeing from the war in Mozambique would flood into this camp in Zimbabwe on the border with Mozambique.

As we discussed the whole operation, the subject came up concerning snakes and wild animals, such as lions — this being Africa.

Someone asked the camp director, "With all of that meat and food stuffs, doesn't it attract snakes? Have you had any black mamba snakes in this area? I was told they live in the rocky hills and savannas of southern and eastern Africa where we are right now. Isn't it considered the deadliest snake in the world?"

"Why, yes, this is the region where the black mamba snake is found," the director said. "The only other snake in Africa that is more deadly might be the puff adder viper of central and west Africa. Black mambas, though, are Africa's longest venomous snake, reaching more than 14 feet (4.5 meters) in length. They are also among the fastest snakes in the world, slithering at speeds of up to 12.5 miles per hour (20 kilometers per hour)!

He went on educating us about the deadly snake. "They don't get their name from their skin color, which tends to be olive to gray, but rather from the blue-black color of the inside of their mouths, which they display when threatened. Black mambas are shy and will almost always seek to escape when confronted. However, when cornered, these snakes will raise their heads, sometimes with a third of their body off the ground, spread their cobra-like neck-flap, open their black mouths, and hiss. They even crawl into houses, huts, or tents where people live, with the warmth of these dwellings drawing them while they look for food. If an attacker persists, the mamba will strike not once, but repeatedly, injecting large amounts of potent neuro- and cardiotoxin poison with each strike.

"Before the advent of black mamba antivenin, a bite from this fearsome serpent was 100 percent fatal, usually within about 20 minutes. Unfortunately, antivenin is still not widely available in the rural parts of the mamba's range, and mamba-related deaths remain frequent."

Someone else asked, "Once one bites you, you mean in just 20 minutes the person can die?"

"Yes, they're deathly dreadful," the camp director said. "We try to keep a watch out for them and protect the refugees from them."

When we asked if he had seen this type of snake in the camp, the director said yes.

"I had an encounter with one a few weeks ago. A boy came running to my dwelling here toward evening and said a huge black mamba snake was seen slithering down from the rocky mountainside toward the infirmary. I quickly grabbed a long handled shovel that was outside the back door and went running over toward the infirmary. It had started slipping along the bottom of the outside wall. I waited around the corner at the end of the same wall and when its head slithered out around the corner, I quickly chopped its head off!"

"Were you scared?" I asked.

"You better believe I was scared," he said. "My knees were literally knocking against one another. I knew if I missed its head and it sank its fangs into me, I would have 20 minutes at best to live since we had no antivenin in the camp at that time — now we do. Brother Swaggart, would you like to see its skin?

"You still have the skin?" Brother Swaggart asked.

"Yes, I dried it out and rolled it up. Wait just a minute; I will be right back."

The camp director disappeared into another room behind where I was seated and returned with a huge roll under one of his arms. It was so big that his arm could barely wrap around it. He then stopped and went to the door to the right of where I was seated and started unrolling the dried skin of the black mamba snake. Flattened out, the skin was at least two feet wide, which meant that when it was alive and in the form of the snake's tubular body, the diameter was thicker than a man's thigh, maybe even twice as thick. As he unrolled the skin, it kept going and going, clear across the room in which we were gathered (which was approximately 12 feet by 12 feet) and into the hallway on the other side of the room. It must have stretched out more than 14 feet in total length.

As we contemplated the snakeskin spread across the floor, the realization of the giant size of this deadly reptile hit us: living out here in this part of Africa was no picnic. Then we looked at the brother who directed the camp and could appreciate his dedication to work among these refugees.

As we were leaving, I asked him, "Have you ever wanted to get back to Chicago to be away from all of this?"

"What, and leave the dear people I love?" he said. "No way. I will stay and help as long as there is a needy refugee. God sent me here and until He says to return to the States, I will be here."

This man of God was really helping these people. As we headed for the Land Rovers (Jeeps) that had brought us to the camp, the camp director introduced us to the young African pastor who preached to the refugees and had led thousands of them to the Lord. He had his Bible in his hand and a huge smile on his face. You could sense the burden this man had for these refugees.

Also, the camp director had instituted a work-training program where every person learned a skill in agriculture or some other area. In cooperation with the Zimbabwean government, as each person acquired the skill, he would eventually be put on his own piece of land to farm (if agriculture was what he learned) or placed in a job using other skills he or she had acquired.

In other words, after being treated by our medical staff and recovering from rounds of malnutrition, and after acquiring a skill, the refugees would not be staying in these refugee camps all of their lives. They would be working with their own businesses and families, and they would be serving the Lord. This was one of the best operational and effective refugee camps I had ever seen in the whole world.

The real change that propelled the people to have a better life was the gospel of Jesus Christ, which they had accepted while in the camp listening to the dynamic preaching of that dear African brother with his Bible.

I had seen many so-called Africa aid programs raising funds for victims of famine in war-torn, stricken Africa. If donors were to know the truth, only about 1 to 5 percent of the millions of dollars they gave ever reached the Africans in need.

But on this day, I saw firsthand all of the funds (and more) that were donated through Jimmy Swaggart Ministries go directly to the people. I also witnessed how it lifted them out of the cold night of despair and sin and planted their feet on the solid Rock, Christ Jesus! It gave these Africans hope and a new life of blessing from God. This was made possible because of His dedicated workers in the harvest fields and the people back home who loved and cared enough to help with their offerings to Jimmy Swaggart Ministries. The same can be said for the multiple hundreds of thousands (really millions) of lives changed all over the world through the television ministry.

Whenever Brother and Sister Swaggart raise funds — then or now — I can attest to the fact that 100 percent of every dollar given has gone and is going to that for which it was raised. This is the real story of Jimmy Swaggart Ministries all over the world.

NO MISSIONARY

Upon returning from Mozambique, I began to investigate the possibility of contacting a missionary in Zambia to arrange a meeting with Zambian television. But I found that there was not one resident missionary in Zambia at the time! I also found that the country was more than 65 percent Muslim and totally under communist political rule, not to mention the Satanist practices that were rampant across the country. The people of Zambia lived in perpetual fear for their lives.

Then I was told (by contacting a missionary in a neighboring country) that Zambia had a Marxist-socialist oriented government, and the national television network was government-owned and operated. The situation looked more impossible by the day. However, II Chronicles 16:9 states:

"For the eyes of the LORD run to and fro throughout the whole earth (and this includes Zambia, which is in the very heart of Africa), *to show Himself strong."*

This would be another perfect opportunity for the Lord to do the impossible.

TRIP INTO ZAMBIA

Upon arriving in Lusaka, the capital of Zambia, I was met by a dear Zambian pastor, John Chisa, who had come over from Harare, Zimbabwe, where he was finishing his training for ministry at the Bible school there. I could sense the tremendous burden this man of God carried in his heart for the lost of his native country of Zambia. He and his lovely wife had sacrificed much so that John could finish Bible school.

During the evening meal, he told me, "We have pleaded for years for a missionary to come and help us in Zambia, but no one would come to stay. We prayed and prayed until God told us what to do. My wife would go to work, and I would travel to Zimbabwe to prepare for full-time ministry."

John continued, "If a missionary won't come, then it is up to us to do the best we can because we know that someway God is going to open this nation of ours to the gospel as never before, and we need to be ready to bring in the harvest. We are convinced that the Jimmy Swaggart telecast, if aired in Zambia, will open the door to this great harvest!"

At that moment, I realized just how important this trip to Zambia was. I pulled out the audition tape we would take to the television station the following day. The eternal fate of more than 6 million dear Zambian people was hanging by a thread — a thin videotape with a Spirit-anointed gospel message on it. This would be all that would stand between time and eternity for most of these people.

I returned to my hotel room and wept uncontrollably. What an awesome responsibility God had placed upon Brother Swaggart — and upon you and me — to reach this generation with the gospel of Jesus Christ.

H. B. GARLOCK

Years ago, I had heard how Missionary H. B. Garlock had been on this same continent of Africa preaching the gospel under unmentionably adverse conditions. He would travel hour after backbreaking hour into the most savage bush to preach among some of the fiercest tribesmen Africa had ever known. He went back into the very darkest recesses of this great land.

After conducting a short service that brought the people in a certain village the first gospel message they had ever heard, H. B. Garlock and a few of the Africans with him on this particular trek spent the night in a hut before the return trip the next day. About midnight, they were suddenly awakened by the sound of tom-toms (drums) and blood-curdling screams.

A huge group of black cannibals, each carrying a weapon, had just come bursting into the village, screaming and yelling at the top of their voices, "Where is the white man? We have come to kill the white man! We know he is in town, and if you don't tell us where he is, we'll burn your town to the ground!"

At this point, Brother Garlock felt impressed to go outside the hut and face the angry mob. His friends begged him not to go out, but he stepped out anyway into the opening. They made a mad rush toward him, with drawn knives, shouting, "Kill him, kill him!" The leader rushed at H. B. with his cutlass raised to behead him.

Brother Garlock described it later:

"When it seemed the end had come, and my head was about to be severed from my body, I closed my eyes and committed myself to God, repeating over and over again that one name that is above every name, 'Jesus, Jesus!'"

Suddenly there was a death-like stillness! The tom-toms stopped beating, and all screaming and yelling halted abruptly. H. B. opened his eyes to see the savages standing with their weapons raised ready to strike, but they were all frozen in their tracks, including the would-be executioner. They relaxed and withdrew from H. B. and the hut.

The leader then came back toward H. B. and seized his ankles and began pleading for mercy, saying, "We see the white man's God fights for him."

God had delivered Brother Garlock from certain death.

OUR GOD CAN

Here I was standing on the same soil of this continent in another time, in another generation; it was holy ground. H. B. Garlock had given his all to reach these dear people so long ago. Not only that, but God gave His all when He sent His Son to die on the Cross of Calvary. Now God was giving us the opportunity to reach this generation of Zambians' entire country with this glorious gospel by means of television.

AT THE NATIONAL TV NETWORK

At Zambia TV, John and I were met by a most gracious man who served as the program director. After giving some background information concerning our program, we gave this kind gentleman the audition tape.

Now the moment arrived to ask, "When will the program be aired on Zambia TV?" The director responded with, "I will get an answer to you within a few days."

When the reply came, it stated, "As soon as you can send us the tapes, we will be able to air the Jimmy Swaggart telecast. We will be more than happy to air this fine quality program free every Sunday!"

RESPONSE

The telecast had been airing almost one year in Zambia, and the response was phenomenal. John Chisa graduated from Bible school and served as the administrator of our JSM outreach office there.

So many people bombarded the local newspaper with questions concerning the new telecast in their country that one of the reporters wrote a rather lengthy article. In it, he was trying to answer the questions that were sent in, even though he had no information concerning this ministry at that time. They had never heard of Jimmy Swaggart or of the gospel message he preaches over television.

In his article, the reporter stated, "From the many letters received, the viewers either love or hate him." Of course, we know that truth will be either received or rejected.

RESULTS

Many dear Zambian people had given their hearts to the Lord as a direct result of watching the telecast. Our problem then was not that the response was meager, but it was so great that we had difficulty getting enough booklets and materials to Brother John to give to the growing number of people who wrote to our outreach office in Lusaka.

What was written off by man as an impossible situation became God's opportunity. The door to Zambia was now open!

The new converts in Zambia would make pleas similar to this one: "Jimmy is our missionary every Sunday, but we do trust God to send us a missionary who will live here in Zambia and help us continue on in the Lord."

The Jimmy Swaggart gospel telecast had such an impact that the country of Zambia now has become more than 85 percent Christian with less than 5 percent Muslim and no communism to speak of, and Satanism has been banned by the government. A Pentecostal gentleman was even elected president of Zambia!

The vision of the fields that *"are white already to harvest"* (Jn. 4:35) is still being fulfilled.

"The people which sat in darkness saw great light; and to them which sat in the region and shadow of death light is sprung up" (Mat. 4:16).

Man says it can't be done—reaching the whole world with the gospel. All the demons of hell are arrayed against the fulfillment of this vision, but *"this gospel of the kingdom shall be preached in all the world for a witness unto all nations; and then shall the end come"* (Mat. 24:14).

Think of it—reaching the whole world with the gospel!

Our God can and will! We just need to continue to believe and obey Him, the Lord of the harvest.

As we look all around us,
All the fields are white,
They're ripened unto harvest,
Yet so quickly comes the night.
Christians must get busy,
There's so much work to do.
Here's an urgent task awaiting you.

Souls are crying, men are dying,
Won't you lead them to the Cross?
Go and find them, please help to win them
Win the lost at any cost.

Check your fold, my Christian brother,
See if all your children are in.
Are there some still straying in the
Darkened fields of sin?
You must go out and win them,
Go quickly without delay,
Soon the trump of God shall end the day.

Go out and win, rescue from sin,
Day's almost done, and the battle's almost won.
Souls are crying, men are dying,
Win the lost at any cost.

CHAPTER 24

41° 54' 10" N
12° 29' 46" E

THE MOST
MEANINGFUL GIFT

"But God commendeth His love toward us, in that, while we were yet sinners, Christ died for us."

— Romans 5:8

THE MOST MEANINGFUL GIFT

41° 54' 10" N | 12° 29' 46" E

IN SOUTH AMERICA, IT was nearing the Christmas holidays, and a particular woman was having problems with her husband, her children, and her work. Tormented by poor health and these difficult problems, she decided to attempt suicide, crying out from the bottom of her heart, "Doesn't anyone care about my life? Is there any help for such a troubled, lonely person as I?"

Just as she was going to end it all, she passed by the living room where the television was on, but the volume low. As she went over to turn it off, the man on the program said something like, "You may feel all alone. You may try to end it all, but don't turn off that TV set. You are about to meet One who can change your life and set you free. I'm talking about Jesus. He will give you hope."

She continued to listen and knelt to pray the sinner's prayer with Brother Swaggart. Afterward, she wrote:

"I accepted Jesus Christ as my Saviour that Saturday afternoon, and He saved and healed me the very same moment. My family saw the change in my life, and now none of us will miss one of your programs. I was saved just in time. I feel as though I was snatched from the jaws of death."

Thank God, the Jimmy Swaggart telecast was on and this woman could hear the gospel before it was too late. How many others have not had this opportunity and instead have thrown up their hands in despair, thinking, "What's the use? No one cares about my life. The problems are too great. The bondage hurts too much. I'm incurable. I might as well end it all."

LOWEST POINT

Recently, I stood looking out over the Dead Sea — the lowest spot on the face of the earth. As I looked west toward the wilderness of Engedi and up toward the mountainsides riddled with caves and caverns and a small waterfall, I realized that this was the place where a prominent man in Old Testament times reached what was probably the lowest point in his life. Surrounded by the armies of a jealous enemy and hidden in one of these dark caves, this man cried out in desperation, *"No man cared for my soul"* (Ps. 142:4).

Yes, even David, a man after God's own heart, felt a moment of utter despair — seemingly having no help, refuge, or security — when his father-in-law, King Saul, was searching to kill him. Just like David, there are millions who are tucked away in lonely, dark, prison caves of fear, sickness, pain, sin, abuse, and death, crying out, "No man cares for my soul!"

Perhaps you have felt this same frustration at some lonely, desperate moment in your life. Please know that there is One who cares, who understands, who can deliver you from the enemy of your soul, and who can set you free and heal your body — One who is Himself the giver of life. He exclaimed, *"I am come that they* (you) *might have life"* (Jn. 10:10). Who is this One? It is Jesus Christ, the Saviour of the entire world! Romans 5:8 says,

"But God commendeth His love toward us, in that, while we were yet sinners, Christ died for us."

Jesus took your sin and sickness and bore it in His own body on the Cross. He received the full death blow of the judgment of God for your sin and mine by paying sin's penalty with His own innocent, spotless, and undefiled life's blood on the Cross of Calvary.

"For He hath made Him to be sin (a sin offering) *for us, who knew no sin; that we might be made the righteousness of God in Him"* (II Cor. 5:21).

Thank God, this wonderful story does not end on the Cross that made all of this possible, or even in the tomb. The glorious message of the gospel is that He lives! And because of what He did on the Cross, you and I can come to Him by the means of the Cross and receive Him and His free gift: eternal life. This precious gift of God is offered to all, including *you*. It is the greatest gift of all!

So many have found Jesus as a result of the Spirit-anointed gospel being preached on Jimmy Swaggart Ministries' Son-Life Broadcasting Network all over the world.

This is why we trust the Lord to fight this battle for us to get the programming on in country after country. Without this gospel witness, hundreds of thousands locked in spiritually darkened caves of fear, famine, doubt, guilt, and sin will die without hope of escape.

For instance, in Peru, a country of 20 million people, we tried to get on several national networks, but they were not interested. The largest network quoted us a rate so high that not even an advertiser could buy time.

THE TELECAST(S)

Then it happened! Bruno Frigoli, one of the most dedicated and fervent missionaries I know, called our Baton Rouge office, saying, "An appointment has been arranged with the government network here in Peru. Can you travel down to negotiate a contract for airtime?"

"Of course," was my instant reply, although I knew I already had four trips scheduled that same month. This meant that between two of the scheduled trips, I would have to squeeze in another 9,000 miles and not be able to come home to Baton Rouge for three long weeks. More than 20 million souls hung in the balance. I knew that if I delayed and put it off for a more convenient time for both my family and me, the opportunity would not be there.

You might say, "That's just a little too intense; you're trying to dramatize the situation too much." Well, is it too intense for the man standing in the middle of the road at night in the drenching rain, yelling to others that just around the curve, the bridge has been washed out? Is he too intense if, armed with a flashlight, he waves both arms and yells a warning at the top of his lungs to oncoming cars, "STOP! The bridge is out"? Is he too dramatic? I don't think so.

And, if I do not go and do it, who will?

I arrived in Lima, Peru, in the early morning hours after my last stop on another continent more than 4,500 miles away. I had a splitting migraine headache that had already caused me to dry-heave at least eight times, sapping my body of all strength and causing some temporary blindness in my left eye. In spite of this, Brother Frigoli and I went to the government television headquarters building in the capital's downtown business section.

The Peruvian government had been ruled for more than 15 years by a communist-Marxist, military junta dictatorship during the time my family and I had carried out missionary work in Peru. We were preaching the gospel, winning souls, and establishing churches in southern Peru. So, it was a tough go to try to negotiate with the powers that be who were still ensconced with a communist mind-set, and who wanted to nationalize everything and did not want anything foreign.

FINALLY A CONTRACT TO
AIR THE GOSPEL TELECAST

After many trying meetings, we finally agreed on a time slot and a reasonable rate. Then we were told that this particular network covered more than 300 cities and towns in the major part of Peru! From the very first airing of the one-hour telecast, letters by the hundreds began pouring into our outreach office in Lima each day. These letters were miracles in themselves. You see, since my wife, Jean, and I were missionaries in Peru for 11 years and knew that Peruvians generally do not write letters in response to television and radio programs, these letters were phenomenal.

Frances Frigoli, Brother Frigoli's wife, called our office in Louisiana about a month after the program began airing and said, "This is fantastic. We are receiving so much mail from dear Peruvians who are coming to Christ while watching the telecast that we need an emergency shipment of the ministry's Spanish version of the booklet, *There's a New Name Written Down in Glory*. We also need to add two more secretaries to help answer the letters pouring in!"

The people began to ask when Brother Swaggart and the team could come for a nationwide crusade. The date was set, and the Alliance Stadium in Lima was secured. About six months before the crusade dates, our contract for the weekly telecast was to be renewed. When Bruno and I met with the station management, we told them that the contract would not be renewed unless our daily telecast, *A Study in the Word*, was included. They finally accepted. For the first time, the gospel started going out over television daily into many towns tucked away in the high Andes Mountains and the jungles of Peru.

THE CRUSADE

Enthusiasm was at a boiling point when the crusade began. Brother Swaggart relates how that during the day before the first night of the crusade, he was walking and praying in a park near the downtown hotel. During the prayer, he cried out, "Oh Lord, what do you want me to give this dear people of Peru in the messages of these crusade services?"

The Lord spoke to him, saying, "Tell them not to look to America and the supposed almighty dollar for their help. Don't look to anything else but to Jesus. He loves you and is sufficient for your every need. He alone will save you. He alone can change you. He alone can meet your need. He is the most important gift of all that I can give you."

The 45,000-seat stadium was filled to overflowing each night. During the three nights, we saw more than 150,000 people in attendance, with more than 20,000 giving their hearts to the Lord. Many in attendance had already come to the Lord while watching the telecast.

For instance, one young man told us, "I had been running from God. I am 25 years old, and my father pastors a small church in the mountains. I came to Lima to attend the university, where I received a degree in electronic engineering. I went to work for the television network that aired your program. I felt as though no one really cared if I lived or died. I watched your telecast each week, and during one of your programs, I prayed and asked Jesus to be Lord of my life. I felt the call of God into full-time ministry, and now I attend the Bible Institute in Lima.

"Thank you for preaching the gospel over television and in the crusade at the Alliance Stadium. Our great country of Peru will never be the same! You've given us the most meaningful gift of all — the gospel of Jesus Christ!"

PROBLEMS

Immediately following the crusade, the Roman Catholic Church printed articles in the newspapers downgrading all that happened. The headlines in one leading paper read, "False Prophet Offends Church." What had been said to upset the ecclesiastics?

The article stated that Jimmy Swaggart actually preached that "Jesus Christ is the only way to get to heaven. If you confess your sins to Him, and Him alone, He will forgive you and set you free. Jesus will give you eternal life, and you can live with Him forever in heaven."

Is that so offensive? That is the gospel that will save souls and change lives! Does that make someone a false prophet? I would say that the person who stated the above concerning Christ Jesus is a true, God-called prophet, which Brother Swaggart definitely is!

Evidently, pressure was put on the TV network to take our program off because it was canceled. The switchboards of the network were jammed for several days after the telecast was not aired, with viewers asking why their favorite program was taken off. The management still would not put the programs back on. It looked as though the other networks had the same pressure. We kept trying, but every door was seemingly closed.

We decided to try the network that had originally given us the outrageous rate. What a surprise when the man in charge told us that he would be delighted to air our program! He had seen the crusade and the good results it brought for the country.

He said, "I don't care who or what puts pressure on our television network, we will air the Jimmy Swaggart telecast, no matter what!" A reasonable, fair market rate was agreed upon, along with the times and days.

This network covered the entirety of Peru, reaching into 486 cities and towns — many more than the previous network!

Was it worth it to keep fighting to get back on television? Yes!

Thousands of souls came to Jesus. Churches were built throughout the capital and all over the country. Children's schools went up, and a medical van began ministry in the out-of-the-way places. Workers were trained in the Bible schools to bring in the harvest. Not only did this happen in Peru, but it happened in scores of countries all over the world. Bruno described it like this: "JSM has speeded up missions in Peru by a whole decade or more."

At that time, the ministry supported on a monthly basis 610 missionaries in 117 countries. We had helped to build 110 Bible schools, more than 200 churches, and 144 children's schools, and we fed more than 450,000 impoverished people daily, with most of them being children. Seventy medical units treated more than 150,000 people each month. More than 1.5 million gospel booklets were sent out from 65 International Outreach Center offices. The telecast aired over 3,000 stations in half of the world. In fact, 195 countries were touched substantially in some way by the total mission's thrust of Jimmy Swaggart Ministries, for which we give God all the glory.

Why did we do all of this? It was because, like the psalmist of old, there are souls crying, *"No man cared for my soul!"*

Do you care enough to pray?

To give?

To go, if called of God to do so?

God cared and loved you enough that He gave the best heaven had — His own Son. Will you give Him your best so that others may have the privilege of the most meaningful gift of all?

"The Lord is not slack concerning His promise, as some men count slackness; but is longsuffering to us-ward, not willing that any should perish, but that all should come to repentance" (II Pet. 3:9).

Far away on distant shores many souls are in despair,
For their hearts are sad and weighted down with sin;
And their tear-stained faces plead for relief from all
  their care,
Persecution from without and fear within.

Poor lost souls with blinded eyes grope about in sin's
  dark night,
Kneeling down before their gods of wood and stone.
Can we see them dying there, still denied the gospel light,
Let them go into eternity alone?

Lord, I've heard the millions cry and my life to Thee
  I give;
Winning souls for Thee, dear Lord, will be my goal.
Send me out to distant shores, let me labor there and live,
Let me tell each one, "Christ careth for your soul!"

"No man careth for my soul," thus cry the millions!
"No man careth for my soul," O hear their plea!
Won't you give your life today to spread the gospel,
So that Christ can save their souls and set them free?

CHAPTER 25

51° 30' 30" N
0° 7' 32" E

THE FAILURE
OF THE CHURCH

"It pleased God by the foolishness of preaching to save them that believe."

— I Corinthians 1:21

THE FAILURE OF THE CHURCH

51° 30' 30" N | 0° 7' 32" E

The train came to a dead stop in one of the most remote spots on earth. I was met square in the face by a friendly gust of sandy desert wind. After rubbing the grit out of my eyes, I discovered that the town in which the train was detained was located in the midst of the Gobi Desert in Asia. In fact, this was part of Inner Mongolia.

Being in such a remote part of the world, I wondered if a television station or even a church could be found here on the backside of the world. After an exhaustive investigation, I discovered that there was, in fact, a television station in the Gobi Desert with thousands of TV sets receiving its signal, yet I could not find a single church.

Later, I discussed my findings with the leader of a prominent mission, and he revealed that there never had been a single known believer in Jesus Christ within the Inner Mongolia area. In fact, years earlier, he had specifically asked a North American friend to try to locate even one Christian in this far removed region of Asia. After an arduous search, his North American friend concluded that not one reported Christian could be found in Inner Mongolia, and there was no documentation that there had ever been one.

Knowing Inner Mongolia's past spiritually barren condition, the same leader of this prominent church mission's department later told me: "Your having the Jimmy Swaggart telecast aired throughout Mongolia is a first!"

Think of it — no church! What happened? Why wasn't there a church or a single believer in Inner Mongolia?

Why? It is because the church of past generations failed to obey God and *"earnestly contend for the faith"* (Jude, Vs. 3). They did not "go" and preach the gospel. They embraced a gospel of easy living and popular acceptance, which prevented the lost from hearing the true gospel of Jesus Christ. It happened then, and it's happening now — right under our noses!

GREAT BRITAIN — AN ISLAMIC STATE?

During one of the first times I was in London in the early 1980s, I was told by a prominent citizen, "At one time, this empire was so vast and extensive that the Englishman could boast, 'The sun never sets on the British Empire.'"

Yet today, the sun has set on a people who, as a nation, have turned their backs on God, establishing policies outlawing the preaching of the gospel, as the United States is doing little by little. Yes, there are godly people in the British Isles, but they will be the first to admit that their fellow countrymen need God as never before just as we admit in the United States.

This Brit went on to say, "Around 1960, you could count the number of mosques in all of Great Britain on your two hands. Today there are over 1,500 mosques and over 2.7 million faithful Muslims who attend them (2011 census). There are over 100 Sharia law courts in the U.K."

What can the Anglican Church (Great Britain's state religion) do about this situation when only 1.5 million of its more than 22 million baptized members actually practice their faith?

All active Christian denominations in Great Britain are challenged today, trying to hold their own, while Islam and satanic cults are experiencing rapid growth. The same could be said about the growth of satanic cults in the United States.

So, do not think that Great Britain is the only nation with this scourge growing. France is in dire straits as well. Many times a nation will try to supposedly be "equitable" in regard to religious freedom, but they actually restrict the preaching of the gospel of Jesus Christ to a back room, or to no freedom at all, by enacting rules and laws against the gospel.

THE BBC LONDON

With a few days between trips, I worked from my office at JSM headquarters and, at the invitation of Brother Swaggart, participated in the ministry's daily program, *A Study in the Word*. While working in Baton Rouge, I received a telephone call from the British Broadcasting Corporation in London, England.

The person on the other end of the line was the producer of the weekly, Sunday evening, prime time program called *Everyman*. This was a British television documentary series on BBC One that aired between 1977 and 2005. Its main subject matter was usually about moral and religious issues.

The *Everyman* series producer related that they had seen the Jimmy Swaggart telecast in many countries of Europe. In fact, their correspondents around the world reported that the same weekly telecast was being aired in different languages in the various countries where they were stationed.

The producer explained that it was quite a phenomenon to be on in so many countries of the world. Some way they had tracked down that I was the person responsible for putting it on so many national television networks in all of these countries of the world. This person said that the BBC wanted to do a special on my travels and try to answer the question: "Why is the Jimmy Swaggart telecast so popular with the viewers in most every country it is on television?"

I was asked if I could, on my next trip to Europe, plan to come to London and be their guest for this interview over BBC One, the main channel of their huge multi-channel network.

I said I would, of course, and looked at my calendar for the dates of my next trip to Europe and gave them the date I would be available.

That date finally came and as I arrived into London after a long flight to other places around the world, I was able to get to the hotel a little after midnight of the same morning

I was to go to the BBC headquarters. There was a note left at the reception desk of the hotel stating that a taxi would come to pick me up at 7 a.m. to take me to the BBC main production complex.

It's important to note that the BBC then was not just another small network among many. At that time, it was the largest television network in the entirety of Western Europe and actually spanned the entire globe. In the U.K. alone, it employed more than 30,000 people.

As I reached my hotel room, I have to confess that my strength was totally depleted. My head ached with an acute migraine causing my eyesight, at times, to completely fail. Nauseated from the severe headache, I immediately regurgitated in the bathroom and realized I would not be able to sleep since lying down only made the migraine worse. Fortunately, there was a huge wing-tipped chair in the room where I could sit and lean my head against the wing tip and try to sleep.

I do not relate all of this to you to make you feel sorry for me, but to let you know that traveling to many different countries and carrying out the Lord's business is not some exotic excursion or tourist fantasy, but a test that only the Lord can pull you through.

That entire night, I was unable to sleep from the intense pain in my head and nausea that caused me to regurgitate 20 more times. By 5 a.m., I decided to start my day, as is my practice, with morning devotions with the Lord before getting ready for the taxi that would pick me up.

It was my understanding that I would be picked up and taken to the London BBC Television Centre, meet some people, have a brief 10-minute filmed interview, and then say good-bye and be on my way. Was I ever mistaken!

THERE WAS A SECOND TAXI

I staggered into the hotel elevator, thanking the Lord that the temporary blindness I had experienced all night was finally gone. As I stepped out into the lobby, I found an entire camera crew waiting for me.

"We will be filming you all day," the crew director explained. "We will follow you in a second taxi after filming how you entered the first taxi at the hotel. We will then travel across London, showing how you arrive at the BBC Television Centre, just as you have done in all the countries around the world where you have put the Jimmy Swaggart telecast on a television network. This is what I was instructed to do. This is a documentary about you and your incredible journey of putting the most viewed gospel program on television around the world. They say it is a phenomenon, to which I agree."

Stunned, I said, " I thought this was just an interview with the program director of BBC about the telecast."

"This is going to be viewed at prime time on a Sunday night when BBC One has the most viewers of the week," the director said, opening the taxi door for me. "They want to tell your story."

This was different. I wasn't anybody but a messenger boy from the sticks of Arizona, and they wanted me to speak to the entire BBC world television audience at prime time! Besides that, from the last look I had in the mirror at the hotel, I looked like a pallid, sick corpse.

As my taxi pulled away, I glanced out the back window and, sure enough, they had cameras mounted on their taxi, filming the whole thing. I turned back around, sat back, and with what little strength I had left, sighed this prayer: "Oh my wonderful Father, You have planned all of this. I belong to You, Lord, and I need a touch from You. For Jesus Christ's sake, please give me Your grace and favor with these authorities at the BBC Centre today and with the viewers of this BBC special when it is aired. May they see Jesus in some way. Thank You for hearing this request. I ask it all in the name of Jesus. Amen."

THE BBC CENTRE

We pulled into the circular drive in front of the main high-rise building on the BBC Centre complex grounds, and I saw another film crew, all set up with strong flood lights, near the front glass doors. They were waiting to capture my entry into the main lobby.

Once inside, I was met by a lady who introduced herself as the director of a certain department of BBC, and she asked me to follow her for our first appointment.

I would spend the next two to three hours meeting with many different producers and directors of different divisions of the BBC and visiting one of their many film-video editing centers. When making a special project for television, before airing, the BBC first filmed everything they did and then transferred it all from film to video in the editing center.

THE DIRECTOR GENERAL OF RELIGIOUS PROGRAMMING

Finally, while walking to our next appointment on one of the top floors of this building, the host told me that I would now meet with the person who had the authority to either put our telecast on the air or not. The host said that I should be prepared for a negative response because at that time, the programming policy did not permit any live gospel preaching, but only documentaries of churches or reporting of happenings in the religious world.

Before this meeting, the film crew asked for a few minutes to set up in the office of this head of religious broadcasting.

As the cameras rolled and the bright lights bore down on us, I was introduced to John (I will only use his first name since we were on a first name basis for this interview), the head of programming for the BBC. He was a very congenial person, and the weight of his responsibility was tangible.

He began by explaining how the programming of BBC was set up with the required censorship that conformed all programming to their technical standards, which were very high. Then he talked about the content restrictions of their broadcast policies.

"We respond directly to the governing board of the BBC that maintains strict adherence to our broadcasting policies," he said.

Then it was my turn to speak.

I said, "John, how long have you been in this position with the BBC? You carry much responsibility for the success of its broadcasting."

"About 12 years now. I have seen a lot in these few years," he replied.

"Well, congratulations," I said, "I can see you have done a superb job in administrating such an important network's programming for the enjoyment of the viewers."

Then John asked me about the scope of Jimmy Swaggart Ministries.

I gave him a brief synopsis of all the different effective ministries in which JSM was involved around the world, with the respective statistics of each outreach. This included Child Care International to the underprivileged in third world countries, the medical van ministry, the citywide and nationwide crusades, *The Evangelist* magazine, the building construction projects of hundreds of churches and evangelistic centers in third-world countries, the famine relief program, the Calcutta, India, feeding program and hospital of Missionary Mark Buntain, the monthly support of more than 600 missionaries worldwide, and most of all, the coverage and viewership of the weekly Jimmy Swaggart telecast of more than 300 million people in 150 countries.

"Well, thank you for this overview of the ministry," John said. "It certainly is extensive, to say the least. We know from our correspondents in almost every nation around the world that your television program enjoys a very great coverage. Actually, it is the largest in the religious broadcasting world, and it has the second most coverage in a number of countries — next to the *I Love Lucy* comedy show, which has the most outlets as far as programming is concerned. Jim, you have certainly done an excellent job in extending this telecast into most of the countries of the world."

"Thank you," I said. "You are very kind, but I feel that I have not done very much to bring this about. It has been the Lord who has made it possible. So many lives have been changed as a result of Brother Jimmy Swaggart's preaching. Invariably, in most any nation in which the program is aired, the telecast becomes the number one rated program, even over all secular programming. The people see right away that the program really does not have much to do with religion, but more so with a person — Jesus Christ, the Son of God — and a personal relationship by faith alone, no matter what the religious background of the individual. Even in the predominately Muslim and Buddhist countries, where it airs currently, it has become the most viewed program, not to mention the many communist nations where it airs. The political leaders of many countries have told us that the telecast has actually saved many countries from utter chaos by giving the people hope and a new life in Christ. We would want the dear people of the U.K. to also enjoy the blessing of the gospel of Jesus Christ preached over this telecast over BBC TV."

PREACHING OF THE GOSPEL PROHIBITED OVER THE BBC

At this point, John began to quote the BBC broadcasting rules and regulations concerning religious broadcasting.

He said, "Proselytizing is not allowed over the BBC, nor is the airing of entire preaching programs. We can report on a church service or religious gathering and include a brief excerpt of what is said, but talking straight to the public is prohibited. We follow the guidelines of the Church of England, the Anglican Church, in these matters,"

By this time, John and I had established a pretty good rapport with one another. We both knew that what the other believed was in direct opposition. Still, there was a deep respect for one another that the Lord had put there.

The conversation had somewhat heated up and, all of a sudden, I felt the Lord would have me ask him a rather direct question.

I said, "When do you think you will begin airing the Jimmy Swaggart telecast on a weekly basis over BBC?"

"Under our current policies, never!" he said.

ANOTHER DIRECT QUESTION

Undeterred by his last answer, I said, "Well, John, may I ask you a question?"

"Yes, of course."

I said, "Let's suppose that Jesus Christ came in person to the BBC today and asked you for time to preach over the BBC network. Would you give Him the program slot?"

John hesitated and then, with a twinge of sadness, said, "No, I could not give Jesus Christ any time over the BBC."

There was a simultaneous, almost audible, shudder from the crowd of BBC technicians, producers, and directors watching and working our interview.

"This is most unfortunate," I said. "The nation that gave the world some of the greatest missionaries and Christian statesmen of all time and experienced some of the greatest moves of God in the history of mankind cannot even let the best Man whoever lived — the Saviour of all mankind, who died on the Cross for us — speak over BBC. I am so sorry to hear that."

John hesitated a moment and then, rather sarcastically, asked me point blank, "Jim, do you really think that Jimmy Swaggart will ever preach over any BBC-owned television network in the future?"

All of a sudden, I felt the presence of the Lord and without hesitation responded, "I not only think he will, but I know that some day the gospel Jimmy Swaggart preaches will air all over the United Kingdom because God loves the British people too much to let them go to hell without having the opportunity to hear the blessed gospel of Jesus Christ!"

"Well, we'll just see about that," John said.

As the interview finished and we shook hands, I thanked John for this privilege to be with him and the cordial people of BBC. As the host director and I were walking out to the elevator, I asked, "You don't think your people will air that last segment do you? It was pretty strong."

"I know they will," she said. "That is why we wanted you to come because we knew you would tell the truth and put what we all want here to the head of BBC. It is not right that all these other countries in Europe, not to mention the rest of the world, can have the Jimmy Swaggart telecast airing weekly, and we here in what is supposed to be a free country with free speech guaranteed not to be able to have Jimmy Swaggart preach over our national television network, or any other preacher for that matter. It is just not right. We need the gospel message desperately here in the U.K."

After the interview with John, we still had several other meetings with different departments of the BBC. Finally, as we headed to the main floor to have the last filming of me leaving the BBC for the day, a strange thing happened.

BBC film crews had set up their equipment both inside the lobby by the main door and on the outside where the taxi was standing by, waiting for me to enter it. In the process, half of the entire lobby was cordoned off. No one could enter or exit the building until this last segment of me saying good-bye at the door, entering into the cab, and driving off was filmed.

A CELEBRITY MADE TO WAIT FOR JIM WOOLSEY

Just as the clapperboard was sounded to synchronize the video with the sound of this filming segment, a man came down the main stairway and into the lobby. He wanted to exit the building but was denied. The incident seemed to be drawing attention and when I looked across the lobby at the man, I understood why: it was the famous English singer and former Beatle, Paul McCartney.

Filming quickly resumed, but in the distance I heard a member of the crew explaining to Mr. McCartney why he could not yet exit the building.

"The *Everyman* special documentary with Jim Woolsey is being filmed," the staffer told McCartney. "It concerns the possible airing of the preaching of the gospel of Jesus Christ over the BBC. You will have to wait until they finish this last segment."

The film crew continued, capturing my formal departure from the BBC — my handshake with their representatives at the door as I exited the BBC London Centre and a wave good-bye from the taxi.

As I was chauffeured off, I turned and looked out the window at all of the equipment set up there and the people involved in this documentary special, and I knew that God had done something that day in His great plan of redemption. I thought about the interview with John and wondered if I had overstepped my invitation by putting him on the spot like that and my response at the end — the prophecy that came forth.

The Sunday arrived when the *Everyman* special was aired prime time all over the U.K., Europe, and elsewhere. The last segment, I noticed, was left in, unedited.

A couple of weeks later, word came to me that when the *Everyman* special aired, the BBC had the highest rating of any one program ever on its television network. The day after it aired, calls jammed BBC phone switchboards all day and most of that week from viewers asking when the special would be replayed. A few weeks later, by popular demand, the documentary played again with the same results — the highest rating ever of any program ever aired over the mighty BBC.

PROPHECY FULFILLED

In 2012, the SonLife Broadcasting Network (SBN) channel was included in the BBC-owned Sky Television network coverage for the U.K. Sky TV airs SBN programming, featuring Jimmy Swaggart and others preaching the gospel of Jesus Christ and Him crucified, 24 hours a day, seven days a week, with more than 14 million households receiving this channel in the U.K.

God fulfilled His Word! He did the impossible! Even though the BBC stated emphatically that it would never be possible to air this preaching of the gospel, God knew this in the one plan He had already designed before the foundation of the world:

So shall My word be that goeth forth out of My mouth: it shall not return unto Me void, but it shall accomplish that which I please, and it shall prosper in the thing whereto I sent it" (Isa. 55:11).

ELSEWHERE IN EUROPE

Bob Mackish, who was a veteran missionary to the Eastern Bloc countries of Europe, told me: "They have erected a giant Buddha along the Danube River here in Vienna! Additionally, a large Muslim mosque has been constructed and recently opened. I feel so burdened when I see these things permitted in a 'Christian' country. I can't believe this is happening here in the great country of Austria!"

Recently, I was in Brussels, Belgium, visiting the huge Belgium BRT television network center. Before going over to the network headquarters, I walked through an open-air shopping mall where thousands of people were going into a variety of shops, theaters, restaurants, and bookstores.

I had walked a couple of blocks when I heard the loud gong of a church bell. Right there, tucked away in the heart of this huge metropolitan city, was an old church, its bell calling people to worship. I stood and watched to see how many people would enter through the ominous gothic doors. After the longest wait, guess how many went inside to worship. None! Yet, hundreds flooded into movie theaters and places of entertainment.

What a graphic picture of the modern church. The whole extent of its evangelism is a gonging bell, falling on the spiritually deaf ears of a pleasure-seeking generation:

"Lovers of pleasures more than lovers of God; having a form of godliness, but denying the power thereof" (II Tim. 3:4-5).

But even now, powerful forces are still at work to silence the gospel, and the result will be the same — the loss of countless souls for all eternity!

HOW CAN THIS BE?

The director of our German JSM office at the time told me, "Yours is the only actual 'preaching' program allowed on this German TV network. Many people are being saved as a direct result, but there are powerful forces at work trying to take it off the air because most Europeans hate the preaching of the gospel."

The same was true in several other countries at the time. They view preaching as foolishness and a waste of good airtime. Many networks do not allow preaching, yet they air programs depicting pornography, violence, murder, rape, and every type of filth that gradually tears down the family unit and deteriorates the very moral fabric upon which all nations are built.

THE ONLY ANSWER

"It pleased God by the foolishness of preaching to save them who believe" (I Cor. 1:21).

Thank God that in the midst of this whole sordid mess, there is at least one network that is preaching the gospel of Jesus Christ and Him crucified and seeing unprecedented results because of the anointing of the Holy Spirit. This is the *only* answer for a lost world the church has failed to reach. In many countries, this is the only voice preaching the Message of the Cross.

In the 1980s, Missionary Warren Flattery, our JSM Belgium director, shared this:

"The Jimmy Swaggart telecast, being broadcast into Belgium over RTL-TV Luxembourg, is reaching the people in their own living rooms with the gospel. Never have so many responded to preaching of any kind here. The phones continue to 'ring off the hook' all day long in our offices in Waterloo, and letters are pouring in from people who have been touched by the singing and preaching.

"One lady contacted us, saying that she was so thankful for a program that preaches the true gospel. You see, her husband was an atheist most of his life. During the war, his parents were killed, and he blamed it on God, becoming bitter and turning his back on God to become a hardened atheist. A man in his late 60s, his wife found him in the living room with tears running down his cheeks at about midnight one Saturday night just a few weeks ago while watching the weekly telecast.

"'You should kneel down and lift your hands toward God like they do on that program and repeat the prayer they pray,' she told him. He knelt down with his hands toward heaven and repeated the sinner's prayer.

"'God came into his life, and you could see the change come over his face,' she said. 'The next morning, he fell over dead of a heart attack. He just made it through! If that telecast, anointed of God, had not been on television the night before, my husband would have died lost for all eternity. Thank you for the only preaching we have on television in Belgium.'"

A lady wrote our office in Baton Rouge, saying:

> "We in Trinidad have only recently begun to receive your television broadcast, and already it has turned our nation upside down. Everyone I know sets aside that hour in the morning when the broadcast comes on the air and feasts upon every word."

AN AWESOME RESPONSIBILITY

God is literally propelling this Spirit-anointed Message of the Cross of Jesus Christ today over insurmountable obstacles into all the world, saving souls, breaking bondages, and changing lives. For many, this is the only true gospel they will ever hear. Our responsibility is great — even awesome — when you think that this will be the only voice millions of people will hear on television between here and eternity.

There are now more than 3 billion people who have access to this gospel programming each day, if they want to tune in, by way of cable and satellite networks, electronic devices, and the Internet.

What the historical church failed to do — preach the gospel to the whole world — this ministry is doing by the help and grace of God. While dead religious hierarchies are banging their hollow bells of emptiness, God is blowing the wind of His Spirit across unreached thresholds so that this vital message of Jesus Christ and Him crucified may reach every person in this generation in every nation of the world.

"And this gospel of the kingdom shall be preached in all the world for a witness unto all nations; and then shall the end come" (Mat. 24:14).

With more than 7 billion people in the world today, *"There remaineth yet very much land to be possessed"* (Josh. 13:1).

Let's give the winds a mighty voice and flood every nation with the preaching of the gospel of Jesus Christ and Him crucified!

We have heard the joyful sound: Jesus saves! Jesus saves!
Spread the tidings all around: Jesus saves! Jesus saves!
Bear the news to every land, climb the mountains, cross
*   the waves;*
Onward! 'tis our Lord's command; Jesus saves! Jesus saves!

Give the winds a mighty voice: Jesus saves! Jesus saves!
Let the nations now rejoice: Jesus saves! Jesus saves!
Shout salvation full and free; highest hills and deepest caves;
This our song of victory: Jesus saves! Jesus saves!

CHAPTER 26

41° 54' 10" N
12° 29' 46" E

NOW IS THE TIME

"And that, knowing the time, that now it is high time to awake out of sleep: for now is our salvation nearer than when we believed."

— *Romans 13:11*

NOW IS THE TIME

41° 54' 10" N | 12° 29' 46" E

Some people told us it was useless to try to reach the people behind the Iron Curtain. They tell us that most iron curtain countries are atheistic in official belief and communistic in political ideology.

In the natural, it seemed utterly impossible to do anything behind these man-made barriers, whether it was the Iron Curtain, the Bamboo Curtain, or whatever. However, God delights in doing the impossible. He knows no closed doors!

I remember one cold wintry morning when the Aeroflot Soviet plane on which I was traveling landed in the capital of the largest communist country on the face of the earth — Moscow, Russia, the former Soviet Union. While we had been sending program tapes to several other communist countries for quite some time and airing over national networks, we had been unable to even distribute any video program tapes among the churches of the great land of the Soviet Union.

Through a series of miracles, God opened the door for me to meet with the maximum authority relative to the churches in this great land.

As he watched the Russian demonstration tape I carried with me, he became excited and asked, "Could you wait a moment while I ask the other leaders of the work who are in a prayer meeting in another part of the building to come and view this tape with us? Their meeting will be over in another 45 minutes, and then they will be able to see this great service in the Russian language."

"Yes," I said. "I will be more than happy to wait, but while I'm waiting, I can run over to the duty-free shop and purchase more video equipment for the brethren to view the programs in their own churches."

By taxi, I hurried across town to pick up the equipment and more tapes from my hotel. Of course, when the brethren viewed the program, they became excited and elated that there was such a powerful gospel program available in their language.

I left the tapes and equipment with them and went on my way. Months passed without any word from them.

VERY SPECIAL VISITORS

After almost a year, a group of Russian brethren on a tour of the United States stopped by our offices in Baton Rouge. These particular men were not present that day I left the tapes and equipment in the capital city of their country. I purposely didn't mention the tapes. If they volunteered the information, I would know for certain if the tapes had been distributed throughout the land.

The first day of their visit to Baton Rouge, nothing was said. However, on the second day, when we went into the main television studio, the brethren viewed the huge world map that was the backdrop for the daily program, *A Study in the Word*. They noticed that the Soviet Union was not colored in red (which means Jimmy Swaggart Ministries is involved in some way in those particular countries).

The spokesman for the group asked, "Why isn't our country painted in red?"

I told them that we were not involved to much extent in their country and felt we must be honest in what we place on the map concerning our world outreach involvement.

"But you are involved considerably in our country," the man said, somewhat puzzled at my lack of knowledge.

As our discussion continued, he asked me, "Do you know program number 1264? That program has been such a blessing to our people in the Russian language, but we only have Part I. We were instructed not to return to our country without Part II. Is there any way you could give us the second part in the Russian language also?"

At this point, I realized that the tapes were being used and were being a great blessing to the work of the Lord in their country. I also knew that the program to which they were referring was a crusade service from Hawaii.

The brethren went on to tell us that the Jimmy Swaggart programs were being used and spread throughout the country. They had already been through the southern and western parts of the country and were now penetrating the far reaches of the eastern part into Siberia.

As the programs were played on the VCR television units in each church, people with other VCR units were recording them, and the ones who didn't have video recording units were using their audio cassette players to record the messages and send them to other churches and relatives across the country. God was using them to help stir the churches and bring revival to that great land.

The group leader asked, "Please, can you give us some more programs as soon as possible?"

While our production team rushed to duplicate more programs and send them to Russia, I was making plans to contact the national television network of that great country to have this glorious message of the gospel broadcast across that entire land!

WHEN GOD GETS READY?

Many people think that when God gets ready and wants us (His church) to take the gospel to a specific nation or area of the world, then He will change the political situation to make it possible. They say that we should wait until all the political, social, economic, and religious conditions are right and then take the gospel to the people; that we should wait until the television networks contact us to air the program.

My friend, that will never happen. Jesus said, *"Go ye into all the world, and preach the gospel to every creature"* (Mk. 16:15).

This means every single nation — whether closed or open, rich or poor, democratic or communistic, or near or far. The gospel is more than politics, religion, or a philosophy, and it's much, much more than a culture. It is an *ultimatum* — believe or perish. It is God offering every person *eternal life*, and this eternal life is in Jesus Christ! He is the *only way* to heaven. He purchased this passport to heaven at a great price. He died on the Cross of Calvary and paid the sin debt for you and me. This He did with His own precious, innocent, spotless, and undefiled life's blood, which set us free from the penalty of the broken law and the judgment of a thrice-holy God. This is ours by faith alone in Jesus' finished work of the Cross.

"For He has made Him to be sin (a sin offering) *for us, who knew no sin; that we might be made the righteousness of God in Him"* (II Cor. 5:21).

God's Word states emphatically: *"Behold, now is the accepted time; behold, now is the day of salvation"* (II Cor. 6:2).

In prayer, I asked God about the concept given above (really an excuse) that, as they say, "We should wait until all the political, social, economic, and religious conditions are right and then take the gospel to the people. We should wait until the television networks contact us to air the program."

I began praying something like this, "My most gracious, kind, and loving heavenly Father, hallowed be Your name. I come to You in the name of Jesus. Lord, I know You are not willing that any should perish. You heard this unbelief that says it is no use trying to take the gospel to Russia over television. 'You should wait until conditions are just right,' they say. Should I wait until conditions are more favorable? You see how difficult it is to even acquire a visa to visit Russia, but there are more than 300 million dear souls in the Soviet Union without Christ. Lord, I have no strength and don't know how to even approach this impossible obstacle of the Iron Curtain of communism built around Russia. Should I wait, Lord?"

Almost immediately upon ending with the word 'Lord,' He responded. The Lord said to me, "Conditions will never be just right in this sin-cursed world. I have called you to offer My message to every nation of the world. I have set before you an open door, and no man can shut it. I will lead you in My way to go, and you will behold the hand of God at work. Follow Me! Now is the perfect time. When it is the most impossible is the moment I can work and move if you will just believe I can do it, and all the glory is Mine!"

Very seldom has God spoken to me so clearly. I wept. I knew then beyond a shadow of a doubt that God could and would, by His design, open the Soviet Union to the gospel over television.

BROTHER AND SISTER SWAGGART
INVITED TO COMMUNIST SOVIET UNION

In the early part of 1985, Missionary Bob Mackish (a missionary to eastern Europe) called me and said his contacts in communist Russia wanted to invite Brother and Sister Swaggart and my wife and me to visit the Soviet Union. Also, he said the brethren behind the Iron Curtain in Hungary and Poland would like us to visit them in their countries on the same trip.

Brother Mackish said he would help me with all the formalities of acquiring visitors' visas for us. He would have the leaders of the officially recognized churches in Russia extend an official invitation letter that was needed to facilitate authorization of our visas. Please understand that at this time, all travel to and from the Soviet Union was very restricted, with almost no travel permitted. It was even more difficult for United States citizens to acquire a visa.

Immediately I asked Brother Swaggart if he would accept such an invitation. He did accept, but it would be months after our return trip home that I learned of his struggle in making this decision to go to the Soviet Union.

"To be frank with you," he said, "I was somewhat nonplussed in my spirit because I've been very hard on the communistic philosophy over our nationwide (even worldwide) telecast; perhaps harder than anyone has ever been, and we were reaching millions of people. However, after praying about the situation, I felt that God would want us to go. I sought the Lord earnestly about our safety and protection, and I felt the assurance of the Holy Spirit that everything would be satisfactory. Sure enough, it was exactly as the Lord spoke it to my heart, and I'm so glad that we went."

After Brother Swaggart told me that he consented to go, I responded back to Missionary Bob Mackish that Brother Swaggart said that he would accept the invitation to visit the Soviet Union and the other countries behind the Iron Curtain. Brother Mackish was delighted. I gave him the list of names of the small group going on this trip, which were Brother and Sister Swaggart, my wife, Jean, and me, and a couple of others. Only the six of us would be going.

BOB AND BONNIE MACKISH

Brother and Sister Swaggart closed a crusade in Denver, Colorado, on a Sunday afternoon and flew the next morning to New York City, where they met us. We then flew on to Vienna, Austria, where we met Bob and Bonnie Mackish.

Bob and Bonnie Mackish were certainly two noble souls. If ever there were noble souls, then Bob and Bonnie fit the description perfectly. At the time of this trip, they had been laboring in eastern Europe for nearly 20 years. Tremendous revivals had taken place in those eastern European countries, and Bob had helped to spearhead them. Also, he had made nearly 30 trips into the Soviet Union, aiding and strengthening the brethren the very best that he could. He was one of the godliest men my wife and I have ever known.

A long time ago, when our Saviour met Nathanael, He said, *"Behold an Israelite indeed, in whom is no guile"* (Jn. 1:47). The same could be said for Bob Mackish. He was truly a man with no guile.

We stayed all night in Vienna and left for Moscow the next morning.

MOSCOW

The Moscow airport was built by the West Germans for the 1980 Moscow Olympics. It was jammed with people, but to be frank with you, it was not a very inviting place to be.

We were unaccustomed to seeing soldiers with guns slung over their shoulders, but we saw this constantly in the Soviet Union. They were everywhere — on street corners, in shops, etc. Their presence seemed to be a constant reminder that the Soviet Union was an armed camp.

Later Brother Swaggart would write: "I couldn't help but think of the so-called peace activists here in the States who constantly fight against our weapon systems in America — and the Army, the Navy, the Air Force, and all other branches of military service. They seem to favor the philosophy of the Soviet Union. And I found myself wondering what they would think should they ever go into Moscow or any city in the Soviet Union and observe soldiers on every corner."

THE BRETHREN MET US

When we finally cleared customs — and that was an experience in itself — we were met by brethren from the Baptist church in the Soviet Union. Let me explain to you a little about the church in the Soviet Union.

At that time, they had what was called the registered church, which included churches of most denominational affiliations. They were all called Baptist (I assume the Eastern Orthodox Church was not included in this). However, in this so-called Baptist union, there were Pentecostals, Methodists, and all types of others as well. They had another type of registration of churches that was not included in the Baptist union. Then they had what was called the unregistered church.

There were probably about 5,000 churches in the Soviet Union, and there may have been 1,000 to 2,000 more that were unregistered.

THE UNDERGROUND CHURCH

Naturally, the question comes to mind about the underground church. Most of this information came from Missionary Bob Mackish. As mentioned, he had more experience in the Soviet Union than most, having made more than 30 trips into it and having preached innumerable times all over the Soviet Union. Actually, Bob is Russian. His parents, if I remember correctly, were born in White Russia, where Minsk is the capital. He still had relatives there.

According to what we saw and the information that Bob Mackish gave us from nearly 20 years of experience, there was very little underground church in the Soviet Union. Once we were there and able to observe it, it became more understandable.

After this trip, Brother Swaggart wrote what he believed about freedom and religion in the Soviet Union, and I agree:

"The Russians have what they call a Freedom of Conscience Act. When it comes to religion, briefly, it means freedom of religion — which means a person can belong to whatever church he desires.

Secondly, it means the freedom of no religion — which means a person can be an atheist or whatever he desires.

Thirdly, it means freedom from religion.

Now, the second freedom is somewhat peculiar to the Western mind, but to the Russian, it's a very sensible proposal.

Before the revolution under the czars, everybody had to belong to the state church, which was the Eastern Orthodox Church. If you didn't belong to the Eastern Orthodox Church, it was very difficult to feed your family. The situation was dictatorial. The people grew to abhor, to literally hate the Eastern Orthodox Church, hence, what they call freedom of no religion.

The last freedom in their philosophy is the most damaging of all. When they say 'freedom from religion,' it stops all evangelization. It simply means that if you have no religion, no one can approach you and witness to you; it's against the law. Of course, all evangelization of any type is stopped, including such things as literature, door-to-door witnessing, or just witnessing to somebody on the job, radio, television, or whatever. So this makes it very difficult for the church. Yet, the Holy Spirit has a way of getting through all of that.

If someone makes a personal inquiry, an individual is free to share his faith, but even then, he has to be very careful.

The people seem to be free to go to the churches as they desire. There are no apparent restrictions. However, the preachers cannot say anything against the government, and they cannot speak out against any difficulties or problems in the country. They are strictly limited to preaching the salvation message of the Lord Jesus Christ and Christian growth. Nothing can impact the government in any way. If anyone does that, he's in trouble.

So the preachers restrict themselves to preaching the gospel."

EVERY CHURCH WE ATTENDED WAS FILLED

On this trip, Brother Swaggart was invited to preach in one Mennonite church, two Baptist churches, and a Pentecostal church. Incidentally, according to the men who were with us, the Pentecostal faith is the fastest growing and is probably the largest in the Soviet Union, with many thousands having been saved and baptized with the Holy Spirit.

Some reading this will say everything was staged for our benefit on that visit, and I'm sure those things could have been done.

Brother Swaggart put it this way, "I cannot answer for some churches, but I can answer for the Pentecostals. I know these brethren have been baptized with the Holy Spirit. I know their spirit, and I sensed the moving and operation of the Holy Spirit."

The Pentecostal church where we preached on a Sunday morning was in Minsk, Belarus. It was packed to capacity, and the Spirit of God moved in a beautiful way. The men and women sat there and wept as the tears rolled down their cheeks.

ABOUT THE SERVICES

The services were a little more orthodox than that to which we were accustomed in the States, but you must understand that they had had very little opportunity to assemble and have church. In fact, this privilege had been granted only about five to seven years previously. Before the Freedom of Conscience Act, the situation was not very healthy; however, it has improved somewhat in the last few years. Contrary to many statements, these churches were filled with young people.

Of course, the Soviet Union had done everything within its power to educate the youth in the atheistic dogma of communism, and I'm sure it has had its effect. As well, they will try to make people believe that only very old people attend the churches, but something was happening that you need to know about.

THE RUSSIANS ARE SEEING A DIFFERENCE

Brother Swaggart described the tense situation: "I believe it was Karl Marx who said, 'Religion is the opiate of the people.' Of course, he was speaking of the Eastern Orthodox Church. That's all he knew, and it was corrupt to the core. To be frank with you, the communist masters in those days had never seen real Christianity in action, and, sad to say, most of the world still hasn't.

"The Soviet Union has a terrible problem with drunkenness, stealing, bribery, and other such sins. Now, with their new religious freedom, the people have noticed that the Pentecostal Christians and many of the Baptist Christians do not drink, steal, lie, or take bribes. As a result, this has made an impact upon many Russian officials. To be frank with you, this is the very thing that overthrew the Roman world of some 1,700 years ago.

"Little by little, the Romans started noticing that the morality and the culture of the Christians were far above that of Roman paganism. Now, many Russian officials are starting to notice that there is a difference between true Christianity and their own philosophy of atheism and others who call themselves Christians but really aren't. One communist official told Bob Mackish, 'Christianity and communism, as far as attainments are concerned, are very similar. We communists work just as hard as you Christians, but the difference is that when we die, there is nothing; when you die, you have something to look forward to.'

IS THE CHURCH FREE?

"Of course, the church is not free. There is no semblance of freedom as we know it. To be frank with you, the whole of the Soviet Union could be described as one giant prison, but it's more a prison of the spirit than it is a prison of the body. There is so much the people and the preachers want to tell you, but they cannot say anything. Once again the question is asked, 'Well, what about the underground church?'

"Now, I doubt seriously that there is an underground church in the Soviet Union, at least as we think of it here in America. I know we hear stories of Christians meeting out in the woods and things of this nature; however, when one starts to think about it, this would be very difficult.

"First of all, there are very few telephones (at least, that Christians have) in the Soviet Union. Secondly, the weather is almost always bad. Thirdly, it would be very difficult to get the news to any appreciable number of people to meet anywhere — and really, it is not necessary. The churches are open and the people can go.

"Every church we saw was being enlarged. It was crude construction, but the places were full, and they needed the space. This one thing I do know: when I preach, I recognize the Spirit of God, and I recognize the moving of the Holy Spirit on the people. It moved beautifully so in the Soviet Union in all the churches we visited."

THE SCHEDULE

We stayed at the Russian Hotel. It was the largest in the world, with more than 4,000 rooms. The rooms were very Spartan. To be frank with you, they were little more than a hostel. We had our meals in the restaurant at the top of the hotel (19th story), and the food was quite good, although it all had a "sameness" about it. We were seated at the same table every day. From that table we could look down on Red Square, the tomb of Lenin, and the Kremlin walls. It was a sobering thought to realize at every meal that when we would look out at those Kremlin walls from 19 stories up, behind those walls men had plotted, and were plotting, to dominate the world. That little 3-acre enclosure had cost the American taxpayers several trillion dollars in tax money and had thrown the world in turmoil.

Brother Swaggart preached in the Baptist church in Moscow on a Tuesday night, and the next day, we flew to Novosibirsk, which is in western Siberia. It was a town of about a million people as compared to Moscow's 9 million. We preached there in a community church pastored by a very gracious Mennonite man; however, quite a number of different denominational people also attended — Baptists, Pentecostals, etc. It was packed, and it was an excellent service.

MEETING WITH THE COMMISSAR IN EACH CITY

Upon arriving in each city, Brother Swaggart and I would have to go meet with the Soviet government commissar in charge of internal affairs and religion. In this one particular city, we went to one of the top floors of the huge Stalin-built skyscrapers. When we entered this Russian gentleman's office, he was somewhat cold in his greeting and asked us to sit down in front of his desk.

The commissar did not waste any time in getting to the point. He said, "Mr. Swaggart, you preach in your country against our country, calling it what your president calls it, an 'evil empire.'"

As we sat there listening, Brother Swaggart noticed the man had several service medals pinned to his suit jacket from the Great Patriotic War (World War II) and said, "I see you have several medals there," pointing to one in particular. "What is that one?"

The commissar looked down and said, "It is for being in the Battle of Kursk."

"I just read a book on the great tank Battle of Kursk," Brother Swaggart said. "You mean you were in that tank battle, one of the biggest ever fought?"

"Yes, I was in the very thick of the battle," he said, and then plunged into a very detailed description of the entire battle, pausing only to answer the questions Brother Swaggart asked about the commissar's war experience.

Their conversation went on for a good 40 minutes. By the end, the man had forgotten about the belligerent remarks with which he had opened and came around to our side of his desk. We stood up, and the commissar embraced Brother Swaggart's hand with both of his and told him, "If there is anything I can help you with while you and your people are visiting, please let me know. I hereby grant you complete freedom to visit any place you would like with your group."

We thanked him for his kindness and went on to visit the churches and brethren of the city. They even let the brethren of the Pentecostal underground churches show up to the meetings with no trouble from the commissar or the authorities. It was just great! Thank the Lord that He showed Brother Swaggart what to say.

We flew back to Moscow the next morning, a distance of about 1,800 miles. That night, we caught a train from Moscow to Minsk (it was a sleeper), and we traveled all night. Brother Swaggart said that he had never traveled by train before.

THE INTERPRETER

We arrived in Minsk on Sunday morning right about daylight. Brother Swaggart preached in the Pentecostal church that same morning, where there were about 500 to 600 people present.

The interpreter assigned to Brother Swaggart for the entire trip and for all of the church services was a KGB agent; he was not even saved. After he was first introduced to Brother

Swaggart, and we were told that this interpreter came from the KGB, Brother Swaggart later asked Bob Mackish and the brethren if it were possible to get a different interpreter. They said no, it would not be possible. He would have to preach through this interpreter. Throughout the preaching itinerary, this interpreter had done a fairly decent job at the previous churches we had visited.

Our next stop was this large church in Minsk. As Brother Swaggart was preaching, right in the middle of the message, he said something, but there was no interpretation. He thought that the interpreter, who always stood a step back and to the right of Brother Swaggart, could not hear him. So he repeated the sentence, but no interpreter's voice followed.

Brother Swaggart turned around and looked at his interpreter. Tears were streaming down the man's face. This KGB interpreter said, "I want to accept Jesus as my Saviour."

Right there in the middle of Brother Swaggart's message, he gave his heart to the Lord and was gloriously saved. (A few days later, when we were back in Moscow and leaving from the airport, the brethren came to the departure concourse, and the KGB interpreter came with them. He embraced Brother Swaggart to say good-bye and said, "When you came, I did not know Him, but now I know Him; I'm saved! Thank you, thank you, thank you!" Every one cried tears of joy and thanked God for this new brother in the Lord. About six months later after returning to the States, Brother Mackish called me long distance and asked me to tell Brother Swaggart that the interpreter had passed away of cancer, but he was saved!)

As Brother Swaggart continued to preach to that congregation in Minsk, all of a sudden, he held his Bible high into the air and declared under a heavy anointing of the Holy Spirit, "One day soon this gospel is going to be preached in every single city, every town, and every village of this great land of Russia!"

Later, back at the hotel, he told Frances, "Did you hear that? Do you think it was of the Lord? How can it be? This country is closed."

It looked in the natural that it would be absolutely impossible for that prophecy to be fulfilled. There were so many souls who needed to hear; nearly 1.5 million in the beautiful city of Minsk alone.

However, in my heart of hearts, knowing God's love for the dear Russian people, that He is *"not willing that any should perish"* (II Pet. 3:9), I believed this prophecy to be from the Lord. In the many, many trips I would take back to Russia over the next five years, I would recall what the Lord said through Brother Swaggart and know that it would be fulfilled.

Sunday night Brother Swaggart preached in the Baptist church, and the attendance was about the same. However, many of the Pentecostals had come over to the Baptist church, having dismissed their own services to do so. The next day (Monday), he spoke to a Bible school gathering in the same Baptist church. It really was not a Bible school as such; it was a correspondence school, and once a year, they brought the students in. He preached to them, and the Spirit of God moved so graciously and touched their hearts and lives. It left a great impact on them.

That evening, we caught another train back to Moscow, traveling all night.

DEPARTURE

When the brethren took us to the Moscow airport to leave for Budapest, Hungary, and we were saying good-bye, it was one of the tenderest moments I've ever experienced. They literally put their heads on our shoulders and sobbed. I don't mean just a tear, I mean a literal breaking and weeping. There were reasons for this. One, they had sensed the moving and the presence of the Holy Spirit; two, they were pleading with us to come back; and, three, when you looked into their eyes, these preachers wanted to tell you so much — but they couldn't say anything. It was like going from one world to another.

BUDAPEST, HUNGARY

Even though Hungary, at that time, was a communist country, ruled by the Soviet Union, it was like coming out of darkness into light. Hungary was controlled by the Soviet Union, but she looked to America. Her eyes were ever westward.

Our preaching schedule took us to Budapest, one of the most beautiful cities on the face of the earth. The beautiful Blue Danube flows right through the center of it.

When we met the pastors there, and Brother Swaggart preached in the service that night, there was an outpouring of the Holy Spirit that literally flowed in the place. Scores responded to the altar call, lining the front, with tears rolling down their cheeks as the Spirit of God moved.

God told Brother Swaggart then that He was going to move greatly in the eastern European countries in the future. With the SonLife Broadcasting Network now covering these countries by satellite and several cable TV systems, I believe we are going to see that great move take place in countries such as Hungary, Poland, Czechoslovakia, Slovakia, Yugoslavia, and Romania.

WARSAW, POLAND

In the late 1980s and 1990s, most Americans had seen Poland on their television sets more than any other country in eastern Europe simply because of the solidarity effort. In Warsaw, God gave us a great service, and the next morning, just before leaving, Brother Swaggart, Brother Mackish, and I, along with the leader of the Poland church, went to visit the construction site of the combination Bible school-church that we were building there.

The construction workers were laying the foundation. On completion, our facility would stand some four stories high, right in the shadow of a giant building constructed by Joseph Stalin in the early 1950s. More than a year before this trip, we had been asked for finances to help construct this Bible school and church facility, and by the help and grace of God, Jimmy Swaggart Ministries was able to do it. The building is now up, and the ministry emanating from it has touched the hearts and lives of untold thousands of people in Poland.

LEAVING THE AIRPORT

Our trip to the Soviet Union had come to a close, and it was time to return to the States. The people we had met and the lives we saw changed deeply affected us, but probably Brother Swaggart most of all.

He shared the following from our last day of the trip:

"When we were in one of the airports (I believe it was in Budapest) getting ready to leave and were walking to customs — having said good-bye to the pastors — a terrible sadness overwhelmed me. I asked, 'Lord, is it fair? We have so much freedom, and they have so little.'

But then the Spirit of God started to move on my heart. Right there in the airport, I sensed the presence of God so mightily, and the Lord said to me, 'Yes, it is difficult now, but shortly, it will be over.'

All of a sudden, the words of David Engles' beautiful song started to come to me.

There's a whole lot of people going home,
By the signs of time it won't be very long.

In the twinkling of an eye we'll all be gone,
There's a whole lot of people going home.

God said, 'I have a lot of them who have not bowed the knee to Baal, even under their communist masters, and a lot more are going to be added.'"

THIS WAS THE REAL REASON FOR OUR TRIP

Brother Swaggart continued:

"We wanted to do whatever was possible to try to find a way to help the brethren there and to get the gospel of Jesus Christ in a greater way to these people. We have some plans, but I cannot divulge them all. I will say that I believe God is going to help us somewhat in the Soviet Union with television. No, we won't be able to be on their television stations right now, but there is another way that it may be done. It will be legal, and we are working on it."

Little did we know how mighty our God really is!

"But as it is written, Eye hath not seen, nor ear heard, neither have entered into the heart of man, the things which God hath prepared for them that love Him" (I Cor. 2:9).

There will be those who are missing,
You'd think ev'ry body would know;
But they'll still be too busy going nowhere,
They won't even notice that we're gone.

Some will go into a panic,
Crying sing another verse of that song;
Saying, "Lord, here am I now I'm ready,"
But their last opportunity is gone.

I can see Him at the table,
Almost ready to say come;
Knowing well there will be no vacant settings,
'Cause the rest of the family's coming home.

There's a whole lot of people going home,
By the signs of time it won't be long;
In the twinkling of an eye we'll all be gone,
There's a whole lot of people going home.

CHAPTER 27

55° 45' 20" N
37° 37' 2" E

BACK TO MOSCOW

"Lead me in Thy truth, and teach me: for Thou art the God of my salvation; on Thee do I wait all the day."

— *Psalm 25:5*

BACK TO MOSCOW

55° 45' 20" N | 37° 37' 2" E

The Aeroflot plane touched down on the runway at the Sheremetyevo International Airport just as the sun set in western Russia. It was my first trip back into Moscow alone, and the day happened to be quite dreary and rainy.

I was somewhat apprehensive about finding anybody at the Moscow TV Center to whom I could talk about the telecast. I had no appointment and knew no one. I sighed a prayer, "My Father in heaven, Your name is glorious. You have led me these many, many miles into country after country on the face of the earth and opened door after closed door to the gospel over television. Here I am Lord, coming into the largest country on the face of the earth with no appointment and no contact to help me know what to do. Please have mercy on me and the dear Russian people and show me the way. Please Lord, what should I do? Thank You. In Jesus precious, holy name I ask this of You. Amen."

It was already dark and as the plane taxied toward the terminal, we had to wait on the tarmac for a considerable time. After awhile, some of the passengers became anxious and asked the flight attendant in very loud voices, "What's the hold up? We've been waiting out here for more than 30 minutes!"

"No hold up," the attendant said. "We just have to wait for the next available guide to lead us to the proper concourse to park."

"What's a 'guide?'" a passenger asked.

"It is a motorized utility cart that meets every plane that lands here and leads them to the terminal and their parking spot," the attendant said as he continued to walk toward the front of the plane.

FOLLOW ME

Sure enough, as I looked through the small window of the plane, dripping down with streaks of rainwater on the outside, I could see a small, covered cart that looked like an oversized golf cart. It pulled up alongside the plane on my side where I was seated and continued to travel forward — parallel to the length of the plane — in order to get out in front of the plane. As the cart passed my window, a huge sign on the back of it read in big English block letters: "FOLLOW ME."

All of a sudden, I had the answer from the Lord to my prayer.

Little did I know that this would be the first of many trips to Moscow. For six years, I would spend one week of every month in Russia. For those first 30 months, I spent my weeklong visits working with them to try to see how we could get on TV for the first time. This was in no way an easy undertaking.

You have to remember that this was monolithic communism; the mentality was very, very closed. There had never been a foreign religious program over television. They actually called it "religious broadcasting," which was a misnomer. It is gospel broadcasting, so this was the start of working through all kinds of situations both in Russia and in the United States.

WRONG SIDE OF THE STREET

In 1985, on the trip when Brother and Sister Swaggart and some of us were invited to visit churches in Russia, I broke away from the group one day and went to the Ostankino TV Tower Center in the heart of downtown Moscow.

I didn't realize it at the time, but the tall building I visited that day was only part of the television center's huge complex.

The best I was able to do was to give someone who came down to the receptionist counter a Russian Jimmy Swaggart telecast on a broadcast quality videocassette tape and my business card. No authority of any kind met with me. There was no response from Russian television after I returned to the States.

Now, a few months later, I was getting out of a taxi in front of the same Russian television headquarters building I had visited in 1985. By now I had learned that this building was just one in the long stretch of properties crowding both sides of the street and leading to the Ostankino TV tower two blocks down — all owned by the Moscow Ostankino TV Center.

I approached the same office counter again, where several people were waiting in line to talk to one of the receptionists. So, I joined a line and struck up a conversation with a young man in a suit who came and stood behind me.

After some small talk, in which I discovered he spoke perfect English, he asked, "Who are you here to see?"

"I really have no appointment with anyone," I said. "I need to see the people in charge of programming and the placement of programs over Russian television."

"Oh, well the people who do that are in the other building on the other side of the street. Let me take you over there. Please follow me." With that, he started toward the huge doors that led out into the street. I turned around and decided to follow him through the large foyer out of the building.

He led me across the street and instead of entering into what looked like the main entrance to that building, he turned left, paralleling the building, and walked down a ways to a smaller entrance. Pointing toward it, he said, "Go in there and sign in at the cage-looking counter, and they will have someone in charge see you."

"Thank you so much," I said, shaking hands with him. "I really appreciate this. Thank you so much."

As this young man left, I noticed he did not return to the building where we met. Instead, he turned and disappeared down the street, never to be seen by me again.

I went on in through the small door that was propped open.

After signing and giving my passport to the person behind the caged-in counter, I waited quite awhile until finally, a rather nice man, who introduced himself as a producer, led me inside and to his office upstairs. We walked through an array of office spaces and equipment all along the way with scores of people working.

During a very amiable conversation with him, I found that he had been the head producer in charge of the Olympics that had been held in Moscow with more than 280 different national networks from around the world. He had coordinated the entire Olympics' TV transmission for all of the countries represented in the 1980 Olympics, which, by the way, the United States boycotted at that time. His task was no small undertaking. He accepted the Russian audition telecast tapes I had and asked if I could come back at the end of the following month. "We need time to review these programs and would like to meet with you again next month."

"Yes, I can plan on coming back next month," I said, thanking him for meeting with me.

NEXT MONTH

The next month I was back, and this kind gentleman introduced me to a Russian Jewish director of television. Little did I know that these two Russian gentlemen would work tirelessly with me over the next couple of years to try to get the Jimmy Swaggart Russian telecast on TV-1. At the end of this meeting, they asked if I could come back the last week of the following month and, of course, I said I would. This went on month after month, with me coming back each time to meet with a different authority working in the vast Russian television system.

Finally, after about two years of traveling back to Moscow for meetings every month, we were able to meet with the Kremlin's maximum head of communications for all Russian radio and television. When we asked him if the gospel telecast could be authorized for airing over Russian television, his answer was a simple but pointed, "Nyet."

NYET!

The answer was the same month after month in meetings with censorship review people with whom the head of communications had us meet: "Nyet, nyet, nyet." The situation looked more helpless and impossible than ever. Before another monthly trip for meetings in Moscow, I prayed and asked the Lord what to do. He impressed upon me to go into the Baltic countries of Latvia, Lithuania, and Estonia — part of the old Soviet Union and countries in the Russian Confederation — and offer the gospel telecast. If one of these countries would accept the Russian gospel telecast, then Moscow would be more likely to accept.

NO FUNDS FOR TRIPS

After traveling back to Moscow only a few times, Brother Swaggart had to break the news to me that the ministry was no longer able to pay for any travel expenses — no airfare, no lodging, and no meals. (Remember, these were not the only trips I was taking. I still had to travel to countries all over the world that aired the telecast, manage an international outreach office, and tend to a myriad of other responsibilities related to worldwide ministry.)

I asked Brother Swaggart if I was able to raise the travel funds on my own, could I still continue making the necessary trips. He said that would be all right.

Not only was I confronting insurmountable odds in Russia and other countries, but now I would also have to trust the Lord for the entirety of all travel expenses. This amounted to the tune of more than $65,000 per year, which I did not have, but God was faithful.

Miraculously, God would answer my prayers each month for the expenses and provide the extra funds in some way outside of any of those who already supported the ministry. He would do this for the next five years!

I still traveled more than 50,000 miles each month and continued to fulfill all the responsibilities and appointments on the ground at the same time, which amounted to more than 2,000 hours a year. I was in the air more than 2,000 hours per year, and at the same time, I was carrying out the Lord's business more than 2,000 hours per year on the ground in nations around the world.

Souls were still coming to the Lord by the thousands, for which I give Him all the glory and credit. Why do I relate the numbers 2,000 plus? Well, it is meant to give you a perspective as to how much time this is; a normal working person works 40 hours each week. I believe that adds up to 2,080 hours per year, more or less. So, basically, I was traveling and working double this amount every year for nearly 14 years! Actually, I am trusting the Lord to be able, by the grace of God, to squeeze two, if not three, lifetimes out of this one puny life of mine with the help of the Holy Spirit. You say, "That's too much! You are overdoing it! No one can do that!"

My answer is: I would rather have the Lord tell me on that great day around His throne in heaven, "Jim, you trusted Me to enable you to try to do too much for the cause of Christ," than to hear Him say, "Why didn't you trust Me enough to enable you to do more for the cause of Christ?'"

I only relate this to let the reader know that as a missionary, I was on no extended vacation but was actually hazarding my life for the gospel. It was a great privilege to follow the Holy Spirit and see Him at work in hearts and lives! I also want to demonstrate God's faithfulness, for which I give God all the glory. He had done so much for me on the Cross of Calvary, how could I do less than just continue to follow Him into the mouth of the bear, the lion, the serpent, or even the very mouth of hell itself to rescue the perishing! C.T. Studd, a missionary to Africa, put it this way: "Some want to live within sound of church or chapel bell, but I want to run a rescue shop within a yard of hell!"

"Also I heard the voice of the Lord, saying, Whom shall I send, and who will go for us? Then said I, Here am I; send me" (Isa. 6:8).

Rescue the perishing, care for the dying,
Snatch them in pity from sin and the grave;
Weep o'er the erring one, lift up the fallen,
Tell them of Jesus, the mighty to save.

Rescue the perishing, care for the dying,
Jesus is merciful, Jesus will save.

Though they are slighting Him, still He is waiting,
Waiting the penitent child to receive;
Plead with them earnestly, plead with them gently;
He will forgive if they only believe.

Down in the human heart, crushed by the tempter,
Feelings lie buried that grace can restore;
Touched by a loving heart, wakened by kindness,
Chords that were broken will vibrate once more.

Rescue the perishing, duty demands it;
Strength for thy labor the Lord will provide;
Back to the narrow way patiently win them;
Tell the poor wand'rer a Saviour has died.

C H A P T E R   2 8

56° 56' 58" N
24° 6' 18" E

DOOR TO BALTIC NATION OPENS

"Say not ye, There are yet four months, and then cometh harvest? behold, I say unto you, Lift up your eyes, and look on the fields; for they are white already to harvest."

— John 4:35

CHAPTER TWENTY-EIGHT

DOOR TO BALTIC NATION OPENS

56° 56' 58" N | 24° 6' 18" E

On my very next trip to Moscow, I stopped over in Riga, Latvia, on the way. There are two television networks in Latvia: the Latvian Language Network and the Russian television network. They are two completely separate networks and are no small operations. Each has huge, multistory buildings. The Lord led me first to go to the Latvia Language Network.

While standing in the reception area of the Latvia network building, a young television producer came out to meet me and conducted me back through the building and upstairs. On the way to his office, we had to step over a myriad of cable connections strewn throughout the edifice. Truly, this was a working television operations center.

The young man was very cordial and inquisitive; he showed much interest in the Jimmy Swaggart telecast. At the end of the meeting, he asked me to come back the next month for another meeting.

For the next several months, I included a stop in Latvia on my trips to Moscow. After about three meetings in three different months in Latvia, the young producer asked, "Are you able to be in an interview over primetime Latvian television during the next trip so that we can introduce Jimmy Swaggart to the Latvian people?"

I said, "Wouldn't it be better to just air the gospel telecast and the people can then get acquainted with Jimmy Swaggart firsthand? They will then know what the telecast is about."

"So sorry, but we do not do things that way here," he said. "We introduce any new program with an interview and try to answer any questions concerning the purpose of such a program so that the viewers will know what to expect. It will then be more unlikely that the program will be taken off."

With this, I acquiesced and said, "Well, I guess so, if you really think it is necessary."

So, with that, on the next trip to Latvia the following month, I found myself on primetime Latvian television, talking directly to the Latvian people all across that great land. The host of the program was the same young producer. He began by asking questions about Jimmy Swaggart and the ministry's involvement around the world. As I was answering his questions, he noticed that I was using the word *gospel* every once in a while to explain what Jimmy Swaggart preaches and what the ministry does. We were to only go about 20 minutes with the interview, but he interrupted me when I used the word *gospel* again and asked, "You use 'the gospel,' when answering these questions we have, but just what do you mean by the word *gospel*? We do not know that word."

I was stunned. They did not know what gospel meant? I reached in my back pocket where I carried a small New Testament and pulled it out and asked, "May I use this to explain what the word *gospel* means?"

"Of course, by all means," he said. "Literally everyone in the entire country of Latvia is watching this program tonight, and we would like to know."

I opened my New Testament to Mark 1:15 and stated, "First of all, when Jesus Christ started preaching, He said:

'The time is fulfilled, and the kingdom of God is at hand: repent ye, and believe the gospel" (Mk. 1:15).'"   ⟵

I said, "The word *gospel* literally means 'good news.' The gospel of Jesus Christ is the explanation of who He is and what He accomplished for you in His death on a cruel Roman cross almost 2,000 years ago. It's good news because it's the answer to a problem every person has. Have you ever done something wrong and felt really bad about it? You let someone down or you told a lie. You felt so sad and guilty afterwards. That is the problem — we all have done bad things to some degree. That is called sin. But there is good news that someone did something for us to get rid of our sin.

"But to truly comprehend how good this news is, we must first understand the bad news. As a result of the fall of man in the garden of Eden, every part of man — his mind, will, emotions, and flesh — have been corrupted by sin. Because of man's sinful nature, he does not and cannot seek God. He has no desire to come to God and, in fact, his mind is hostile toward God."

I then read Romans 8:7, which says,

"Because the carnal mind is enmity against God: for it is not subject to the law of God, neither indeed can be."

I continued on, "We know that we have all sinned. We just have to ask ourselves, 'Have I ever told a lie?' and we know we have. This is what the Word of God says in the Bible:

'For all have sinned, and come short of the glory of God' (Rom. 3:23).

"God has declared that man's sin dooms him to an eternity in hell, separated from God. It is in hell that man pays the penalty for sin against a holy and righteous God. This would be bad news indeed if there were no remedy.

"But in the gospel, God, in His mercy, has provided that remedy, a substitute for us — Jesus Christ — who came to pay the penalty for our sin by His sacrifice on the Cross."

"For the wages of sin is death; but the gift of God is eternal life through Jesus Christ our Lord" (Rom. 6:23).

"In I Corinthians 15:2-4, Paul explains the means of the gospel by which God saved us — the death of Christ on a

Cross, God's only begotten Son, on our behalf. He was buried and rose again from among the dead and He lives; He lives seated at the right hand of God. When we put our faith in Christ Jesus as our Saviour, in God's eyes we died with Christ on the Cross and were buried with Him. Then we were resurrected with Him to a new life."

I then read the following from my little New Testament:

"Know ye not, that so many of us as were baptized into Jesus Christ were baptized into His death? Therefore we are buried with Him by baptism into death: that like as Christ was raised up from the dead by the glory of the Father, even so we also should walk in newness of life. For if we have been planted together in the likeness of His death, we shall be also in the likeness of His resurrection" (Rom. 6:3-5).

I said, "Paul tells us to 'hold firmly' to this true gospel, the only one that saves. Believing in any other gospel is to believe in vain. In Romans 1:16-17, Paul also declares that the true gospel is the power of God for the salvation of everyone who believes. By this, he means that salvation is not achieved by man's efforts but by the grace of God through the gift of faith."

"For I am not ashamed of the gospel of Christ: for it is the power of God unto salvation to everyone that believeth; to the Jew first, and also to the Greek (Gentile)" (Rom. 1:16).

"Because of the gospel, through the power of God, those who believe in Christ are not just saved from hell."

I read again out of the Word:

"That if thou shalt confess with thy mouth the Lord Jesus, and shalt believe in thine heart that God hath raised Him from the dead, thou shalt be saved" (Rom. 10:9).

"We are, in fact, given a completely new nature with a changed heart and a new desire, will, and attitude. Let me read it:

'Therefore if any man be in Christ, he is a new creature: old things are passed away; behold, all things are become new.'" (II Cor. 5:17).

"We cannot earn our salvation," I said. "Works are never the means of salvation. The only means of our salvation is by faith in the Cross of Jesus Christ; by what He did there in His finished, completed work on our behalf. Those who are saved by the power of God will always show the result of salvation by their changed lives. God does all of this for us. The only One who can change our lives is Jesus. He wants to come into our hearts and live His life in us.

"His Word says:

'Behold, I stand at the door, and knock: if any man hear My voice, and open the door, I will come in to him, and will sup with him, and he with Me.'" (Rev. 3:20).

After I read this verse, the producer asked, "How do we invite Jesus to come into our hearts?"

"Just repeat after me this prayer," I said. "Is it alright to go ahead and pray?"

"Why, yes."

"Okay, just repeat out loud after me: Dear God in heaven."

The producer and everyone in the studio began to repeat after me, with the viewing audience doing the same.

"Our Father in heaven, I come to You. I confess that I am a sinner and need Your salvation. I am sorry for my sin. Wash me of all my sin and unrighteousness in the blood of the slain Lamb of God, Jesus Christ. Dear Jesus, I invite You to come into my heart. I accept You as my Saviour and Lord. According to Your Word, which cannot lie, I confess You with my mouth as Lord of my life and believe in my heart that God raised Jesus from the dead and according to God's Word, I am cleansed; I am saved. Thank You, Lord, for coming into my heart. Amen."

When I opened my eyes and looked up, the producer and just about everyone there were wiping tears from their eyes.

The interview that was to only last 20 minutes turned into a good 50 minutes and aired prime time. Yet even with this special about the Jimmy Swaggart telecast, I still did not have a promise to air the program over Latvian television.

However, the Russian television network had seen the special and contacted me, asking if I could visit their facilities to talk about airing the gospel telecast. Of course, I said I would and set up a date to meet with them the next month on my next trip to Moscow from the States.

LATVIA RUSSIAN TV CENTER

When I arrived at the Latvia Russian television center, I signed in at the base of a huge tower with an unusual elevator inside. The front desk said that this was the third tallest tower in all of Europe. When I entered the elevator, I found it was very modern, and as I ascended upward, it actually went at an angle to the side as it pulled us to the top of this high-rise building.

The director of Russian television in Latvia met me at the elevator on the top floor and explained that the design of the elevator was taken from the Eiffel Tower in Paris, France, and was by an architect from Georgia, Russia.

The director was very friendly and after a few questions, asked me straight out, "Are you able to send us enough Russian Jimmy Swaggart programs to air once every week?"

We really only had about two pilot programs in Russian but had not yet produced any more. By faith, I said, "Yes, we will prepare them immediately and send them. What will be the start date?"

"We would like to start airing in eight weeks," the director said.

"Good. I will leave these two audition programs with you to begin and have our television production department start sending the rest as they are produced," I stated.

The director and I signed a contract. Now I just had to convince Brother and Sister Swaggart to have the Russian programs prepared for airing.

MINISTRY STRAINING TO
MEET AIRTIME OBLIGATIONS

You see, back home in the States, the ministry was so far-reaching and involved in so many television outlets that we were struggling to meet expenses.

Back in Baton Rouge, I met with Brother Swaggart with the good news that Latvia Russian television had accepted the telecast, but we would need to produce programs in Russian. This meant finding a voice to interpret, purchasing all of the necessary equipment, and hiring more people in the TV department. We would also need translators to put the Russian script together of Brother Swaggart's preaching for the Russian voice to read. This was no small thing!

"Yes, we will do it," Brother Swaggart told me. "But you will have to locate a Russian voice."

AN INTERPRETER'S VOICE

After many phone calls, I located a brother with an excellent voice living right there in Baton Rouge. He attended a large charismatic church in town. So, he asked me to ask his pastor for permission to do the lip-sync voice. This meant I would have to call the senior pastor to get his permission for this brother to be the voice that would reach an entire nation with the gospel, and possibly the entirety of the Soviet Union of more than 300 million people.

Over the phone, I explained to his pastor who I was and the door God had opened in Latvia for the gospel over Russian television. I gave him the name of the brother in his church with the excellent Russian voice and then asked him, "Is it all right with you if this brother serves as the Russian voice for the Jimmy Swaggart gospel telecast?"

I was not prepared for his answer.

"What?" the pastor exclaimed. "There is no way I will give my permission for him to be the Russian voice!"

I said, "But sir, the souls of more than 300 million dear Russian people are at stake."

"I do not care about any of that," he retorted. "They can all go to hell for all I care!"

Realizing the evil spirit that was in this supposed 'man of God,' I just replied, "Thank you, sir, for your time. I will be in prayer for you."

His last words to me were, "I don't need your prayers. Good-bye," and he slammed the phone receiver down.

Wow! I must admit that I never expected a man so well respected among charismatic believers across the country and looked up to as a Christian leader to be such an outright fraud with absolutely no concern for souls and their salvation.

A different leader of another denomination I called basically said the same thing.

Finally, I was put in contact with Brother Walter Bagrin who lived in Tennessee and spoke impeccable Russian. After he tried out, the result was excellent. He agreed to serve as the voice for Jimmy Swaggart over Russian television. The programs were produced and started airing over Latvian Russian television. It was a first — the first time anywhere in the Soviet Union territory that the gospel had aired over television! Praise God! The network in Latvia said the switchboards at the headquarters were jammed for days with calls from people wanting to know when this great telecast would air again. They liked it!

TROUBLE FROM THE KGB

About six weeks into the airing of the telecast, the Russian network in Latvia contacted me and told me that the KGB from Moscow had flown in to Riga and came to the network management, telling them to take the Jimmy Swaggart telecast off the air. The network objected, "Who will confront the Latvian public when they complain?"

The answer they received was, "Well, you will have to respond, but there probably will not be anybody complaining because no one likes the telecast anyway."

"You are wrong about that," a manager said. "Be here tomorrow — Sunday morning — and when the telecast does not air, then we will see what happens."

The next morning, the KGB arrived early and went up to the top floor and waited with the network management. The usual time for the Russian Jimmy Swaggart telecast arrived and there was no telecast. Since the switchboards at the network did not operate on Sundays, no incoming calls could be received. However, about halfway through the usual time that the telecast would air, people in cars, on bicycles, carts, motorcycles, mules, as well as on foot began to converge on the network headquarters. In a short time, thousands of people were out in front of the building, demanding that the Jimmy Swaggart telecast be put back on television.

One of the managers turned to the KGB agents and said, "You can go down there now and tell Latvians the program is off."

A KGB agent asked, "Is there a back door where we can leave out of this building?"

"So, we can put the telecast back on the air?"

"Do whatever you want but get us out of this building," the KGB agent said. "Our plane back to Moscow is waiting for us at the airport." And with that, they left, or should I say, escaped. The telecast was back on to the cheers of the public outside and the people in their homes all across Latvia!

Praise God! The Lord had performed an important victory.

"Fear thou not; for I am with thee: be not dismayed; for I am thy God: I will strengthen thee; yea, I will help thee; yea, I will uphold thee with the right hand of my righteousness" (Isa. 41:10).

I am weak, but Thou art strong;
Jesus, keep me from all wrong;
I'll be satisfied as long,
As I walk, let me walk close to Thee.

Just a closer walk with Thee,
Grant it, Jesus, is my plea,
Daily walking close to Thee,
Let it be, dear Lord, let it be.

Through this world of toil and snares,
If I falter, Lord, who cares?
Who with me my burden shares?
None but Thee, dear Lord, none but Thee.

When my feeble life is o'er,
Time for me will be no more;
Guide me gently, safely o'er
To Thy kingdom shore, to Thy shore.

CHAPTER 29

55° 45' 20" N
37° 37' 2" E

FINAL SHOWDOWN

"That they may know from the rising of the sun, and from the west, that there is none beside Me. I am the LORD, and there is none else."

— Isaiah 45:6

FINAL SHOWDOWN

55° 45' 20" N | 37° 37' 2" E

On my next trip into Moscow to meet again with the man I called the "Russian Bear" (the director of all communications for Russia), I was able to tell him that the Russian Jimmy Swaggart telecast was now airing in Latvia and was the most viewed television program there and would be starting to air in other republics.

From that time on, instead of his answer being "Nyet," it was, "We agree with you in principle that the program should be on."

Trip after trip, he said the same thing that he had said to me for months and months: "We agree with you in principle that this program should be on."

Each time I would ask, "Well, when do you think it can go on?"

The director and his staff had seen it, and they liked it. But at the end of each of my meetings with them, I heard, "Well, we agree with you in principle, so we'll see."

Finally, after many trips, many meetings, many "nyets," and many, "We agree with you in principles," I was in that familiar place in the meeting, with the Russian Bear sitting at the head of the table with all the other authorities. We had come down to that part of the contract about a start date. Then, like so many times before, I asked, "When will the telecast start?"

The Russian Bear said the same thing, "Well, Mr. Woolsey, we agree with you in principle. This is a very good program, well produced ...."

Suddenly, something in me (forgive me) made me get somewhat rude.

I blurted out, "No offense, sir, I respect you, and I've enjoyed being with you and your people so many times, but I didn't travel 6,000 miles around the world and come here this many times just to hear you tell me once again, 'We agree with you in principle.' I want to know when the telecast will go on TV-1."

This got a reaction. The lead director put his hand over his mouth and said, "Uh, let me get back with you, let me get back with you!" Then things began to move.

During my next trip to Moscow, they said that I would have to be interviewed live over TV-1, prime time, at the Moscow Cultural Center, a huge marble building. The interview would be with all of the intelligentsia—authorities of the government there and leading university professors and students. This was before the telecast ever went on.

I would later learn from local authorities that not one American, not even a president, had ever been on TV-1 to talk to the Russian people. After 70 years of communism, I would be the first American English-speaking person to address the Russian people directly.

For now, I still had questions. "Why do they need me to have an interview?" I asked.

A director said, "You need to go on with this type of interview so we can introduce the Jimmy Swaggart telecast to the people of Russia."

"Wouldn't it be better to just put the telecast on?" I countered. "They'll find out right away then just who Jimmy Swaggart is."

"No, no, no, no!" he said. "We don't do things that way here."

So, finally, I acquiesced.

THE CULTURAL CENTER

On my next trip to Moscow, I really wasn't prepared for what happened. I thought there would be the TV crew, a panel with a host asking questions, and a small group of people invited to listen in one of the small conference rooms on one side of the cultural center. Was I ever mistaken!

After arriving at the huge, downtown cultural center, we went into the main floor (walking on the beautiful marble floor), past several thick, marble columns down the side colonnade. Then we stopped, and they introduced me to the woman moderator, who had me follow her into the main, large, cavernous auditorium filled with people.

"Who are all of these people?" I asked.

She said, "There are some here from what used to be the Komsomol, the youth division of the Communist Party. These are the leaders of youth groups, who were called before when they were younger the All-Union Lenin Pioneer Youth Organization. The cultural center is also jammed full of university students, their professors, Russian intelligentsia, scientists, political authorities, and some religious people from the Russian Orthodox Church."

Lit by the bright stage lights, I had a good view of this enormous, beautiful, marbled, columned auditorium. We sat down with three other people on the panel facing a multitude of people that stretched so far back that I could barely see the last row.

Suddenly, the TV cameras were rolling with their powerful spotlights. We were going out live over all 7,000 TV-1 television stations and repeater stations that evening. We were airing across the entirety of Russia's 10 time zones, all 15 republics, and into every Russian home with a television set. It was total coverage!

This was an incredible opportunity, but I couldn't help thinking, "Who am I to speak to all these Russian citizens?" Here I was, just a hick from the sticks of Arizona sitting before all the Russian people, representing one of two nations whose conflicts and challenges had strained their relationship for decades now, and I was not even an ambassador of the U.S. State Department.

Then I remembered that I was an ambassador of heaven with the gospel of Jesus Christ. I whispered a quick prayer, "Oh, God, help me now. I do not know what to say, Lord.

Please, may the Holy Spirit take control and speak to this dear people in wisdom. In Jesus Christ's precious name, Amen."

The panel interview started, and they began to ask me about Jimmy Swaggart Ministries. I explained all the different outreaches in which we were involved, including the child care in third world countries, the building of schools, our evangelistic centers, the support of more than 600 missionaries and their families around the world, the construction projects, and, of course, the television coverage around the world.

Periodically, the host would interject, "Wow! It's mammoth what this ministry does in so many nations of the world!"

"Yes," I thought, "by the power of the Holy Spirit."

I summarized the Lord's use of the ministry by saying, "The sun never sets on the Jimmy Swaggart mission's outreach around the entire world."

Then they rolled a clip of Brother Swaggart preaching the gospel in Russian that I had given them on one of my earlier trips. I must admit that they picked a really good segment of the program tape. As we watched Brother Swaggart walk back and forth on the platform, waving his Bible in the air and preaching in perfect Russian, you could feel the anointing. The cultural center filled with excitement.

WHAT IS THE GOSPEL?

I was only supposed to be interviewed about 20 minutes, but the host continued asking excellent questions, and panel and audience were very attentive. Well, it got to be 30 minutes and still more questions, and everybody was so very interested. Finally, about 40 minutes into this interview, in the midst of all of these questions, the host turned to me and said, "Mr. Woolsey, you keep referring to 'the gospel,' but we don't know what the gospel is. Could you tell us what the gospel is?"

"Well, I tell you what, if I could use this," and I pulled my small pocket New Testament out of my back pocket, "if I could use this, it's the Bible, I can explain it to you very quickly from this book."

"Please do," she said. "Please go ahead."

So I started explaining, going through the Scriptures, showing how man is depraved and born a sinner, completely lost.

I said, "Have you ever done something wrong that afterward, you felt bad about? You've sinned against somebody, or you told a lie, or you stole something? You did something, and you really felt like a miserable scrounge afterward? That's what sin does. It makes you guilty, and you know you're guilty. We're all guilty before God."

I continued explaining from the Scriptures how God sent His only begotten Son to die on the Cross for us to take our sins away. It would be by means of this sin offering of His only Son, who was sinless. I read John 3:16:

"For God so loved the world, that He gave His only begotten Son, that whosoever believeth in Him should not perish, but have everlasting life."

I said, "The only thing God could accept was the sacrifice of a sinless man, and Jesus was the perfect man and, at the same time, God. He paid our sin debt with His own poured-out, innocent, spotless, and undefiled life's blood and died on the Cross outside of Jerusalem. He was buried, and our sins were buried with him, but He rose again, and He lives, and He is seated at the right hand of God!

He says in Matthew 11:28-30:

"Come unto Me, all ye that labour and are heavy laden, and I will give you rest. Take My yoke upon you, and learn of Me; for I am meek and lowly in heart: and ye shall find rest unto your souls. For My yoke is easy, and My burden is light."

I told the Russian people, "And this is His invitation to everyone who comes to Him by faith."

The host asked, "Well, what should we do with this invitation?"

"In prayer, just accept Him by faith into your heart and your life as Lord and Saviour," I said.

All of a sudden, someone sitting near the back row, who looked like a very distinguished university professor, jumped up and shouted, "Hey! Hey! Why are you telling us about this 'gospel' when by tradition, we are Russian Orthodox? Why do we as Russians need this 'gospel'?"

You see, before the Bolshevik Revolution in 1917 (that happened 70 years before this moment), Vladimir Lenin took over Russia, and the atheistic, Marxist-communist hammer and sickle ruled across that land. Then later, in 1924, Joseph Stalin became premier of the Soviet Union. During all of that time, the Russian Orthodox Church had held sway over the people as the official religion of Russia, even though somewhat suppressed by communist atheism.

In response to this man's question, other people in the cultural center began to murmur out loud, "Yah, yah, what about that? We're supposed to be Russian Orthodox. We don't need any foreign religion!"

Thinking he had me there in front of all of these thousands of people, the same man hollered again, "No, we should have our own religion! We don't need this import of this, this so-called gospel. Why do you think we need this gospel?"

As he spoke, silently, inside my heart, I cried out to God, "Oh, my Lord, please have mercy and help me. Please give me Your wisdom as how to answer."

Fortunately, the moderator spoke for a moment, then turned to me and said, "Yes, Mr. Woolsey, what do you say to that?"

The Holy Spirit told me to just ask him a question.

I said, "Kind sir, what is the name of your flag, the Russian flag?"

"Well ... Well ... Well," he hesitated, and then said, "It's the Flag of Andrew."

"Yes! One of your flags is called the Flag of Andrew," I said. "Do you know who Andrew was?"

He said, "Well ... Well, I ...." I saw he was hesitating, and I didn't want to make him look out of place.

I said, "Well, Andrew was a disciple of Jesus Christ. He came to the Lord, accepted Him, was baptized with the Holy Spirit, and went forth preaching the same gospel under the same anointing of the Holy Spirit that Brother Jimmy Swaggart preaches on the telecast. Andrew came up through the Caucasus into what is now part of the Russian Federation, in this general area, and preached the same gospel Jimmy Swaggart preaches on the Russian telecast. People came to the Lord, they got saved, their lives were changed, and the church was formed. The early church was formed on what is now Russian soil. That's how your ancestors had a true faith, the real gospel." (I wanted to say that over the centuries, the church degenerated into the Russian Orthodox Church. It was taken over by all kinds of icons and idolatry, which were added to the Word of God, and the gospel was lost. They were not preaching Jesus Christ and Him crucified — the gospel that the early apostles of the church preached. Instead, I continued.)

I said, "It is the gospel that preaches Christ and Him crucified that's right here in this book, the Bible. This life-changing message the early Russian church preached was lost over the centuries. So, we just want Jimmy Swaggart to bring back to Russia the same message that Andrew preached to this great land ...."

I was interrupted at that point; everybody just started clapping and cheering, and I thought they were thanking the Lord, but they were shouting, "Yes! Yes! We want this program! Yes! That's what we want! Why not? This is what we are ... these are our true roots!"

B19

The poor guy who started all this just sat back down, sort of ashamed that he had even said anything. The people were excited about the Jimmy Swaggart telecast coming to TV-1, and the host thanked me for appearing to answer these questions.

I was told that a few weeks later, due to popular demand, this interview aired twice more on prime time television all across Russia.

THEN IT HAPPENED

Two trips later, I was in the hotel room in Moscow on a Sunday morning. I was getting ready to go to another business meeting aimed at getting the telecast on, just as I had done on so many trips before. Each time, I would be there for an entire week, going to one meeting after another. Some of the meetings were held at the Ostankino TV Center, which, at the time, was the largest and tallest point of any structure in the Soviet Union at 1,772 feet tall (540.1 meters). It is a sphere in the sky, similar to Seattle's Space Needle, only this is the Russian Television Network. It's no small thing; it's huge!

I had spent countless hours with producers and directors figuring out how to get the telecast aired—to broadcast it over 7,000 or more television stations, across one-sixth of the earth's land surface, and into 11 time zones of the world — almost half of the world. This was no small undertaking.

In the bathroom of my hotel room while brushing my teeth, I thought, "Lord, how long? How long are we going to have to wait for these people to stop saying 'nyet,' or 'I agree with you in principle' — till the millennium?"

Then all of a sudden, while standing in this hotel room in Russia, I heard the opening notes of a song very familiar to me:

Sometimes alleluia,
Sometimes praise the Lord,
Sometimes gently singing,
Our hearts in one accord.

Oh let us lift our voices,
Look toward the sky and start to sing
Oh let us now return Thy love.
Just let our voices ring,
Oh let us feel His presence,
Let the sound of praises fill the air,
Oh let us sing the song of Jesus' love to people everywhere.

In a few quick steps, I was standing in front of the TV set in my room, watching Brother Swaggart play the piano and sing:

Oh let our joy be unconfined,
Let us sing with freedom unrestrained,
Let us take this feeling that we're feeling now,
Outside these walls and just let it ring!
Oh let Thy Spirit overflow,
Lord we're filled from head to toe.

I love you Father, Son, and Holy Ghost,
I want the world to know.

The Jimmy Swaggart telecast was on the air in Russia!

For the first time in this country's 70-year history under the hammer and sickle of communism, the gospel of Jesus Christ was finally reaching the people of Russia!

Before this, these precious people had had no official outside contact with any gospel. Think of it, a population living in one-sixth of the earth's land surface with no freedom of press and no freedom of worship, caught in a spiritual prison of atheism and communism, until now.

As I watched Brother Swaggart thundering across the stage, holding his open Bible high and preaching in Russian, it was clear that the blessed gospel of Jesus Christ and Him crucified had come to this dear Russian people through television.

I remember thinking how fitting it was that the first message Brother Swaggart preached in Russian was titled, "The Miracle of the Changed Life." What an astounding miracle God had just performed against all odds!

Yes, the Russian Jimmy Swaggart telecast began to air that day and would continue to air every week for three and a half years! It was the very first foreign secular or religious program to air over TV-1! What a miracle!

In my whole life, I had never really ever danced in the Spirit, but I want you to know that I danced in the Spirit all over that room that day—praising the Lord, shouting, crying, laughing, and rejoicing in our great God and wonderful Saviour Jesus Christ!

MEMO TO BROTHER SWAGGART

To give you some idea of the conditions existing in the Soviet Union at that time, here is a memo that I sent to Brother Swaggart upon returning from one of my many monthly trips to Russia:

MEMORANDUM TO: BRO. SWAGGART
SUBJECT: MOSCOW, RUSSIA TRIP UPDATE

"After landing at the Moscow International Airport, I was greeted by the director general of the Centre of Russian Commercial Television and the vice president of this television network. This is the network, TV-1 (formerly Communist State Television), over which our telecast is broadcast every week.

As these kind gentlemen drove me from the Moscow airport directly to the Moscow TV center, the director played a Jimmy Swaggart music cassette on his car tape deck all the way to the TV center. In fact, every time I rode in his car this particular week, he had your music playing with the volume up almost as loud as it would go. Even in the TV center, he had your music playing in his offices. Different people would come to me at different times asking for a copy of the new Jimmy Swaggart music cassette, *The Healing Jesus*. They love it.

The ride through the center of Moscow reminded me of just how bleak the current situation is for the people here during this cold Russian winter. With all the snow on the ground, it causes a continuous spray of mud to fly from the tires of all the cars transiting these streets. Consequently, every vehicle is coated entirely with mud. The windshield wipers only function in removing the mud from the windshield, as long as the small supply of water in the windshield spray container lasts. Then, it's forget roadway visibility and drive by pure instinct.

On previous visits, we would pass shops with long lines of people waiting for the chance to purchase some food. On this visit, I noticed that the lines had changed instead to huge mobs of people jostling one another to get the last few quantities of items available that day in each shop. We passed many, many of these big mobs of people gathered outside stores and shops throughout Moscow. This situation, combined with the rather characteristic, drab-colored buildings, created a very gloomy atmosphere under a dense, winter cloud cover. The whole situation in Russia is rather depressing right now in the natural. Just think, the average wage of a worker (whether blue-collar or white-collar) is only about 50 cents per day!

Be that as it may, on every stop we made for various reasons, these TV network leaders would always ask the clerks, technicians, workers, and so forth if they watched the Jimmy Swaggart telecast. Invariably, their faces would light up with a big smile as they told how much they appreciated the telecast. Even the director general said the telecast gives the Russian people hope in the midst of these critical, trying times.

As we pulled into the snow-packed parking lot of the Moscow TV center, once again I saw that ominous Moscow TV tower (the tallest structure in Moscow) over which the signal that carries our telecast to these 300 million people of the 15 republics is broadcast each week. What a miracle! When we saw this TV tower about five years ago, it looked utterly impossible to be able to broadcast any gospel whatsoever from this place since communism would never allow it. But there we were, going into the once impenetrable TV center to continue our discussions concerning the continuance of the Jimmy Swaggart telecast.

These leaders of the network began to tell me about the TV ratings and the many, many viewers watching Jimmy Swaggart preaching in Russian. The director general said, 'We appreciate so much the Jimmy Swaggart telecast and want you to personally tell him so. We want to apologize for the way we had to juggle the time-slot a few weeks ago from the weekend to Fridays, but since the program was changed from Friday back to the weekend, the ratings have gone up dramatically from what they were!'

Then they explained to me that when the program was on Sunday mornings at 8 a.m. after being on each Friday for a few months, most of the audience that wanted to see it were not up yet. However, since many are off from work on Saturdays, they still get up as early as they do during the week. Therefore, the TV officials thought it wise to put our telecast on the air on Saturdays. They told me that since they made this change, the ratings have soared. You see, once a program's ratings fall, and it is taken off TV-1 or TV-2, it cannot be put back on under any circumstances. This is why these network leaders are just as excited as we are about the large viewing audience the Jimmy Swaggart telecast has on Saturdays. In fact, they told me that according to the ratings, more than 200 million viewers are watching the telecast each week now! Praise God!

The next day, I was taken to the central post office in Moscow where we have the post office box where the people write after watching the telecast. The mail is coming into our box in huge bundles. I asked Brother Anatoly, the Russian pastor who picks up the mail, if he would choose some outstanding letters for me to bring back to Baton Rouge. He said, 'Outstanding letters? They are all outstanding! Every one we read makes tears come to our eyes. They tell of praying with Brother Swaggart for various needs and salvation at the end of each telecast. Many have been saved and delivered and many needs have been supplied. Families have been put back together and drunks set free from bondages to vodka and alcohol.'

The same day, I interviewed a Russian pastor concerning the telecast. He said his church had about 200 to 300 in attendance each week. Then he started receiving people into the services who said they are watching the Jimmy Swaggart telecast. He said he now has more than 1,000 people in attendance at this church each week as a direct result of the telecast.

There was a large pile of mail on the table in front of him from viewers from all over the 15 independent states of the former Soviet Union who had written to our Moscow address. As he was talking, he reached his hand out and pulled a random letter out of the pile, and to his surprise, the letter was written to Jimmy Swaggart from a viewer in the same town where he is pastoring. Was he ever excited!

Next, he related how one of the many viewers who now comes to his church got saved. The particular man he told about drank an excessive amount of vodka every day — not just in the evenings, but in the mornings, at noon, and then from the time he came home from work until going to bed each night. His wife had long since given up on chiding him for his drunkenness. Then the man started watching the Jimmy Swaggart telecast. His wife brought the customary bottle of vodka to him at the same time the telecast was on, but he told her he didn't need it. He said, 'I believe what this man on TV says. It is much better than this old vodka.' From that day forward, he has not been drinking, and he gave his heart to the Lord!

The pastor then went on to relate some other testimonies. I had the privilege of watching the Russian telecast over nationwide TV-1 the weekend while I was in Moscow, and I must say, it makes me want to jump and shout, to say the least. Even though it is in the Russian language, you can still sense the power of the Holy Spirit during the whole telecast. The editor in chief of the network told me that they certainly appreciate the fine video quality of the program and said, 'Please do continue to send us these programs that are so much needed by our country at this critical juncture in our history.'

The director general of the network then handed me a personal letter to give to you, Brother Swaggart, in which he thanked everyone involved for the telecast, and he also wanted us to know how important the telecast is to their country at this time. He states that the Jimmy Swaggart telecast is still the only gospel telecast on TV-1 each week covering the whole of the 15 republic states. He also asked me to personally remind Brother Swaggart that they are awaiting his and Sister Swaggart's and the team's visit to Moscow for a crusade meeting in the large stadium there.

We have been trying to install an outreach office to minister to the large number of people who write as a result of the telecast. The pastors across the country have practically begged us to answer the many letters and help channel the new people who come to the Lord into existing churches. We have located an office space in downtown Moscow that would help us bring in this great harvest. However, it will take a monthly budget of several thousand dollars for the expenses of printing, postage, rent, and utilities. I told the pastors that we will trust God to lay a burden upon hearts to help us bring in possibly the largest harvest of souls ever known."

Brother Swaggart's response to my memo was an approval of funds needed for the outreach office in Moscow.

TESTIMONIES 20 YEARS LATER

Some 20 years later, I was in a Campmeeting service at Family Worship Center in Baton Rouge, and after the service, I met three Russian pastors and a missionary on their way from Russia to a conference in Dallas. For these pastors, it was their first visit to America. All four men had stopped by to be in one of the Campmeeting services. As they introduced themselves, the three Russian pastors began to tell me where they were on that Sunday so long ago when the Jimmy Swaggart Russian telecast was first aired. All said they were completely lost and without God.

One of them said, "I was seated there in front of my TV set, already completely drunk on vodka by 9 o'clock that morning. In the one hand, dangling over the arm of my easy chair, was a bottle of vodka, and in the other hand, a cigarette. I was in a daze, but all of a sudden, I heard something different. I started listening. After the music, a man came on in front of a large crowd of people in a coliseum and began to read out of the Bible and preach in Russian. I had never heard a man speak as this man spoke."

SOMETHING GOT A HOLD OF ME INSIDE

He continued, "Something got a hold of me inside. I now know it was the Holy Spirit. By the time he finished preaching, I had thrown my half-empty bottle of vodka away, put out the cigarette, and was repeating the sinner's prayer after Brother Swaggart with tears running profusely down my face. Jesus came into my heart and life! I was saved, changed by the power of God! From then on, I listened to every program and recorded them on my VCR, and I would play them over and over again. Many of my friends, who were once just as much a drunken derelict as I was, gave their hearts to the Lord while watching the telecast. Later, while watching one of the programs, I was baptized with the Holy Spirit and called to preach. I have been pastoring now for over 15 years. Please tell Brother and Sister Swaggart that we are so grateful for the telecast and this Spirit-anointed ministry. It has changed our lives!"

The other two pastors had about the same testimony as to how they gave their hearts to the Lord. One of them was saved at the end of that first telecast. The other was saved at the end of the second telecast because his mother saw the first telecast and told him about it and said to watch it the next weekend. He did and was gloriously saved.

PERESTROIKA

What this pastor went on to say was startling. He said, "Our entire country was in chaos. Sometime after the program started airing over television, Gorbachev's 'perestroika' (restructuring) and 'glasnost' (openness) was initiated. It introduced profound changes in our society, with the entire economic practices changed, along with changes in internal affairs and international relations. From 1988 to December 1992, these changes in the country had left us all with no hope and no place to turn. Gorbachev's promises did not come to fruition."

DESPAIR SET IN ON A NATIONAL SCALE

The pastor continued with his report on the situation at that time, which I believe is a true assessment of the situation. He said, "Despair set in on a national scale. More people saw no hope of a future, and more turned to drink and drunkenness. If it weren't for Brother Swaggart's preaching, which came on Soviet television TV-1 in 1989, we would have been plunged into complete chaos as a nation and as a people. The

Soviet Union officially collapsed in 1992, along with the collapse of communism in the 15 individual republics. However, so many people came to the Lord while watching Brother Swaggart's program that it rescued us from total anarchy and gave us hope. The telecast saved our nation."

The other Russian pastor standing there that day said, "The Russian Jimmy Swaggart telecast stayed on the air weekly until the end of 1993. It gave us hope and brought to our nation for the first time over television the Lord Jesus Christ."

From the very start of the Russian Jimmy Swaggart telecast, our makeshift outreach office in Moscow began to fill with letters from viewers all across Russia, writing to say that they had accepted Jesus Christ as their Saviour. Pastor Anatoly Sokolov, who served as director of that outreach office in Moscow, said this was incredible because the Russian people on the whole do not write many letters; they didn't want to spend money on stamps. However, there were so many letters coming in that we could not answer them all due to limited funds.

More than 1 million letters stacked up in that little outreach office from people who had accepted Christ as their own personal Saviour! That is no exaggeration.

SATAN CONTESTS

Of course, with such a great victory and so many people coming to the Lord, the Devil was not going to just take it lying down. He tried to take the telecast off Russian TV-1 by inciting old communist sympathizers to try and turn Russia back to communism and take over the government. The world saw this moment over television—the huge crowd of protesters outside of the Russian parliament's multi-story building and the artillery that had been shot into the side of the building and exploded, tearing away that part of the edifice.

The old-line communists wanted to take back the country and were protesting in front of the Russian parliament, which they call the Russian White House. Demonstrators took over the mayor's offices and tried to storm the Ostankino Television Center, but they were unsuccessful in this attempt.

A 10-day conflict ensued and became the deadliest single event of street fighting in Moscow's history since the revolutions of 1917 when Marxist-communism took over. According to government estimates, 187 people were killed and 437 wounded; non-governmental sources put the death toll as high as 2,000. This was no small uprising and a very serious situation.

Outside Moscow, the Russian masses overall were confused and disorganized. This uprising was called the Second October Revolution, with the first, of course, being the 1917 October Revolution.

I was there, jogging down along the river in front of the parliament building. The Moskva River runs through Moscow, with paved roads and sidewalks running parallel to it in somewhat of a depression from the surrounding landscape. I had left the hotel in the early morning, jogging toward the area where the river runs past the parliament building a block or so away. Anyone down by the river cannot see what is going on up where the buildings and streets are because the whole river is in a defile a considerable distance below the main streets up above this area of town.

So, from the river, I could not see all the demonstrators and army that had gathered there that morning.

THE IMPACT OF THE EXPLODING
TANK SHELLS HIT MY LUNGS

As I was jogging, all of a sudden I heard a huge BOOM! Tanks of the Tamam division of the armed forces were shelling the parliament building just up above me. I felt the impact of the exploding tank shells hit my lungs. I stopped dead in my tracks.

"What was that?" I thought, and I turned toward the embankment going up to the area in front of the parliament and ran up the sidewalk to see.

I ran up the embankment on the side of the street that led to the huge intersection in front of the Russian White House. From there I saw how the huge mass of people and army troop carriers and tanks had swarmed the whole area. The situation was tense.

Most of the world was looking at the same scene I was, live over worldwide television. Several floors on the right side of the parliament building were spewing out huge clouds of smoke where the tank shells had exploded.

A critical confrontation was taking place. The first president of the Russian Federation, Boris Yeltsin, stepped into the thick of the crowd, climbed up onto what looked to be a troop carrier, and started to talk down the protestors with a little megaphone speaker like those used at sporting events. He began to calm down the crowd.

And what did they put on television to calm down the entire nation of confused, bewildered masses of Russians and all of Moscow? They played the Jimmy Swaggart telecast in Russian over and over and over again for all the rest of that day and night, straight through to the next day. The whole population calmed down, and the communists couldn't take over.

The Holy Spirit knows what He is doing. I believe the Russian Jimmy Swaggart telecast not only saved more than 1 million souls from all across Russia and the many Russian commonwealth nations while it was aired during those three and a half years, but it also saved an entire nation from total anarchy, chaos, and a return to communism.

Some 20 years later, those Russian pastors visiting Family Worship Center in Baton Rouge attested to the same.

ONLY GOD

Some say that the most Muslim country on the face of the earth today is the Middle East nation of Turkey. I have been told by well-meaning ministers and laymen that it would be impossible to air our telecast in this Islamic country. One well-meaning mission's leader in that part of the world chewed me out for even attempting to put a gospel program on Turkish television!

However, we are commanded by Jesus Himself to take the gospel to every nation, and that includes Turkey. To not go would be wrong. We must go; we have no alternative.

After talking with the representatives of the TV network in Ankara—the capital of Turkey and the Bible region of Galatia — and agreeing to send the program tapes to them, we experienced another miracle. In the fall of that year, our telecast began airing over the national Turkish TV network. This was the first time in the history of that great country, as far as we know, that a program of this nature had aired over television.

How could it be? Only God!

Only God could go before us in the face of seemingly insurmountable circumstances and make a way where there seemed to be no way. Please understand that this is only a start. And, please continue to pray for Turkey that God will open the door even wider.

WE ARE RECEIVING THE MESSAGE

Once, while traveling up country from Lagos, Nigeria, to a state of that beautiful country that was primarily Muslim, I drove to the government-owned and operated television network that happened to be across the street from the largest and tallest Islamic mosque in all of Africa.

You might say, "Why would you even try to put the Jimmy Swaggart gospel telecast on in what is obviously an area diametrically opposed to the gospel? It would be a waste of time, in fact, utter foolishness to even try."

Yeah (excuse the slang), and so what do we do, just let Satan have his way and take these dear Muslim people to hell without a warning? Go ahead and keep on in your unbelief, but I believe God. Jesus is bigger and better than anything else on earth, even bigger than Satan! Who am I to limit God? He called me to at least offer the gospel of Jesus Christ to every person and nation on this planet Earth. What they do with the invitation is up to them, but I cannot fail my Lord. If I do not offer the blessed gospel to them, pray, tell me, who will? If I do not offer the gospel, it will not be offered, and people will not have access to hear the greatest story ever told!

As I drove past the front of the huge mosque on my left, I breathed a prayer, "Oh, Lord, my God, my Father in heaven, please help me now and take me to the person responsible for placing programs on this powerful TV network and give me the words to say."

I parked the rental car in the parking lot, but there was no one to tell me where to go. Inside this huge television complex, I started out down one row of offices, reading the titles on the doors until I came to "Director of Programming" on the top of a door. I opened the door and asked the secretary if I could see the director. In a moment, I was conducted into his office.

A rather heavy Muslim man dressed in his typical garb sat behind a large desk. He was very congenial and asked, "What can I do for you?"

I introduced myself and gave him my business card and said, "I am with the Jimmy Swaggart telecast that airs over the greater part of the world. On most of the networks that carry it, this weekly one-hour telecast has become the number one rated program of all programming on the networks."

"Do you have a sample tape of the program?" he asked.

"Yes, would you like to view it?"

He had a videotape player and monitor available, so he pushed the tape in and started playing it. As he watched, he made several comments like, "Wow, this is really great production quality! Nice music." When Brother Swaggart started preaching, he became very quiet. At the end of the program, he said, "This is a very well-produced program that would be great to have broadcast over our network, but it is a Christian program. We are Muslim, and I would be putting my job on the line if I authorized the airing of the telecast."

"Yes, I have heard that said before," I said, "but after the telecast began to air, it became the number one rated program liked by people of all different kinds of backgrounds, including Muslims."

"But I might lose my position with the network," he retorted.

"Well, why don't we do this? Put the telecast on for six weeks as a pilot project, and if the Jimmy Swaggart telecast does not become the number one rated program in six weeks, I will personally come and take it off myself."

The Muslim thought for a minute and then said, "I think I can do it that way for six weeks as a pilot project to test viewer's choice ratings. Okay, let's do it." He signed the contract and gave me the physical address and the way to send the programs to him. I shook hands with him and thanked him for the opportunity to meet with him.

From my home base, I planned another trip six weeks out that included a stop in Nigeria to meet again with this Muslim director.

When the trip came and I arrived in Nigeria, I gave the director a long-distance call from Lagos to let him know about what time I would be arriving to see him. When I returned this time, as I was nearing the huge mosque and the TV network, I remembered that before, there was no one to meet me. This time, as I drove into the television network parking lot, the program director was waiting on the curb with a great big smile on his face.

As I got out of the car, he came over to shake my hand and welcome me back, and with some excitement in his voice, said, "You were right. The Jimmy Swaggart telecast has become the most viewed program on our network in just six weeks! And I want you to know, we are receiving the message!" Of course, he meant the gospel of Jesus Christ!

As a result, many, many thousands of people came to the Lord and were saved by the grace of God as a direct result of Brother Swaggart's Spirit-anointed preaching. Praise God! We give all the glory to Him!

Should I have not attempted to introduce the gospel of Jesus Christ in this predominantly Muslim part of Africa, to people who were wallowing in unbelief? My God is bigger than Islam, Buddhism, communism, Confucianism, and all other "isms." Christ Jesus is the only one who died for our sins and made a way for *"whosoever will"* to be saved from eternal perdition. It behooves us to do all we can to get the

Message of the Cross of Jesus Christ to everyone in this generation on the face of the earth.

THE DOOR IS OPEN

The doors of the nations of the world are open as never before. I believe this is the moment in history that God has chosen to reach an entire generation with the gospel of the Lord Jesus Christ. However, it is up to you and me to walk through those doors.

"For a great door and effectual is opened unto me, and there are many adversaries" (I Cor. 16:9).

Yes, there are many adversaries, but God has opened the door. We go through that door by interceding in prayer for the lost, by believing God to do the impossible, and by giving to enable the gospel to be aired in every country of the world so that men, women, boys, and girls of all colors, cultures, and creeds may come to know Jesus.

Yes, it takes prayer partners, first of all, who will intercede with us, and who will travail for the lost of the world and not just their own circle of family and friends. Ask God to have mercy upon this untoward generation and on those who sit in darkness. Pray for the advancement of His kingdom into their hearts, lives, and homes by using SonLife Broadcasting Network to bring the light of the gospel of Jesus Christ and Him crucified into more cable, satellite, and IP TV systems all over the world.

It takes all of us believing together that God will do the impossible, and that He will remove the obstacles and walk through the closed doors before us and make room for the Son-Life Broadcasting Network channel on every cable, satellite, and IP TV system in the world. It would be a sin not to use the technology God has put into place that enables us to offer the greatest story ever told to every home on the face of the earth.

And, yes, it takes money. It takes great amounts of money to accomplish world evangelization. If we will respond by obeying what the Lord impresses on our hearts to give each and every month, then the needs will be met, and the Lord will continue to multiply His blessing upon those who do. He said:

"I have shewed you all things, how that so laboring ye ought to support the weak, and to remember the words of the Lord Jesus, how He said, It is more blessed to give than to receive" (Acts 20:35).

The mandate God gave Brother Swaggart most recently was to send the gospel by television all over the world and to do it quickly. It is one and the same plan — God's plan — that He called Brother Swaggart to fulfill more than 50 years ago. God has called each one of us to participate in His plan of redemption for our generation. You have a vital part to fulfill by the grace of God. The Lord said He would open the door wide and when God opens the door, no man can shut it. It is no small thing to air programs over the entirety of the world. We must believe God and accelerate our efforts.

If all of us will do our part, then we can help send the gospel to those who sit in darkness. There will come a glorious day around the throne when these precious people from behind the seemingly closed doors will tap each one of us on the shoulder and ask, "Are you one of those who supported the Jimmy Swaggart SonLife Broadcasting Network that was sent to our country? Without your help we would not be here, for it was through this network that we heard about Jesus. Thank you, thank you, thank you!"

Jesus said, *"I must work the works of Him that sent Me, while it is day: the night cometh, when no man can work"* (Jn. 9:4).

Yes, night is coming. A storm is on the horizon. The doors are now open as never before, and, thank God, today is the day of salvation—when all who call upon the name of the Lord can be saved. Let us work while it is day! Let us sacrifice and rise to the occasion of this moment in history to reach a lost and dying world with the gospel of Jesus Christ. It can be done. The Holy Spirit is doing it through consecrated believers like you and me who follow His leading. Now is the perfect time!

I've seen the lightning flashing and heard the thunder roll;
I've felt sin's breakers dashing, trying to conquer my soul;

I've heard the voice of Jesus telling me still to fight on;
He promised never to leave me, never to leave me alone.

No, never alone, no, never alone,
He promised never to leave me, never to leave me alone;
No, never alone, no, never alone,
He promised never to leave me, never to leave me alone.

The world's fierce winds are blowing, temptations are
    sharp and keen;
I feel a peace in knowing my Saviour stands between;
He stands to shield me from danger when earthly friends
    are gone,
He promised never to leave me, never to leave me alone.

"No, never alone, no, never alone,
He promised never to leave me, never to leave me alone;
No, never alone, no, never alone,
He promised never to leave me, never to leave me alone."

"When in affliction's valley, I'm treading the road of care,
My Saviour helps me to carry my cross when heavy to bear;
My feet entangled with briars, ready to cast me down;
My Saviour whispered His promise never to leave me alone.

"No, never alone, no, never alone,
He promised never to leave me, never to leave me alone;

No, never alone, no, never alone,
He promised never to leave me, never to leave me alone.

He died for me on the mountain, for me they pierced His side,
For me He opened that fountain, the crimson, cleansing tide;
For me He waiteth in glory, seated upon His throne;
He promised never to leave me, never to leave me alone.

No, never alone, no, never alone,
He promised never to leave me, never to leave me alone;
No, never alone, no, never alone,
He promised never to leave me, never to leave me alone.

He gives me the sweet promise that He will come again,
And when He reigns in glory and I to heaven attain;
I shall in that dear country be numbered with His own,
And live with Him forever, never, no never alone.

No, never alone, no, never alone,
He promised never to leave me, never to leave me alone;
No, never alone, no, never alone,
He promised never to leave me, never to leave me alone.

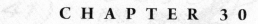

CHAPTER 30

55° 45' 20" N
37° 37' 2" E

THE LAST TRIP
TO MOSCOW

"Yea, though I walk through the valley of the shadow of death, I will fear no evil: for Thou art with me; Thy rod and Thy staff they comfort me."

— *Psalm 23:4*

THE LAST TRIP TO MOSCOW

55° 45' 20" N | 37° 37' 2" E

In traveling all over the world, I have seen the powerful forces of darkness arrayed against the advance of the gospel of Jesus Christ. You see, every time people are won to the Lord as a result of the Spirit-anointed preaching of the gospel of Jesus Christ and Him crucified, the enemy of man's soul does not take it lying down. He attacks with all fury, but God's promise is:

"Ye are of God, little children, and have overcome them: because greater is He that is in you, than he that is in the world" (I Jn. 4:4).

During my last trip to Moscow in late 1993, I was lodging in the multi-story, downtown hotel on one of the middle floors. The meetings that day were long and exhausting, and I fell in bed rather late after being invited to a restaurant to eat with one of the authorities from the Russian television network. I thought, "Finally I can get some rest because there are no appointments tomorrow morning before going to the airport." Was I ever wrong!

MASSACRE TOOK PLACE

In the middle of the night, I awoke to the sound of several automatic weapons firing. Quickly coming to my senses, I realized that the shooting was coming either from down the hall in the room next to me, or very close to that room.

Instinctively, I threw myself on the floor. Just outside of my hotel room door, I could hear people screaming as the rapid gunfire continued for what seemed like an eternity. Then, all of a sudden, it was complete silence. I dared not move or make a noise.

After another 10 minutes of so, a hotel employee came through the hallway telling everyone to evacuate the hotel and to take their luggage with them. I looked at my watch; it was 4 a.m. I quickly showered, dressed, and packed what few things I had in my carry-on. When I exited my room, there was a hotel employee telling everyone to exit to the elevator at the opposite end of the floor from where the shooting noise had come.

In the hotel lobby, other guests and I were ushered into a rather large ballroom where breakfast foods had been set out on the tables for us to eat. Please understand that breakfast every day is sliced cucumbers and salami. After spending several hours with these guests in the ballroom, we were told that we could either leave or go back to our rooms.

Since it was nearly time for my ride to pick me up for the airport at 10:30 a.m., I went out into the lobby near the front door. Out in the foyer, I could see what looked like several KGB agents talking to the people who guarded the hotel. (Every hotel has these guards that check everybody's documents when they enter or exit a hotel in Moscow.) I was standing there with several other people who were talking about what had happened in the night, but none with information as to what took place. As I stood there, I saw my friend from the television network, the director general, come through the huge front doors. So, I went out to meet him in what was a type of foyer.

After shaking hands with him, we started out the main doors of the hotel. Just then, among the hum of all the talking, I heard one KGB agent say to another: "What a massacre!"

"Yea, they say it was the supposed communist mafia."

"Who were they looking for?"

"They think they heard them say it was for somebody that puts programs on television."

"Somebody must have upset them greatly with their programs."

"Yea, whatever was said made them think that the new enforcement laws enacted were the result of that programming."

The director and I went through the foyer and outside into the drive-up street in front of the hotel and got into his car. I did not say anything to him about the conversation I'd overheard because I wanted to see if he would volunteer any information, but he did not. It looked as though the authorities tried to hush the incident. All the director asked me was, "Would you like to have a good meal in the restaurant on top of the airport before you leave back to the States?"

"Of course," I replied, "That will be just fine. There is plenty of time before the departure of the plane."

NOON MEAL BEFORE DEPARTURE

We arrived at the airport and parked the car. As usual, the airport terminal was very crowded. We went up the elevator to the large restaurant toward the top of the terminal building and entered through the main dining room entrance.

We were gruffly greeted by a rather stout, wide, middle-aged hostess. She informed the Russian television director that we were a bit early and that we would have to wait until the restaurant officially opened. She pointed to some chairs inside the dining room near the entrance and told us to wait there. When she was ready to seat us, she said, she would tell us. Of course, we took a seat where she told us.

Fifteen minutes went by as the director and I conversed about a continuing contract for the telecast. Meanwhile, some new diners showed up at the door. The stout hostess strutted toward them, motioned for them to follow her, and immediately seated them in the dining room. The director watched this out of the corner of his eye, I noticed. This happened several more times — new people arrived through the main entrance, the gruff hostess motioned for them to follow her, and she seated them. By now, the director — a reserved and dignified man — started to get annoyed. After all, we were the first to arrive, and he was irritated because the hostess had made us wait while seating all these other guests who came to the restaurant after us.

The hostess was in mid-strut of meeting yet another group of new people when, still frustrated, the director stood up and motioned for me to do the same. But instead of us catching her attention, the hostess walked right past us and waved for the others to follow her and be seated. This made my friend's neck turn red and his fists clench.

Finally, the hostess strutted toward us and motioned for us to follow her to a table. Walking side by side, my Russian friend and I quietly followed some 10 feet behind her. Suddenly, while pointing to the backside of the stout hostess in front of us, the director turned his head my way. In a low, guttural voice out of the corner of his mouth, he said very slowly: "R-r-r-russian tank!"

It was all I could do to stay composed and not burst out laughing. For this polite gentleman to unload such a humorous remark — a man who had never demonstrated one moment of emotion or humor in all of our past meetings — really helped to relieve the frustration of the moment.

After being seated and making sure the hostess was far away, we both burst out laughing. We were not laughing at the hostess, mind you, for she was just doing her job the best way she thought it should be done. Rather, we were laughing at one another for getting so uptight about our supposed "importance" and the seeming injustice done to us in not seating us immediately.

After boarding the plane and taking my seat, the Holy Spirit seemed to impress upon me, "This will be your last trip to Russia for awhile." And it was.

You see, after Russia began to open up, many supposedly well-meaning groups of Christians, especially from the United States, started visiting, and all kinds of "wackos" came, not to preach the gospel, but to demonstrate their false doctrine and worldly ways. Several had their people dressed up as clowns on the corners, stopping pedestrians and bothering them while the people were on their way to work. Others just got in everybody's way, offering no gospel preaching or even an invitation to hear a gospel message.

Finally, the Russian parliament passed new laws that prohibited any more foreign groups from coming and restricted any further formation of legal church entities. Then they stopped all religious broadcasting because of these supposed "evangelizing Christians." *goATS - cLOWNS*

So, after more than three and a half years, the contract for the telecast was not renewed. But thank God for the million or more dear Russians who had given their hearts to Jesus during that time as a direct result of the Russian Jimmy Swaggart telecast.

THE PLANE THAT FELL OUT OF THE SKY

Well, here I was when we started this journey, on a passenger airplane that had already fallen some 29,000 feet out of the sky and was still in a plunging nosedive.

Just as the face of the immense Indian Ocean was coming closer, I came to my senses. My life was flashing before me, reminding me of some of the many flights and trips around the world I had already been on and would be on for the cause of Christ with Jimmy Swaggart Ministries. (Of course, having traveled to more than 150 countries, only a few such trips could be recounted here.)

WAS IT THE END?

As the end seemed imminent, and the plane rushed toward impact, all of a sudden, the engines started to hum, and the fuselage began to shutter somewhat as the nose of the plane began to pull up from its downward vertical path. Within just a few hundred feet of the water's surface, the pilot was able to pull the plane level over the Indian Ocean. Then he banked right and made a 180-degree turn back toward Mauritius.

Praise God, there would still be more living and more trips to reach the lost in many more countries around the world. After landing, the passengers and I were told that when our plane was at 30,000 feet, a compressor had malfunctioned, cutting off all cabin pressure. If the pilot had not dropped the plane out of the sky as quickly as he did — letting it basically fall straight down to earth — we would have all suffered an acute case of hypoxia and died.

I honestly believe that on that day, Satan had tried to kill me and all the passengers on that plane.

How do I know this?

I know it because when I called long-distance back home to inform my family of the change in the return flights, I was told that on the same day, our house almost burned to the ground. Also on the same day, my daughter, Kim, was badly hurt while riding her bicycle. She was riding at top speed with her twin brother Kevin (they were only about 12 years old at the time) when the front wheel of her bike hit a rain-filled chuckhole in the pavement and threw her to the rugged asphalt. The skin and muscle tissue of her right knee was torn away in a deep cut that ran all the way to the bone.

All of this was happening on the same day that I was falling close to 30,000 feet out of the sky!

You see, during my whole missionary experience (some 30 years at that time), when a significant advance was made by the Holy Spirit for the gospel of Jesus Christ, Satan attacked not only me but also my family as well. If it were just me, that would be one thing, but he had always attacked my entire family. He was trying to kill us all because we were doing considerable damage to his nefarious, dark kingdom all over the earth. He does not want any souls whatsoever to be liberated from his grip of sin and death. So, of course, my family and I became the focus of his counterattack here on the front lines. This is actually a continuous, intense, spiritual battle that is going on over the eternal souls of men. The Scripture describes it as follows:

"For we wrestle not against flesh and blood, but against principalities, against powers, against the rulers of the

darkness of this world, against spiritual wickedness in high places" (Eph. 6:12).

If we let the Lord of Hosts fight the battle that has already been won by Jesus at the Cross of Calvary, we have the great promise of the Lord of the harvest:

"The angel of the Lord encampeth round about them that fear him, and delivereth them" (Ps. 34:7).

You say, "Why go through all of this?" I went through it and my family went through it because it is a great privilege to serve the Lord Jesus who died for us on the Cross of Calvary that *"whosoever will"* can come when they hear the good news. That good news says that we do not have to die in our sins, but in God's great love for us, He has made provision that we may be liberated from sin and death. They must hear! And there are still billions of never-dying souls for whom Christ died who have never heard.

You might ask, "What's the use with so many lost?"

That is the problem. We cop out because the task is too great, but listen to me now, dear Christian friend: God has told me in no uncertain terms that now it is possible through modern technological communications for this generation of Christians to actually reach every nation and every person in this generation with the gospel of Jesus Christ and Him crucified. Did you hear that? It would be a great sin not to take advantage of modern technology — radio, television, and the Internet — that God has made possible by His grace. He wants us to reach everyone with this glorious Message of the Cross of Jesus Christ — the greatest story ever told.

Does this make us someone who is better than anyone else? No, we are just what Christ said we are:

"So likewise ye, when ye shall have done all those things which are commanded you, say, We are unprofitable servants: we have done that which was our duty to do" (Lk. 17:10).

He did so much for us at the Cross. Can we do anything less than obey Him and respond to Jesus' Great Commission to preach this blessed gospel to everyone? I believe all Christians should be doing everything they can to support this God-called ministry of Jimmy Swaggart. It has a successful track record of more than 50 years of unflinching commitment to world evangelization, with Holy Spirit results that speak for themselves. There are literally millions upon millions of souls that testify to coming to the Lord as a direct result of this ministry's outreaches.

Now, my unsaved reader friend who has not yet surrendered to Christ Jesus and His claims upon your life, the Word of God puts it like this:

"For it is written, As I live, saith the Lord, every knee shall bow to Me, and every tongue shall confess to God" (Rom. 14:11).

Clearly, every single person ever born will confess that Jesus Christ is who He said He is: the only Lord and Saviour. If we do not meet Him as Saviour today, it is sure that we will meet Him as judge on the other side of the grave! Unfortunately, those who have never invited Jesus into their hearts and lives on this side of the grave will confess that He is Lord, but it will be too late once in the flames of eternal perdition. You see, all the opportunities to be saved are on this side of death. While we have the opportunity today, each one of us has to decide now to accept the eternal life in Jesus Christ that God has made available to every person in His great love and mercy for us.

The Bible says,

"And as it is appointed unto men once to die, but after this the judgment" (Heb. 9:27).

That's it. It's now or never. Accept Him today, for He has taken that judgment for your sin and my sin upon Himself at the Cross in our place. He did this by dying for us so that, by the grace of God, we may have eternal life in Him and never have to see condemnation or receive the just judgment we all deserve. In your own words, invite Him to come into your heart today, and your passport to eternal life will be extended to you from heaven.

The gospel of Jesus Christ is powerful. Because of the Cross of Jesus Christ, I can say without hesitation that your best is yet to come through faith in the Cross of Jesus Christ alone.

"For I am not ashamed of the gospel of Christ: for it is the power of God unto salvation to every one that believeth; to the Jew first, and also to the Greek. For therein is the righteousness of God revealed from faith to faith: as it is written, The just shall live by faith" (Rom. 1:16–17).

Thank you for traveling with me on this *Passport to the Impossible.* Maybe we can travel together again in the future on another passport, recounting the great things God did during my first 15 years as a missionary with my family. And perhaps we can travel again on another journey through the past 20 years of experiencing the Message of the Cross at Jimmy Swaggart Ministries.

In God's single great plan of redemption, I believe the greatest harvest of souls ever known to man is just on the horizon. With God, all things are possible in this His great plan of redemption in Jesus Christ.

Will you take your part by faith in His plan to continue this journey with the Holy Spirit? He loves you so much.

"And there are also many other things which Jesus did, the which, if they should be written every one, I suppose that even the world itself could not contain the books that should be written. Amen" (Jn. 21:25).

I was sinking deep in sin, far from the peaceful shore,
Very deeply stained within, sinking to rise no more,
But the Master of the sea heard my despairing cry,
From the waters lifted me, now safe am I.

Love lifted me!
Love lifted me!
When nothing else could help,
Love lifted me!

All my heart to Him I give, ever to Him I'll cling,
In His blessed presence live, ever His praises sing,
Love so mighty and so true, merits my soul's best songs,
Faithful, loving service, too, to Him belongs.

Souls in danger, look above, Jesus completely saves,
He will lift you by His love, out of the angry waves;
He's the Master of the sea, billows His will obey,
He your Saviour wants to be, be saved today.

The Woolsey Family: Jim and Jean Woolsey, center; and their children, pictured left to right: Kimberly, Curtis, Shauna, and Kevin. Kimberly and Kevin graduated from the Jimmy Swaggart Bible College. Kimberly and her husband, Tom Roof, have served as missionaries to Peru for the past 20 years, along with their son, Daniel, and daughter, Charity.

Guatemala: Jim Woolsey at his desk in the outreach office of Jimmy Swaggart Ministries in Guatemala City.

South Africa: Jimmy Swaggart Ministries Office Director Kokkie Lock (center, holding paper) with his staff.

International outreach: Volunteers at one of the many JSM international outreach offices pose next to stacks of replies from Jimmy Swaggart Ministries to the thousands of people requesting gospel materials.

Chile: Jimmy and Frances Swaggart, left, and Jim Woolsey, front right, in a meeting with President Augusto Pinochet of Chile. Pinochet was Chile's president from 1974 to 1990.

Baton Rouge, Louisiana: Jim Woolsey in his "home base" office located at JSM headquarters. Globes, like the one next to him, and world maps are still a part of Jim's office décor, keeping the countries of the world, and their need for the gospel, a part of every work day.

462

Africa: Evangelist Jimmy Swaggart, left, with a missionary and Jim Woolsey, right.

Africa: Evangelist Jimmy Swaggart (right) interviews Pastor Donnie Swaggart (left), Missionary Jim Woolsey (center left) and Pastor Don George (center right) about the physical and spiritual needs in Africa.

South America (Left to Right): Evangelist Jimmy Swaggart interviews Missionaries Nick Pino and Jim Woolsey in Chile.

Moscow, Russia: After years of trying, Jim Woolsey, center, finally gets Russian TV officials to sign a television contract that put the Jimmy Swaggart telecast onto TV-1 nationwide, to broadcast over more than 7,000 television stations and into 11 time zones.

Latvia: Missionary Jim Woolsey with Pastor Vassily in Riga.

Missionary Jim Woolsey ministers in Baton Rouge, Louisiana, at Family Worship Center, the home church of Jimmy Swaggart Ministries and the headquarters of the SonLife Broadcasting Network (SBN). Church services are broadcast live over SBN to a potential audience of nearly 300 million television households.

Jim Woolsey is a regular panelist on the flagship television program of Jimmy Swaggart Ministries, *A Study in the Word*, which has aired consistently for 40 years. Pictured, left to right: Jimmy Swaggart, Bob Cornell, Loren Larson, and Woolsey.

The Message of the Cross is a live, one-hour daily program that is hosted by Evangelist Jimmy Swaggart, center, and shown exclusively on the SonLife Broadcasting Network. Regular panelists pictured left to right, include Dave Smith, Loren Larson, Swaggart, Jim Woolsey, and Carl Brown.

*"Blessing, and honor, and glory, and power,
be unto Him that sitteth upon the throne,
and unto the Lamb for ever and ever."*

— *Revelation 5:13*

ACKNOWLEDGMENTS

Above all, I am so grateful to my wonderful Saviour, the Lord Jesus Christ, for making all of this possible through His sacrifice on the Cross that enabled the sending of the promise of the Father, the mighty Holy Spirit, to reside in and use this weak, frail vessel of clay.

Words cannot express my gratitude to Brother Jimmy Swaggart and his lovely wife, Frances, for their unflinching commitment to the call of God on their lives to world evangelism. The confidence they placed in me made it possible to carry out the tasks and travel associated with a position in their ministry for these 21 years. Every day that I get to work shoulder to shoulder with this remarkable team is an honor.

Of course, this book would not have been possible without the love, support and encouragement of my family, especially my dear wife, Jean Woolsey.

As for the production of this book, without the expert, professional advice and assistance of managing editor Desiree Jones and editor Cathie Moody in polishing this manuscript, the reader would have had a rather bumpy journey through these pages. Also, special thanks go to graphic designer Tom Coleman for the superb job he did on the cover and page design of this book.

There are countless other employees and collaborators of Jimmy Swaggart Ministries — past and present — whose service to the Lord gained ground for the kingdom of God pushing back the darkness, touching the hearts and lives of people with the gospel in more nations than are mentioned in this book. I personally appreciate the important part each one of them plays in this great team effort to reach the lost.

ABOUT THE AUTHOR **JIM WOOLSEY**

 Jim Woolsey was born in Nevada and raised in Tucson, Arizona. He came to the Lord as a college student while attending the University of Arizona where he graduated with a master's degree in education.

Immediately called to ministry, Brother Jim went first to Peru where he served as a missionary for 14 years.

In 1969, he was the first overseas missionary anywhere in the world to preach and teach on a daily Spanish gospel television program, which aired live every day for several years. He also hosted a live radio program every morning and evening in Southern Peru.

During this same time, Brother Jim also preached every night in open-air "good news" crusades to people who had never before heard the gospel of Jesus Christ. As a missionary in Peru, Mexico, Ecuador, and Guatemala, he preached an average of three to four times a day — more than 1,000 times each year — for several years.

He would preach in one place until his audience grew large and stable enough to establish a church. Then he would move his family to the next city and start again, preaching in the open air until another church was established.

Toward the end of his 20-year tenure as an appointed missionary, Brother Jim accepted a position as the international director for Jimmy Swaggart Ministries. His responsibilities included the oversight of 65 international ministry outreach offices, international childcare (which included a daily feeding program), the construction of all Bible schools, primary schools, and churches; the monthly support of more than 600 missionaries, and helping to coordinate site selection for the ministry's international crusades acquiring both the collaboration with church and government officials in each country. Additionally, he negotiated and maintained more than 5,000 television contracts to get the ministry's daily and weekly telecast on in more than 150 countries and translated into 26 different languages.

The Lord's call on Brother Jim's life has taken him to 182 countries that required more than 4 million miles of travel by air, land, and sea — all in pursuit of venues to distribute the gospel of Jesus Christ to a lost and dying world.

Jim Woolsey lives in Baton Rouge, Louisiana, with his wife, Jean. They have four children and five grandchildren. This is his first book.